CONCISE

ROME

Alta Macadam

Somerset Books • London

Blue Guide Concise Rome. First edition 2010

Published by Blue Guides Limited, a Somerset Books Company
Winchester House, Deane Gate Avenue, Taunton, Somerset TA1 2UH
www.blueguides.com
'Blue Guide' is a registered trademark

ISBN 978–1–905131–30–3

A CIP catalogue record of this book is available from the British Library

Distributed in the United States of America by
WW Norton and Company, Inc.
500 Fifth Avenue, New York, NY 10110

The author and publisher have made reasonable efforts to ensure the accuracy of
all the information in *Blue Guide Concise Rome*; however, they can accept no
responsibility for any loss, injury or inconvenience sustained by any traveller as a
result of information or advice contained in the guide.

Statement of editorial independence: Blue Guides, their authors and editors, are
prohibited from accepting any payment from any restaurant, hotel, gallery or other
establishment for its inclusion in this guide or on www.blueguides.com, or for a
more favourable mention than would otherwise have been made.

All other acknowledgements, photo credits and copyright information
are given on p. 224, which forms part of this copyright page.

Your views on this book would be much appreciated. We welcome not only
specific comments, suggestions or corrections, but any more general views you
may have: how this book enhanced your visit, how it could have been more
helpful. Blue Guides authors and editorial and production team work hard to
bring you what we hope are the best-researched and best-presented cultural,
historical and academic guide books in the English language. Please write to us
by email (editorial@blueguides.com), via the comments page on our website
(www.blueguides.com) or at the address given above. We will be happy to
acknowledge useful contributions in the next edition, and to offer a free copy
of one of our titles.

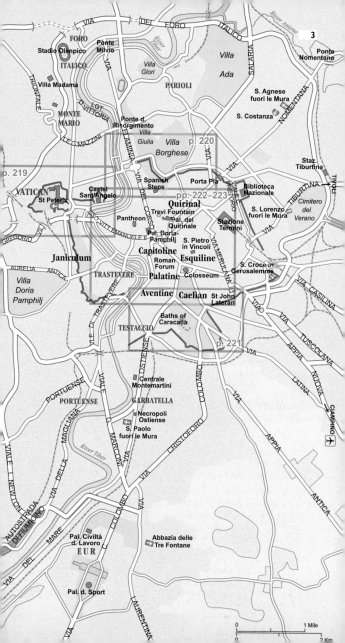

INTRODUCTION

Rome is one of the most celebrated cities in the world: ever since her greatest days as the centre of the Roman Empire, and later as the home of the Roman Catholic Church, she has played a role of the first importance in European history. The Eternal City was the Caput Mundi (Head of the World) in the Roman era, and from it law and the liberal arts and sciences radiated throughout the vast Empire, which stretched from Mesopotamia to Britain. The ancient Roman city, with a population of over one million, was built over the famous seven hills—the Palatine, Capitoline, Esquiline, Viminal, Quirinal, Aventine and Caelian—on the left bank of the River Tiber. The walls built to defend the city by the emperor Aurelian in the 3rd century AD still defined the urban limits of the city in the late 19th century, and it was only in the 1940s that the population began to equal (and then supersede) that of ancient Rome.

The city today preserves numerous magnificent ancient buildings side by side with palaces and churches from later centuries. Its squares are decorated with splendid fountains and Egyptian obelisks. The Vatican, in part of the district which from the 9th century onwards became the stronghold of the popes, has, since 1929, been the smallest independent state in the world.

For centuries Rome has been visited by pilgrims and travellers, and today it is one of the most popular tourist destinations in Europe, not only because of its wealth of art, architecture and cultural patrimony, but also because of its relaxed atmosphere, kind climate, manageable size and friendly manners. The numbers, when looked at as statistics, can seem overwhelming: more than three million people see the Sistine Chapel every year, with up to 20,000 in a single day. For this reason visitors are strongly advised to see not only the most famous sights, but also to spend time exploring the quieter streets and the smaller museums and palaces. This book aims to cover both the major sights of the city and a few of its more hidden treasures.

CONTENTS

THE GUIDE

PRACTICAL INFORMATION

HISTORICAL SKETCH

by L. Russell Muirhead and Annabel Barber

Rome was founded—in 753 BC according to legend and tradition, and probably much earlier—at the spot where the territories of the Latins, the Sabines and the Etruscans met. Its founder was Romulus, son of Mars and the Vestal Virgin Rhea Sylvia, herself a descendant of Aeneas, who had escaped from the burning walls of Troy to found a city among the volcanic hills of Latium. Romulus encouraged his people to intermarry with the Sabines (the famous 'Rape of the Sabine Women') and the fledgling city grew in population and prosperity. Its position was a good one: at the centre of the Italian peninsula, close to the sea and to a crossing place on the River Tiber, and the Romans conquered or formed alliances with the Latins and Etruscans whose territories surrounded them. In these early centuries Rome was ruled by a succession of kings, some of whom were in fact Etruscan: it was an Etruscan who had the marshy valley of the Forum drained and paved as a market-place, and it was an Etruscan architect who built the great temple of Jupiter on the Capitoline Hill. The last and most famous of the kings, another Etruscan, was Tarquinius Superbus. He came to be hated for his lordly ways and was brought down by a Latin plot, led by a man called Brutus, who claimed that Tarquinius' son had raped his virtuous kinswoman Lucretia. Tarquinius was overthrown and Rome declared herself a republic in c. 509 BC. The name Brutus became associated with liberation from tyranny—a later Roman of the same name would famously plot the murder of Julius Caesar.

The Republic was dogged by a long and persistent struggle between the plebs and the patricians, and if this had been its only characteristic, it could never have risen to such supremacy as it did. But Rome had another defining feature: its militarism. Armies trained ruthlessly, discipline was savage, weapons were effective and the men tough. Slowly but surely Rome conquered all around her: the Etruscans, the Volscians and the Samnites. After this, the gateway was thrown open to the south. From the 3rd century BC Rome began to turn her arms against the cities of Magna Graecia, rich and cultured colonies founded by Greeks seeking more fertile terrain than their own at home. The impact on Roman attitudes of this contact with Greek culture, around the Bay of Naples, in Sicily and elsewhere in the south of the peninsula, was remarkable. A hard, austere, martial race, who forbade their women to touch wine on pain of death and who had despised the comfort-loving, uxorious Etruscans, found the sensual luxuries of the Greek world impossible to resist. Their appetites were awakened for precious marbles and statuary. The poetry and the drama charmed and entertained them as much as the philosophy broadened their minds. But though many of the Romans turned Hellenophile, their lust for conquest remained unabated. One obstacle stood in their way: the Carthaginians, a great seafaring nation whose empire stretched from the south of Spain across north Africa to western Sicily. The Carthaginian leader, Hannibal, with his terrifying war elephants, inflicted many defeats on Rome's armies. At length the Romans, who had never been a maritime people, built a fleet and taught themselves the art of naval warfare. After over a century of struggle, Carthage was finally defeated in 146 BC. The Romans now made themselves masters not only of all Italy, but also of Cisalpine Gaul, Illyria, Greece and Macedonia, and finally proceeded to the conquest of the world. While clemency was shown to those who acquiesced in Roman rule, no quarter was given to those who resisted. Disaffection was not tolerated: the so-called Social War in 89 BC, an insurrection of the Italic peoples, was put down, and Rome went on to subjugate Asia Minor, Tauris, Syria and Palestine. Julius Caesar bore the Roman eagles to Transalpine Gaul and Britain.

Yet internal strife robbed the Republic of peace. First there were armed quarrels between the military commanders Marius and Sulla; then leadership disputes between Caesar and Pompey led to civil war. Caesar's faction prevailed—but his triumph sparked fears that he would claim for himself the title of king and return to the ways of the hated Tarquins. His assassination in 44 BC by Brutus and Cassius was followed by the vexed triumvirate of Mark Antony, Lepidus and Octavian (Caesar's adopted son) and ultimately, c. 27 BC, by the founding of the Empire under Octavian (afterwards Augustus), following his defeat of Antony and Cleopatra and the annexation of Egypt. From now on for the next half millennium, Rome was to remain an empire. But Augustus did not share Caesar's fate: he was canny and brilliant and managed to retain the support of the senate, allowing them to believe that they still wielded influence. More importantly, he brought peace, and under him and succeeding emperors the dominion of Rome continued to extend, reaching its maximum expansion under Trajan (98–117). The language and the laws of Rome were accepted as standards by the world, and the solidity of the Roman state was still unbroken in the 3rd century AD, although barbarian pressure was beginning.

The decline of Rome began under Diocletian (AD 285–305), who divided the empire into western and eastern portions. The decline was confirmed when Constantine transferred the seat of government to Byzantium (AD 330). In the 5th century the barbarians descended upon Rome. The imperial city was sacked by Alaric the Goth in 410, by Genseric the Vandal in 455, and by Ricimer the Swabian in 472. Finally, in 476, the Germanic chieftain Odoacer compelled the emperor Romulus Augustulus to abdicate, and thus put an end to the Western Empire. Rome entered the Dark Ages.

The Roman Church, persecuted until the reign of Constantine, now emerged triumphant. Indeed, it can be said to have rescued Latin civilisation from ruin, as the supremacy of the Bishop of Rome was gradually recognised by the Christianised world. At the beginning of the 7th century, Rome came under the temporal protection of the popes, a protection which was later transformed into sovereignty. Determined to reassert the power and position of Rome vis à vis Byzantium, Pope Stephen II allied himself with the Franks, with their help securing territory that was to grow into the States of the Church (or Papal States), the lands over which the papacy ruled until 1870. On Christmas Day 800, the Frankish king Charlemagne was crowned by Pope Leo III in St Peter's as 'Augustus' and 'Emperor', and so began the 'Holy Roman Empire', an institution intended to safeguard an alliance between emperor and pope.

The alliance, as it turned out, was always a shaky one. On the death of Charlemagne a turbulent period ensued, which clouded the fortunes of the papacy as the relationship between pope and emperor and the nature of the power-share between them became more ambivalent. The pope was head of the Church but the emperor was its defender, against pagan barbarians, the Arab infidel and Byzantium. Frequent quarrels broke out over which of the two, emperor or pope, had the better right to consider himself God's representative on earth. Gregory VII (reigned 1073–85) reasserted papal authority, although he was unable to prevent the Normans from devastating the city in 1084. Two later popes, Paschal II and Calixtus II, did much to restore it. In 1309 Pope Clement V, former Archbishop of Bordeaux, was persuaded by King Philip the Fair of France to set up his court in Avignon. Political unrest in Italy made the move attractive to this French pope, who knew that in Avignon he could count on the protection of France. It was not until 1378, at the instance of St Catherine of Siena, that Gregory XI re-transferred the papal seat from Avignon to Rome. Rejoicing in the Eternal City was short-lived, for the Great Schism ensued, a period of uncertainty when popes and rival antipopes claimed authority simultaneously, and allegiances were divided. In 1417 a native Roman was elected, Oddone Colonna. Taking the regnal name of Martin V, he succeeded in establishing the supremacy of a single pope in Rome and began to restore the city, which had deteriorated both physically and socially during its so-called 'Babylonian Captivity'.

The great age of building in Rome came under Julius II (1503–13) and Leo X (1513–21), one a warrior, the other a pleasure-loving Medici. Under both these pontiffs Rome recovered brilliantly, and became the centre of the Italian Renaissance, eclipsing Florence. This was the age of Bramante, Michelangelo and Raphael, the three greatest geniuses of their day in architecture, sculpture and painting.

For much of the 16th century Italy had to fend off the territorial ambitions of two great powers, France and Spain. In 1527 in Rome, another Medici pope, Clement VII, paid dearly for his support of the French faction when the mercenary armies of Charles V of Spain, who was also the Holy Roman Emperor, captured the city and ruthlessly sacked it. Reconciliation followed, and it was another Roman pope, Alessandro Farnese (Pope Paul III), who set about restoring and further embellishing the city, a process which continued to occupy the attention of many succeeding popes, notably Sixtus V, who completed the dome of St Peter's and ordered the siting of the Egyptian obelisks in the positions they occupy today. The mid- and later 16th century was also the age of the Counter-Reformation, the ecclesiastical movement to reform and purge corruption from the Catholic Church in the face of the rise of Protestantism. The Renaissance now gave way to the Baroque, a grandiloquent, sensual, high-flown style which appealed to the emotions and presented the mysteries of the Eucharist as theatre in magnificent surroundings, as exemplified by the great churches of the Gesù, Sant'Ignazio and Sant'Andrea della Valle. The finest exponent of the Roman Baroque was the painter, sculptor and architect Gian Lorenzo Bernini, who enjoyed the patronage of the Borghese family (including Pope Paul V) and of Urban VIII.

The 18th century was a peaceable period in Rome, an age when northern Europeans began to flock to the city to admire its romantic ruins and its Classical statuary. Under Napoleon Bonaparte, the fortunes of the papacy tottered. French troops entered Rome in February 1798 and proclaimed a republic. Pope Pius VI was carried as a prisoner to France, where he died in 1799. In 1803 Napoleon organised the marriage of his favourite sister, Pauline, to Prince Camillo Borghese; in 1809 he annexed the Papal States to the French Empire. In 1810 the French senate proclaimed Rome to be their second capital; and in 1811 Napoleon conferred the title of King of Rome on his new-born son. On the fall of Napoleon, the pope, Pius VII, returned to Rome, to which were restored, also, almost all the works of art that had been removed by the French, thanks largely to negotiations undertaken by the sculptor Canova.

Though Napoleon was defeated, his ghost was not laid to rest. Ideas of nationhood, of independence and of Italian identity had been fomented in people's hearts, and Rome was keenly interested in the agitated period of the 'Risorgimento', when nationalist sentiment coursed through the Italian peninsula and when armies led by Garibaldi were winning victories against the Austrians in the north and against the Bourbons in Sicily and the south. Pope Pius IX, by inclination a theologian, not a politician, and a conservative by instinct, was no match for the radicals. In September 1870, the Italian army under Raffaello Cadorna entered Rome by a breach in the walls to the northeast, beside the Porta Pia. Shortly afterwards, Rome was proclaimed the capital of united Italy, under King Vittorio Emanuele II. Pius IX was relieved of temporal power and confined to the Vatican.

After the First World War (which had little direct effect on Rome), the Fascist movement rapidly developed. The year 1922 saw the 'March on Rome' of Mussolini and his myrmidons, after which King Vittorio Emanuele III invited Mussolini to form a government. Italy entered the Second World War on the Axis side in 1940. In September 1943 the Allied invasion of the mainland began. American troops entered Rome in June 1944. In April 1945, Mussolini was killed after his capture by Italian partisans while attempting to escape into Switzerland. In May 1946, Vittorio Emanuele III abdicated. Less than a month later a general election, with a referendum on the form of government, was held. The referendum favoured the establishment of a republic. The royal family left the country a few days later, and a provisional president was elected. On 22nd December 1947, the Constituent Assembly approved the new republican constitution. Rome was now the capital of the Repubblica Italiana.

THE CAPITOLINE HILL

The compact Capitoline Hill (Campidoglio in Italian; *map p. 222, C3*) is the most famous of the seven hills of Rome. Recent excavations have also confirmed that it was the first of all to be inhabited. Rising to 48m in the very centre of the city, it is the best place to start your visit.

At the top is a spacious piazza with a group of three buildings facing onto it, which were designed by Michelangelo and which contain important museums of ancient sculpture. These are beautifully kept and usually not too crowded. A single lane encircles the hill, from which there are wonderful views of both the ancient heart of Rome—the Roman Forum—and, in the other direction, the later city, with Michelangelo's great dome of St Peter's in the background.

Piazza del Campidoglio

The broad, stepped ramp known as the Cordonata, flanked at the bottom by two ancient Egyptian lions in black granite, was designed by Michelangelo to provide an easy way up to the piazza, whose layout he also planned. He drew up the design of the pavement and the plinth for the famous ancient Roman equestrian statue of the emperor Marcus Aurelius, now replaced by a copy (*the original is described on p. 13*). Michelangelo's grand, beautifully proportioned Palazzo dei Conservatori on the right, and the Palazzo Nuovo opposite it, incorporate the Classical orders of ancient Rome combined with remarkable innovative architectural features. This extraordinarily pleasing urban space was completed when the central Palazzo Senatorio, on a site which has been the seat of the governors of Rome since the 12th century and is still the office of the mayor, was redesigned along the same lines. To the right is the entrance to the Capitoline Museums.

THE CAPITOLINE MUSEUMS

The Capitoline Museums is the general name given to a number of different museums which are all entered from Palazzo dei Conservatori and with the same ticket. Founded in 1471, they constitute the oldest public collection in the world. They are perhaps the most attractive and interesting of all the museums of ancient sculpture in the city.

Open 9–8pm except Mon. It is well worth trying to visit the museums after dark, when the rooms in Palazzo Nuovo are illuminated by chandeliers. The exhibits are excellently labelled, also in English. There is a combined ticket which includes admission to the Centrale Montemartini (see below).

Palazzo dei Conservatori

In the courtyard (**A**) are some fragments, including the head, hand and feet, from a colossal seated statue of Constantine which once sat in the Basilica of Maxentius in the Forum. With a body probably made of wood covered with bronze, this was some 12m high and is the best-known portrait of the first Christian emperor.

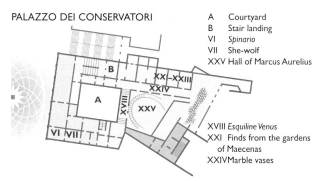

PALAZZO DEI CONSERVATORI

A   Courtyard
B   Stair landing
VI   *Spinario*
VII   She-wolf
XXV Hall of Marcus Aurelius

XVIII *Esquiline Venus*
XXI Finds from the gardens
     of Maecenas
XXIV Marble vases

On the **stair landing** (**B**) are four huge reliefs, three of which are from a triumphal arch set up in honour of Marcus Aurelius, one of the greatest Roman emperors, whose fate it was to carry out many battles to defend Rome but whose humanity and philosophical intelligence are recorded in his *Meditations*. He is here depicted at sacrifice, showing clemency to prisoners who have surrendered to his troops, and enjoying a triumph on his return from battle.

The Appartamenti dei Conservatori display two famous bronzes in two rooms next to each other: in **Room VI** is the statue of the *Spinario*, the delicate figure of a seated boy intent on plucking a thorn from his foot, probably cast in the 1st century BC. Two more exceptional works in bronze are displayed here: a portrait head known as *Brutus*, which may have been made any time between the 4th and the 1st centuries BC, and a bronze vase with an inscription which dates it to the 1st century BC. The next room (**VII**) is named after the *lupa*, or celebrated **She-wolf**, which for centuries was the most famous piece of sculpture in the

Head of the gilded bronze statue of Marcus Aurelius (1st century AD), a masterpiece of ancient sculpture.

from the year of the emperor's death (AD 80) and is the only Roman equestrian statue of this period to survive. It is a masterpiece of Roman art.

Also here are the head, hand and globe from a bronze statue of Constantine, and a gilded bronze cult statue of Hercules.

Close by can be seen part of the massive foundations of the **Temple of Capitoline Jupiter**, dedicated in 509 BC. It is the largest temple known from that time (a model shows its scale, with the tiny parts of it which have survived). It was the temple at which the processions (or triumphs) awarded to victorious generals terminated. The finds made during its excavation

city. It became the symbol of Rome since, as the legend goes, it was a wolf who by suckling Romulus and his brother Remus saved them from starvation so that they then were able to found Rome (the bronze twins were added in the early 16th century). Discussion continues about when this great work was made. Though traditionally considered to be of Etruscan workmanship dating from the late 6th or early 5th century BC, it has recently been suggested that it might even date from the medieval period.

The light and airy modern **Hall of Marcus Aurelius (XXV)** displays the magnificent gilded bronze equestrian statue of Marcus Aurelius, removed from the piazza outside. It may date

Relief from a triumphal arch showing the emperor Marcus Aurelius preparing to sacrifice a bull.

include Bronze Age artefacts (17th–11th centuries BC). Don't miss the exquisite tiny ivory plaque in the form of a lion found in the area of the Forum Boarium (the cattle market of ancient Rome) at the foot of the hill: it dates from 616–578 BC and bears the oldest Etruscan inscription ever found in Rome.

The adjoining galleries contain ancient marble statues mostly found in the late 19th century in the *horti* or grand villas with large gardens once owned by Rome's wealthiest citizens or members of the imperial families.

In the hall (**XVIII**) is the statue of a beautiful young girl known as the ***Esquiline Venus***. We know that she originally was shown tying up her hair before taking a swim, but today her arms are missing. Also

here is the elaborate bust of the emperor Commodus: he is portrayed as Hercules and in his lion-skin bonnet appears rather ludicrous, but the details of the carving are extraordinarily fine.

In Rooms **XXI**, **XXII**, **XXIII** are finds made in the gardens, also on the Esquiline Hill, which belonged to the fabulously rich Maecenas, born c. 70 BC and famous as a patron of the arts. These include a seated dog in rare marble, a charioteer, a low relief of a dancing maenad, statues of the Muses, and a delightful rhyton, a neo-Attic work once used as a fountain. The very beautiful head of an Amazon is a copy of a famous bronze work by Polyclitus. In the gallery (**XXIV**) are beautiful large marble vases, decorated with delicate carvings.

Pinacoteca Capitolina

The picture gallery is on the second floor (don't miss the superb marble intarsia panels of a bull attacked by a tigress dating from the 4th century AD outside the entrance). The gallery is mainly interesting for its 16th–18th-century Italian and foreign works, with the Emilian school (Guido Reni, Guercino) particularly well represented. There is also a delightful early work by Caravaggio (*The Gipsy Fortune-teller*).

The corridor beneath the piazza

Back on ground level, stairs from the entrance portico lead down to the corridor beneath the piazza, lined with some very interesting ancient inscriptions, displayed according to subject matter including the languages of the Empire, burial rites, religion, legal texts, professions and crafts, games, armies.

In the middle of the corridor a passageway leads right to the impressive remains of a huge Roman building which faced the Forum.

Called the Tabularium, it housed the archives of the ancient city. Today its vaulted passageways can be explored and from its loggia there is a wonderful view of the Forum. It incorporated an earlier building, the Temple of Jupiter Veiovis (198 BC), remains of which can also be seen here.

Palazzo Nuovo

Palazzo Nuovo is now, despite its name, the part of the museums which retains the most old-fashioned atmosphere, with its memorable display lit by chandeliers when dusk falls.

The underground corridor emerges by the stairs up to the courtyard. Here is the huge statue of a genial, overweight river god known as Marforio. It has lain in the vicinity of the hill since it was first made around the 2nd century AD, and was moved to its present position in 1596. It was one of Rome's 'talking statues' (*see p. 68*), since anonymous epigrams or satirical comments against the rulers of the day used to be attached to it.

PALAZZO NUOVO

I	Gallery
II	Dove mosaic
III	*Capitoline Venus*
IV	Portrait busts
V	Portrait busts
VI	Pair of centaurs
VII	*Laughing Silenus*
VIII	*Dying Gaul*

The collection on the first floor retains its charming 18th-century display. Amongst the crowd of statues lining the walls of the gallery (**I**) is a drunken old woman clutching a wine flask, typical of Hellenistic realist sculpture. In the hall to the right (**II**) there is a charming little statue of a young girl protecting a dove, a Roman copy of a Hellenistic work of the 2nd century BC. Doves feature also in the exquisite small mosaic exhibited here, which was found in Hadrian's villa in Tivoli. Around the walls are numerous Roman busts. The *Capitoline Venus* is displayed in a little room all on its own (**III**): this is a superbly modelled statue of Parian marble and extremely well preserved, again a Roman replica of a Hellenistic original. After its discovery in

Roman copy of a famous Hellenistic mosaic of doves drinking, found in Hadrian's Villa at Tivoli, east of Rome (2nd century AD).

Rome in the 17th century, it became one of the most admired works in the entire city. **Rooms IV and V** have a magnificent display of portrait busts on shelves round the walls: those in Room IV depict various emperors and their wives and families, while those in Room V include many philosophers. They provide a wonderful sight and this is one of the most evocative places in all Rome where you come face to face with many of the most famous ancient Romans depicted by anonymous artists who invented the great Roman art of portraiture.

The largest hall **(VI)** displays a pair of centaurs signed by two sculptors from Asia Minor, both famous copyists of Greek masterpieces. Against the wall is a very expressive statue of a frightened old woman.

Room VII is named after the delightful statue in red marble of a laughing Silenus. The last room **(VIII)** displays the exquisitely modelled figure of a Celtic warrior (known as the *Dying Gaul*) sitting on the ground, mortally wounded. This is another Roman copy which became particularly famous in the 19th century, when it was identified as a gladiator. Other fine works here are the *Resting Satyr*, a handsome youth languishing against a tree trunk (one of some 70 copies of a renowned Greek original by Praxiteles), and a charming group of Eros and Psyche embracing.

CENTRALE MONTEMARTINI

Map p. 3. Admission 9–6.30 except Mon. Combined ticket with the Capitoline Museums, valid one week. Excellent labelling, also in English. The museum is best reached by public transport: Underground line B from Termini and Colosseo stations to Piramide. In the busy Piazzale Ostiense outside the station, take Bus 23 towards San Paolo fuori le Mura and get off at the 3rd request stop.

Restaurant: La Sella del Diavolo, just outside the entrance. Via Ostiense 102 (see p. 186).

The rest of the Capitoline Museums' collection of antique sculpture is displayed some distance away from the old city centre, in a former electrical plant built in 1912 and which is in itself an amazing monument of industrial archaeology. It now provides a superb setting for the Classical sculpture.

On the ground floor are the earliest pieces, including the well-known statue of a man in a toga carrying the busts of his father and his grandfather. On the first floor the Engine Room has some magnificent works inspired by Greek masterpieces, including statues of Athena, and other female figures in precious

marbles. The reconstructed pediment from the Temple of Apollo Sosianus, which once stood near the Theatre of Marcellus, includes nine fragments thought to date from around 450 BC of a frieze showing a battle between Greeks and Amazons. In the boiler room are more fine statues and reliefs, and there is also a large mosaic with hunting scenes.

Example of a statue of the *Pothos* type ('Yearning'), in the Centrale Montemartini.

The views from the hill

On the far side of Palazzo dei Conservatori, take the very short Via del Campidoglio in order to see the splendid view of the entire Roman Forum, with the Colosseum in the background and the Palatine Hill on the right. On the near side (closest to the Cordonata ramp), go through the archway to the little garden in front of the 16th-century Palazzo Caffarelli. Here there are pleasant places to sit and enjoy the splendid panorama of Rome with the dome of St Peter's in the distance. The door of Palazzo Caffarelli is open to provide access to the museum café, which is on a delightful roof terrace with more lovely views. From here you can follow the narrow road right round the hill, from which paths lead down through gardens to its foot. The precipice at the southern end of the hill may be the notorious Tarpeian Rock from which traitors used to be flung to their deaths. It takes its name from a legendary Roman girl, Tarpeia, who is said to have betrayed Rome when she helped free the Sabine Women, who had been locked up here with a view to increasing Rome's population by forcing them to marry locally rather than in their home territory in the Sabine hills north of Rome.

The road beyond Palazzo Nuovo leads to another little garden planted with pines, cypresses and palms where there are benches amidst a jumble of Roman ruins. From here steps lead down to Via dei Fori Imperiali, where there is an entrance to the Roman Forum.

Santa Maria in Aracoeli

Map p. 222, C3. Usually open 9–12.30 & 2.30–5.30. The most convenient entrance is by the inconspicuous south door (bearing a lovely 13th-century mosaic), reached by steps just behind Palazzo Nuovo. Coin-operated lights essential to see some of the artworks.

In 343 BC, on the highest point of the hill, a temple was dedicated to Juno, which was guarded by geese, sacred to the goddess. In the middle of a dark night in the same century, it was their honking which alerted the Romans to an attempt on the hill by the Gauls, and all was saved. By the 8th century this church had been built on the site. In 1348 an extremely long and steep flight of steps was built from the bottom of the hill up to its main door. Inside, the nave has splendid ancient Roman columns and a lovely pavement in marble inlay in a great variety of geometric designs, one of the best of many such pavements to be seen in Roman churches. The style is known as Cosmatesque, from the name of the family of craftsmen who designed them (and other exquisite marble furnishings for churches). Chandeliers provide the light. At the west end, next to a cardinal's tomb by the 15th-century sculptor Andrea Bregno, is a very worn pavement tomb (set up on the wall) signed by the famous Florentine artist Donatello (1432). Close by is a chapel entirely covered with late 15th-century frescoes by Pinturicchio depicting the life of St Bernardino. Much earlier fragmentary frescoes by Pietro Cavallini, the most important artist at work in Rome at the turn of the 13th and 14th centuries, can be seen in the last chapel in the south aisle, although it has recently been suggested that the *Madonna and Child* could be by Giotto (*light also essential*). The chapel in the south transept contains a Savelli tomb attributed to the great sculptor Arnolfo di Cambio, which incorporates a 3rd-century Roman sarcophagus (and from here you can see a beautiful small 13th-century mosaic on the wall of the adjoining chapel). Off the north transept is a 19th-century chapel with an image of the Infant Christ covered in jewels (the 'Santissimo Bambino'). It receives letters from children all over the world, and the fact that it is, in reality, a modern copy of the original which was held to be miraculous but was stolen in 1994, seems to have made no difference to its popular devotional status.

FOOD & DRINK NEAR THE CAPITOLINE

There is a smart café on the roof terrace of Palazzo Caffarelli, reached through the museums in Palazzo dei Conservatori, or by a separate entrance from Via di Villa Caffarelli just out of the piazza. It has the same opening hours as the museums.

At the bottom of the hill, just across the busy main road, **Ara Coeli Gelateria Artigianale** (*Piazza Aracoeli 9–10*) has excellent home-made ice creams and *granite*. It has a mouth-watering selection of flavours, including *ficchi d'India*, almond, and pistacchio from Sicily.

€€€ **La Taverna degli Amici** (also known as A Tormarganà; *Piazza Margana 37; T: 06 6992 0637; closed Sun evening, and Mon; map p. 222, C3*) is just two steps from the Capitoline Hill, tucked away in a delightful little quiet piazza. By the fountain in Piazza Aracoeli take Via di Tor' Margana. Opposite a 17th-century palace which houses offices of the UN, the restaurant is in a characteristic old russet-coloured house hung with virginia creeper, and has tables also outside. Typical Roman fare and an impressive wine list.

THE ROMAN FORUM, PALATINE HILL & COLOSSEUM

The Forum and Palatine still retain a wonderful romantic atmosphere of fallen grandeur. With very little labelling *in situ*, the feel is neither of abandon nor reconstruction. It is best at first to spend some time simply wandering amidst the ruins and enjoying the sensation of walking on the huge old round paving stones, many of which have lain where they are today for over 2,000 years. The fact that all this still exists undisturbed in the very centre of the modern city adds greatly to the effect.

Map p. 223, D3. Open 9–6. There is a combined ticket for the Roman Forum, Palatine and Colosseum (the ticket is valid until the following day). Ticket offices are at the entrances to all three sites, but to avoid the queues at the Colosseum, buy your ticket either at the Forum or Palatine entrance. With it in hand you go through a separate line.

Audioguides can be hired, although the order of the visit changes according to which parts are temporarily inaccessible. The plan on p. 23 should help you to orientate yourself.

HISTORY OF THE ROMAN FORUM

The first kings of Rome drained the marshes here and paved a rectangular area as a market-place (*forum*) around 625 BC. It became the heart of the ancient city, where the inhabitants would come to see the magnificent temples and triumphal arches built by the rulers of their day, where political assemblies were held, where orators would address the people, where the senate met, where courts of justice sat in the basilicas, where the Vestal Virgins and head of the college of priests who presided over the state cult lived, and where the main religious festivals took place. It was here also that the most important funerals were staged. As Rome declined, so the Forum was gradually abandoned: its monuments were plundered for their stone and the precious marbles were burned in lime-kilns. From the Middle Ages right up until the end of the 19th century the Forum was used as a cattle pasture. Since the end of the 18th century there have been systematic excavations here, and in the 1930s some careful restoration and reconstruction was carried out.

View of the Forum, looking west. The building at the back is Palazzo Senatorio with the foundations of the ancient Tabularium beneath it. The soaring columns of the Temple of Antoninus and Faustina are visible on the right. On the left are the three columns of the Temple of Castor.

Major monuments of the Forum

NB: Excavation work is in progress in the Forum, which results in sections being temporarily closed. If not all the monuments are accessible, they are at least visible.

From the main entrance on Via dei Fori Imperiali a path descends past the immensely high side wall of the Temple of Antoninus and Faustina (*described on p. 25*) and the scant remains of the Basilica Emilia on the right. You are now at the level of the original Forum, and the path takes you out onto the **Sacra Via**, with its huge old round paving stones, the oldest street in Rome, which was the route taken by generals and emperors who had been awarded a Triumph on their way up to the Capitol to offer sacrifice at the Temple of Jupiter. The curved wall of a round altar protected by a roof is all that remains of the **Temple of Julius Caesar (1)**, thought to be the very place where Caesar was cremated when his body was brought to the Forum after his dramatic assassination on the Ides of March in 44 BC and where Mark Antony read out his will. A temple was built here some 15 years later and dedicated by Augustus to the 'Divine' Julius. Because of its association with the most famous of all Romans, this remains a hallowed spot, often honoured by a floral tribute.

The Sacra Via takes you past the site of the **Basilica Julia (2)** on the left. Today all that remains of this basilica, which consisted of a huge hall 82m long and 18m wide surrounded by a double row of columns, are the marble steps and some column bases. It served as a special court of justice which dealt with civil cases. Like many other similar Roman basilicas, the interior was divided by columns into a central nave and aisles and there was an apse at one end, a plan which was then adopted in Christian church architecture. Look out for the graffiti on the steps which served as 'board' games, where the ancient Romans could while away their time while waiting for their case to be heard.

Opposite, on a high base, rises a fluted Corinthian column called the **Column of Phocas (3)**, the last monument to be erected in the Forum (in 608). Where the low fence opens out you can see (under cover) the **Lacus Curtius (4)**, a paved area beside a cast of a bas-relief of a horse and rider. This was once a pond, presumably a remnant of the marsh in this area, but traditionally explained with the charming story that in 362 BC a great chasm opened here which the soothsayers said would only be closed when Rome's greatest treasure was cast into it. A young Roman called Marcus Curtius,

announcing that Rome possessed no greater treasure than a brave citizen, rode his horse into the abyss, which promptly closed.

On the other side of the Column of Phocas, close to the Arch of Septimius Severus, a mound of rubble and brick arches is all that remain of the **Imperial Rostra (5)**, the platform from which speakers would address the crowds in the Forum. It was called thus after the *rostra*, the iron prows of the ships captured in sea battles which used to be set up here as a demonstration of the might of Rome.

At the foot of the Capitoline Hill can be seen the columns of various temples. Eight columns, nearly 11m high with part of the entablature, survive of the pronaos of the **Temple of Saturn (6)**, raised on a high podium. This was one of the most ancient sanctuaries in the Forum, thought to have been inaugurated in 498 BC in honour of the mythical god-king of Italy, whose reign was the fabled Golden Age. The 'Saturnalia' on 17th December was the most important festival of the Roman year, when temporary freedom was given to slaves and presents were exchanged. It later came to be associated with New Year's Day and Christmas. The temple also served as the state treasury where gold and silver ingots and

THE ROMAN FORUM

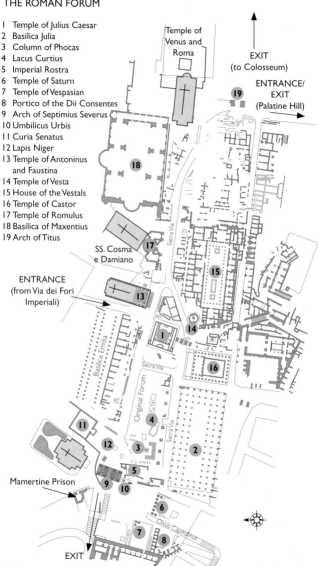

coined metal were stored. The columns that stand today date from a reconstruction in 42 BC.

On the other side of the Clivus Capitolinus, the ancient road which continues up to the Capitol (*fenced off at the time of writing*), are three high columns which once supported part of the pronaos of the sumptuous and elegant **Temple of Vespasian (7)**. To the left can be seen twelve (reconstructed) white columns forming an angle, survivors from the **(8) Portico of the Dii Consentes**, dedicated to the twelve chief gods of the Roman pantheon, the objects of a state cult which had originated with the Etruscans. The gods were first recognised as six male and six female deities who assisted Jupiter in directing his thunderbolts, but the Romans came to identify them with the most important Greek gods. The temple was rebuilt as late as AD 367 by a prefect known for his opposition to Christianity. No other pagan monument was built in the Forum after that time. New excavations have recently been carried out in the fenced-off area on the left, where besides finds from the Archaic period an interesting 12th-century district of the city has been uncovered.

One of the finest of all the monuments in the Forum is the well-proportioned triple **Arch of Septimius Severus (9)**, which has survived its 1,800 years remarkably well. It honoured the tenth anniversary of the emperor's accession. The four large reliefs depict scenes from two decisive campaigns captained by Caracalla and Geta, the sons of Septimius, in Parthia (present-day Iran), an area where a well-organised army and formidable horsemen had constituted a continuous threat to the stability of the Roman Empire since the time of Augustus. In the small friezes are symbolic Oriental figures paying homage to Rome, and at the bases of the columns are captive barbarians.

Just to the right of the arch is a cylindrical construction in brick, the **Umbilicus Urbis (10)**, thought to date from the 2nd century BC and supposed to mark the centre (the *umbilicus* or navel) of the city, and hence of the known world. Close by (covered by a roof) is the site of the **Miliarium Aureum** ('golden milestone'), a bronze-covered column set up by Augustus as the symbolic starting-point of all the roads of the Empire, with the distance from Rome to the chief cities engraved in gold letters on its base. Ever since there has been a familiar saying that 'all roads lead to Rome'.

On the other side of the arch (*roped off at the time of writing*) is the **Curia Senatus (11)**, the former senate house. It was well reconstructed in 1935–39

The bronze doors of the Temple of Romulus are the originals of the 4th century AD.

huge **Temple of Antoninus and Faustina (13)** is one of the most impressive of all the temples left standing today. With its pronaos towering above the steep flight of steps which ascends to ten huge monolithic Corinthian columns fronting the entrance, it gives one the idea of the scale of these huge buildings. It was dedicated to the Emperor Antoninus Pius and his wife Faustina (*the interior, which became a church, is closed*).

Towards the Palatine Hill can be seen a number of columns on high bases (partially reconstructed in 1930) which support a fragment of entablature as well as part of the curving cella wall: this is the **Temple of Vesta (14)**. Just behind it (approached by three or four old marble steps forming a right-angle) you can look into the considerable remains of the **House of the Vestals (15)**. It is built round a spacious courtyard surrounded by a portico and there are ponds in the centre (there is a good view from the Farnese Gardens; *see p. 31*). The task of the Vestals, the virgin priestesses of Vesta, was to keep the fire in their temple, which symbolised the perpetuity of the state, constantly alight: its extinction was the most fearful of all prodigies, as it implied the end of Rome. There were just six Vestals, chosen by the king, and later, during the Republic and the Empire, by the *pontifex maximus,*

to the appearance it had under Diocletian in 283. This was where the senate met, and the interior preserves a beautiful green and maroon pavement in opus sectile and the seating for the 300 senators. In front of it, there are plans to reopen the **Lapis Niger (12)**, where a black marble pavement marks the site of the oldest relics of the Forum, including the ancient sanctuary of Vulcan.

Behind the Arch of Septimius Severus there is an exit from the Forum, up steps to the Capitoline Hill. To see the rest of the Forum you have to retrace your steps and follow the Sacra Via in the opposite direction. The a post which came to be reserved for the emperor himself. Girls between six and ten years of age from patrician families could be candidates. After her election, bound by a vow of chastity, a Vestal lived in the House of the Vestals for 30 years: ten learning her duties, ten performing them, and ten teaching novices. Inside the temple was a venerated statue of Pallas Athena, the *Palladium*, supposedly brought from Troy by Aeneas.

Three tall columns with their entablature are all that now survive of the **Temple of Castor** (or the Dioscuri) **(16)** built to honour the twin sons of Zeus, Castor and Pollux, who according to legend had led the Roman cavalry to victory over the Etruscans at Lake Regillus in 484 BC and who, during the fighting, had miraculously also appeared here beside the Temple of Vesta watering their horses.

Return now to the Sacra Via. The next building on the left is the so-called **Temple of Romulus (17)**, a circular building also converted into a church (a hall of which is visible from the church of Santi Cosma e Damiano; *described on p. 42*). From here you can see its green bronze doors (*illustrated on previous page*) which have, incredibly enough, closed the entrance ever since the 4th century. Continuing slightly

uphill, a path on the left leads to the **Basilica of Maxentius (18)**, which dominates many of the views of the Forum. Here you can stand beneath the three vast barrel-vaulted niches—over 20m wide and 24m high—which are from the north aisle of a basilica 100m long, begun by Maxentius in AD 306 and completed by Constantine. They are one of the largest and most impressive examples of Roman architecture to have survived anywhere. The building used to be the seat of the city prefects.

The Sacra Via leads up to the **Arch of Titus (19)**, a beautiful, perfectly-proportioned single archway (well restored in the 19th century). It is thought to have been erected by Domitian just after the death of Titus in AD 81 to celebrate his victory in the Judaean War, which ended with the sack of Jerusalem in AD 70. The two reliefs inside are well preserved: one shows the triumphal procession bringing the war booty back from Jerusalem, including the seven-branched golden candlestick (or Menorah), the symbol of Judaism, and the other Titus in the Imperial quadriga accompanied by a winged figure of Victory and guided by the goddess Roma. In the centre of the panelled vault the deified emperor is shown mounted on an eagle.

THE PALATINE HILL

On the high hill above the Roman Forum, the Palatine today seems remarkably isolated from the traffic-ridden streets at its foot. It is inhabited by birds (and cats) and is covered with wild flowers in spring beneath its magnificent trees. There are areas where you can wander amidst the ruins and others where excavations are protected by roofs, and you can see some wall paintings in the house where Augustus lived. There are also lovely gardens, well kept and peaceful.

Map p. 223, D3–D4. Open 9–6. For admission, see p. 20 above. The ticket includes admission to the Palatine Museum and House of Augustus. The Palatine, like the Forum, has very little labelling, and can be confusing to visit. It is perhaps helpful to consider it divided into three main areas, described in the order below. The first are the open ruins in the area of the hill around the museum building, including the Palace of Domitian; the second area, including the House of Augustus, takes in the covered excavations on the western part of the hill; and the last area, approached by a cryptoporticus, is that of the Farnese Gardens on the summit towards the Forum.

HISTORY OF THE PALATINE

Research suggests that the hill was inhabited sporadically by the late Bronze Age (13th–12th centuries). Traces of occupation going back to the 9th century BC have been discovered during excavations. It was here that the original city was founded, and legend relates that the twins Romulus and Remus were nursed by the she-wolf here, in a cave at the hill's foot. During the Republican era some prominent citizens, including Cicero, built their houses here. Later, splendid Imperial palaces were built over its slopes, so that the word Palatine came to be synonymous with the palace of the emperor (and hence the word 'palace'). In the 16th century the Farnese family created the gardens on the part of the hill overlooking the Forum, and excavations, begun in the 18th century, continue to this day.

The Palace of Domitian: From beside the Arch of Titus in the Roman Forum, a broad path, on the line of the Clivus Palatinus (the round paving stones of which are still preserved in places), leads

The so-called Stadium, part of the Palace of Domitian.

uphill (on the right steps ascend to the Farnese Gardens; *described on p. 31*). You can just see the Palatine museum building up ahead beyond a cedar tree. Beyond a row of olive trees the path reaches a T-junction where you should take the path to the left. This path continues across the hillside towards the entrance on Via San Gregorio (*see plan overleaf*), but turn right instead towards the solitary pine on a little mound to see the remains of walls and foundations of the Palace of Domitian, a vast collection of buildings brilliantly planned for the emperor by the architect Rabirius. In this area was the peristyle of the emperor's private residence, the so called **Domus Augustana (1)**. Some of the romantic ruins have been left standing above fragments of their once sumptuous marble paving.

Behind the museum building you can look down into a court some ten metres below ground level where there were living rooms and fountain courts. At the eastern limit, again below ground level, is the so-called **Stadium (2)**, which was probably a garden sometimes used as a hippodrome. There is a wonderful view of it from above. On the other side of the museum was the official palace, the **Domus Flavia (3)**. Here can be seen the spacious peristyle with an impluvium in the middle in the form of an octagonal maze surrounding a fountain. The throne room, **Aula Regia (4)**, is to the north of the peristyle and the triclinium or banqueting hall is to the south (close to a 16th-century building), paved with coloured marbles, which are well preserved in the apse. On either side was a court with an oval fountain, one of which still has a magnificent pavement in *opus sectile*.

The Palatine Museum: The museum **(5)** houses material from excavations on the hill. On the ground floor the earliest prehistoric hut village (9th–8th centuries BC) found on the hill is documented. On the upper floor the gallery (IX) has sculptures including a colossal (headless) statue of Cybele found in her temple, and a statuette of a satyr turning round to look at his tail. But the most interesting exhibits are in Rooms V–VII, where there are beautiful painted terracotta panels (28 BC) with reliefs of paired figures, and three black marble herms, and a fragment of a wall painting from the 1st century BC showing Apollo with his lyre against a bright blue ground. In Room VI are fragments of beautiful marble intarsia pavements and panels which once decorated walls, as well as exquisite frescoes of Homeric subjects, all dating from the 1st century AD.

The House of Augustus and covered excavations: Signposted (left) from the museum entrance is the western part of the hill, where all the ruins have been covered with roofs to protect them. They include some very beautiful wall paintings in the **House of Augustus (6)**. The house belonged to Rome's first emperor (r. 27 BC–AD

14). He had his private living quarters here as well as rooms for public ceremonies and two libraries. You can see three rooms on the ground floor with remains of frescoes, where wonderful vivid red and green hues predominate. The first still has a painted barrel vault with green, maroon and red coffers, but the last and smallest is the best preserved. Here the bright red walls have Corinthian columns in perfect perspective in front of them, and above there is an imitation marble frieze and, at the top, a delicate frieze of tritons and sea horses. Outside you can climb the modern iron stairs to look through a glass door into the 'Studiolo', probably used by the emperor as a private study, where the exquisite frescoes are even

Detail of *trompe l'oeil* wall paintings in the House of Augustus.

THE PALATINE HILL

1 Domus Augustana
2 Stadium
3 Domus Flavia
4 Aula Regia
5 Palatine Museum
6 House of Augustus
7 Temple of Apollo
8 House of Livia
9 Temple of Cybele
10 Cryptoporticus
11 Farnese Gardens

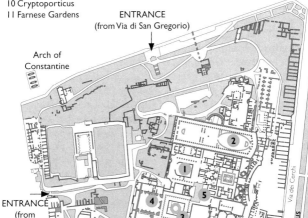

ENTRANCE
(from Via di San Gregorio)

Arch of
Constantine

ENTRANCE
(from
Forum)

Aviaries

better preserved, with a barrel vault decorated with grotesques and winged figures, and on the walls sophisticated architectural perspectives and painted figures. During excavations begun in the 1960s the basement of the renowned **(7) Temple of Apollo**, with Greek and Latin libraries attached, was identified close by. It is known that this was dedicated by Augustus in 28 BC after his victory at the Battle of Actium, when Mark Antony and Cleopatra were defeated.

Return the way you came and follow the path in front of the modern flat-roofed brick building enclosing the so-called **House of Livia (8)** (probably in fact part of the House of Augustus himself, and not that of his wife Livia), with more very fine wall paintings (*but not at present open to the public*) and then left past a round cistern (under cover). A short flight of steps leads up. On the left is the site in 191 BC of the **Temple of Cybele (9)**, the great mother goddess of Anatolia, called *Magna Mater* by the Romans. Hers was one of the many foreign cults introduced into the city. In the large (covered) area of excavations where the path ends you can just make out some round holes in the tufa rock which mark the position of a hut village which occupied this site in the early Iron Age (9th century BC). The cave sanctuary of the she-wolf, known as the Luper-

cal, connected with the legend of Romulus and Remus and sacred to Rome, was also in this part of the hill, as well as a hut known as the House of Romulus.

The Farnese Gardens: You should now retrace your steps to the cistern (ignore the steps signposted left to the Farnese Gardens). In front of the cistern another path leads down to the well preserved **cryptoporticus (10)**. Barrel-vaulted underground corridors were a feature of many grand Roman villas, providing a pleasant means of passing from one area to another without disturbing the rooms above and without having to go outside in the rain or hot sun. This one is still 130m long and its perfectly proportioned space is still inducive to taking a cool stroll on a hot summers' day. Where the vaulting has been preserved, it receives light and air from the windows set high up on the east side. It still has some tiny herringbone paving and simple mosaic floor (but the fragments of stucco decoration in the vault are copies of the originals). It was built by Nero as part of his Domus Aurea (*see p. 35*). At the end it bends right and emerges near the Clivus Palatinus: before this, take the stairs to the left under an arch which lead up to the **Farnese Gardens (11)**. At the top is a pretty little fountain with a papyrus pool and the beautifully planted gardens with box hedges and orange trees and twin pavilions used as aviaries. They were laid out by Vignola in the middle of the 16th century for Cardinal Alessandro Farnese, grandson of Pope Paul III. Delightful paths can be followed through the well-kept gardens. There is a partial view of the Forum and in particular of the three huge arches of the Basilica of Maxentius.

The gardens cover the site of the so-called **Domus Tiberiana**, almost nothing of which is visible here, although its substructures can be clearly seen from the Forum. This area of the hill was a residential area during the Republican period, and then Nero used it for the central building of his huge Domus Aurea (*see p. 35*), which extended all the way across the valley later occupied by the Colosseum up to the Esquiline Hill. The palace here was reconstructed by Domitian (who seems to have called it the Domus Tiberiana) and extended by Hadrian.

It is now best to take the monumental flight of steps down between the twin pavilions to regain the level of the Forum. If you wish to visit the Colosseum (using the same ticket), leave by the gate beyond the Arch of Titus.

THE COLOSSEUM

Map p. 223, E3. Open 9–6. For admission, with the same Roman Forum and Palatine ticket, see p. 20 above.

This famous monument is the largest amphitheatre ever built by the Romans, and it is especially impressive on the northeast side. It has been an emblem of Rome's eternity for centuries. The Venerable Bede (c. 673–735) quotes a prophecy made by Anglo Saxon pilgrims: 'While the Colisaeus stands, Rome shall stand; when the Colisaeus falls, Rome shall fall: when Rome falls, the world shall fall'. The Colosseum was begun by Vespasian in AD 70 and completed just ten years later by his son Titus. Under the emperors the inhabitants of ancient Rome enjoyed coming here to see gladiators (mostly prisoners of war, slaves, or condemned convicts) fight man to man in single combat until one of them was killed; or wild animals, including crocodiles, lions, elephants and tigers, which were shipped to Rome to provide spectacles here. The building was many times restored and has survived damage by fire and earthquake, as well as pillaging down the centuries for its travertine. Travellers to Rome in the 19th

Detail of the Colosseum showing the columns rising through the orders, from Doric at the bottom through Ionic to Corinthian at the top.

century particularly admired the Colosseum's romantic ruined state before the restoration work was begun on it which continues to this day. There are also excavations in progress just outside the southern end.

The exterior

The mighty wall, 545m in circumference, has four storeys. The building used to have 80 entrances, through the archways flanked by engaged Doric columns (beyond these the spectators could easily reach the concentric vaulted corridors which gave access to the staircases and passageways up to their seats). Above, the arches are flanked by Ionic columns in the central storey and Corinthian columns on the upper storey. The top floor is decorated with slender Corinthian pilasters, and here also can be seen a row of projecting corbels. Over two hundred wooden poles used to stand on these which, when inserted through the holes in the cornice above, protruded above the top of the building to support a huge awning which protected the audience from the sun. Where the travertine facing has survived on the exterior you can see the sockets which were made for the iron clamps which originally held the blocks together—but even these were torn out in later centuries.

The interior

Though more than two thirds of the original masonry has been removed, the magnificence of the interior, which could probably hold more than 50,000 spectators, can still be appreciated. The floor of the arena in the centre has long since disappeared so that what you see today are the vaults which supported it and the shafts where the mechanism for the scenery was kept. A wall, some five metres high, would have protected the spectators from the violence taking place in the arena. Above and behind it was a broad terrace reserved for the emperor and distinguished spectators, and the rest of the interior was filled with the tiers of seats. These no longer survive; what you now see are the substructures which supported them and the vaulted passageways which provided access to them. The general populace, including women and slaves, were only allowed access to the topmost storeys.

The valley of the Colosseum

The **Arch of Constantine** (*map p. 223, D3*) is a very well preserved, beautifully proportioned triple triumphal arch erected in AD 315 in honour of Constantine's victory over a rival emperor, Maxentius, at the Milvian Bridge just north of the city centre. Two years previously Constantine had granted freedom of worship to Christians within the Empire and his victory is recorded as 'divinely inspired', though not explicitly by the Christian god. The reliefs on the lower part **(A)** including the victories and captives at the base of the columns and those in the spandrels of the arches, as well as the oblong reliefs above, were all carved at this time. Critics have noted a certain stylisation in the art; it is not as interesting or individualistic as the sculpture of the

earlier Imperial era and seems to prefigure the formulaic norms of Byzantine art. The sculpture on the upper part of the arch **(B)**—the eight large medallions, and the high-reliefs set into the attic, together with the eight statues of Dacians as well as the splendid large reliefs on the inside of the central archway—all dates from previous centuries.

Some columns and a terrace with a garden on a rise towards the Roman Forum are all that remains of the largest temple ever built in Rome, the **Temple of Venus and Roma**, built at the time of Hadrian and thought to have been designed by the emperor himself.

At the junction of Via Labicana with Viale Colosseo and Via Nicola Salvi is a gate into the public gardens on the Oppian Hill, 50m beyond which is the enclosure around remains of Nero's **Domus Aurea** (*map p. 223, E3*), now underground. Although this is extremely interesting for its architecture and fragments of wall paintings and stuccoes, it is mostly closed indefinitely for restoration and only a small part of it can at present be visited by previous appointment (*for information T: 06 3996 7700 and www.pierreci.it*).

FOOD & DRINK NEAR THE FORUM & PALATINE

There are a number of little fountains with running water in the Forum and on the Palatine Hill where you can have a refreshing drink of Rome's excellent water. The Farnese Gardens on the Palatine Hill are a good place for a picnic.

The most inviting cafés and restaurants in the area are in Via Madonna dei Monti (*map p. 223, D3*). To reach it, cross the busy Via dei Fori Imperiali opposite the entrance to the Roman Forum and traverse the little garden at the foot of the stump of a medieval tower towards the Hotel Forum. There are a number of little restaurants here, including the simple **Pizzeria Leonina** at no. 83 (*opposite the end of Via dell'Angeletto; open daily*). This is just a long narrow shop, with a very small counter with stools where you can eat an excellent pizza served on a wooden board, cut into finger-size pieces. No pretension whatsoever. **La Bottega del Caffè** (*Piazza Madonna dei Monti 5*) is a pleasant café with tables outside by the fountain. A place to have a light lunch or enjoy a drink before dinner.

THE IMPERIAL FORA

The area adjoining the Roman Forum (*map pp. 222–23, C2–D2*), where the emperors built other fora with temples dedicated to their favourite gods, was hurriedly and inconclusively excavated by Mussolini before he laid out the wide, processional Via dei Fori Imperiali between the Colosseum and Piazza Venezia. The road has become an important traffic artery and plans to eliminate it have proved impracticable. Nevertheless, systematic excavations are now being carried out and important studies are being made of the ruins for the first time. The busy road itself, the proximity of the popular Colosseum, and ongoing excavation all make this a difficult part of town to visit. The excellent Museo dei Fori Imperiali is a compensation, however. It explains the complicated history of the fora and preserves some of their architectural elements, including sculptures which were, amazingly enough, found here just a year or so ago. Via dei Fori Imperiali is closed to traffic on Sunday, so that is the best day to come here.

HISTORY OF THE IMPERIAL FORA

As Rome's population grew and the original Forum became too crowded, new fora began to be built on land to the north. The first step was taken by Julius Caesar, who built his forum just outside the existing Forum (and with an entrance from it) during the decade preceding his death in 44 BC. The Forum of Augustus was built round the Temple of Mars Ultor, commemorating the Battle of Philippi (42 BC) at which Augustus avenged the murder of Caesar by Brutus and Cassius. The Temple of Peace was erected by Vespasian with the spoils of a military campaign in Judaea (AD 70), and the Forum of Trajan, the last to be built, was completed by Hadrian in honour of his deified predecessor.

By the early 9th century, orchards and cultivated fields had mostly covered what remained of the ruins after they had been rifled for their marbles, and in the 16th century a residential district grew up here. Hasty clearance of the area was undertaken by Mussolini in 1924 to make way for his Via dei Fori Imperiali. It is only in the last few decades that serious studies have begun to be made.

Trajan's Column

This famous column (*map p. 222, C2*), now flanked by two little twin churches with domes (the first built in the 16th and the second in the 18th century), is still almost intact and is generally considered to be the masterpiece of Roman sculptural art, although the name of the artist is unknown. It was dedicated to Trajan by Hadrian in memory of his military achievements in two campaigns (AD 101–02 and 105–06) which led to the conquest of the Dacians (the inhabitants of what is now Romania). The spiral frieze illustrates in detail the various phases of the battles and shows the emperor himself with his soldiers as well as the enemy armies; it is clear that Hadrian wished to emphasise the dignity of the defeated as well as the victors. Numerous naturalistic details include plants and animals. It is difficult to appreciate the beautiful carving with the naked eye today: it is presumed that originally the column would have been clearly visible from the neighbouring buildings which surrounded it. The ashes of Trajan, who died in Cilicia (in modern-day Turkey) in 117, and of his wife Plotina, were placed in a golden urn in a vault below the column. A statue of the emperor crowned the top (replaced in 1588 by a figure of St Peter), and this practice of glorifying a heroic figure was many times copied

Detail from a cast of Trajan's Column showing a group of Dacian prisoners inside a Roman fort.

in later centuries (such as in Nelson's Column in Trafalgar Square in London). Trajan was always acclaimed as one of Rome's greatest emperors—it was during his reign that the Roman Empire reached its greatest extent—and was the first and probably the only emperor allowed burial in the centre of the city.

The Forum and Markets of Trajan around the column are now incorporated in the visit to the Museo dei Fori Imperiali.

The Museo dei Fori Imperiali

Map p. 223, D2. Open 9–6 except Mon. The entrance near the Column of Trajan was closed at the time of writing; steps (close to the Column) lead up to another entrance on Via IV Novembre (and Largo Magnanapoli). Labelling is excellent, also in English.

The area known as the **Markets of Trajan** was built in the first years of the 2nd century AD and became an integral part of the monumental group of buildings which made up the Forum of Trajan, which in the opinion of ancient writers was unequalled in the world. Their architect was almost certainly Apollodorus of Damascus, whom the emperor called to Rome from his native Syria. To make room for them, this area of the city, in the saddle between the Capitoline and Quirinal hills, had to be excavated to a depth of some 30m. Although always known as 'markets', many of these vaulted rooms are likely to have served for official ceremonies and as administrative offices as well as individual shops and workshops, most of which were in the great hemicycle.

The entrance leads straight into an ancient large rectangular hall, two storeys high with six rooms off each side of each floor. The exhibits on the **ground floor** provide an introduction to their history. In the centre of the ancient hall is a fine reconstruction of part of a portico from the Forum of Augustus (the caryatid is a cast). The side rooms contain a particularly significant piece of sculpture from each of the fora. The first room off the right side displays a colossal marble head found in the Forum of Trajan in 2005, dating from the 1st century AD (and reused three centuries later to provide a portrait of Constantine). The third room has a charming frieze of cupids from the temple in the Forum of Caesar (reconstructed by Trajan in AD 113), and in the fourth is a gilded bronze foot found in the Forum of Augustus and thought to have belonged to a winged statue of Victory on the exterior of the temple there.

On the **upper floor** are finds from inside the temple in the Forum of Augustus, including a magnificent capital with winged horses. Some of the most impressive pieces, all from the Forum of Augustus, are displayed in a **central block** of the markets. They include parts of the colossal statue of the deified Augustus, some 11m high, which was kept in a room beside the temple (in the pavement the original paving has been reproduced with the two footprints to give you an idea of the size). Here also are what survives of the very unusual painted decoration, with bright blue and red festoons, made on the white marble slabs which lined the walls of the room.

Outside you can walk along the huge round paving stones of the ancient **Via Biberatica**. Below is the great hemicycle of the markets with its arcaded front. The semicircle ends on either side in a well-preserved apsidal hall. In the upper row there were twelve shops and on the lower level a series of rooms, some of which still have black and white mosaic floors, presumably used as public offices.

The ancient paved Via della Torre leads to the garden at the foot of the **Torre delle Milizie**, a huge medieval tower thought to date from the mid-13th century when it was the keep of a castle. It remains one of the highest buildings in the city centre and is a conspicuous feature on the skyline. It was originally even higher and, on the edge of this part of the medieval town, would have been visible for many miles. It acquired its lean after an earthquake in 1348.

It is well worth climbing up to the terrace high above the market buildings, from which there is a fine view of the Imperial Fora and St Peter's in the distance. The little Renaissance loggia which can be seen here belongs to the **Casa dei Cavalieri di Rodi**, seat of the Roman priorate of the Order of the Knights of St John of Jerusalem.

You can follow the Via Biberatica round the small hemicycle of the markets, back to the exit.

Forum of Trajan

The Forum of Trajan itself can usually be visited (*though it was closed at the time of writing*). The ancient entrance was to the north, behind the Column of Trajan, and the column itself was flanked by two rectangular buildings several stories high, possibly used as libraries. The roofed Basilica Ulpia, with its double row of columns, had an apse at each of its two short ends, and beyond it was the large open piazza of the forum proper, surrounded by porticoes and with exedrae on the long sides. In the centre towards the south was the bronze statue of the emperor, over 12m high. The last element of the forum was a small courtyard (adjoining the Forum of Augustus). When open, you can see considerable remains of the columns of the Basilica Ulpia and part of its pavement in coloured marbles and, lying on the ground

THE IMPERIAL FORA
(RECONSTRUCTION OF THE SITE)

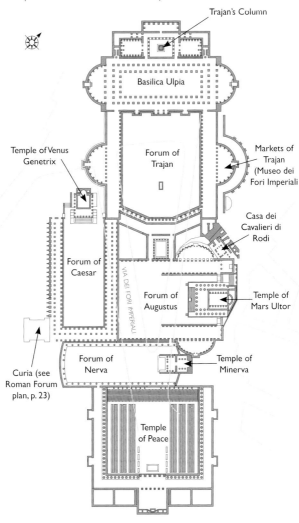

Trajan's Column

Basilica Ulpia

Temple of Venus Genetrix

Forum of Trajan

Markets of Trajan (Museo dei Fori Imperiali)

Casa dei Cavalieri di Rodi

Forum of Caesar

VIA DEI FORI IMPERIALI

Forum of Augustus

Temple of Mars Ultor

Curia (see Roman Forum plan, p. 23)

Forum of Nerva

Temple of Minerva

Temple of Peace

nearer the Column of Trajan, fragments of its colossal grey granite columns, some of the largest ever found in Rome.

Forum of Caesar

The first of the Imperial Fora (inaugurated in 46 BC) was centred round the **Temple of Venus Genetrix**, the most important building erected in the city by Julius Caesar, who claimed descent from the goddess. The temple's high base remains and three of its fluted Corinthian columns have been re-erected. The forum itself was an open piazza surrounded on three sides by two rows of columns raised on three steps and paved in white marble. Well below the level of the temple the three steps of the southwestern colonnade can clearly be seen, and most of the columns are still standing. Excavations in 1998–2006 found tombs of the 10th century BC here as well as various strata of a medieval district of the city. Via di San Pietro in Carcere descends to the church of San Giuseppe dei Falegnami, beneath which is the **Mamertine Prison** (*map p. 23; open 9–5*), a dank underground space where St Peter and St Paul were believed to have been imprisoned before their martyrdom.

Forum of Nerva and Temple of Peace

Begun by Domitian, this forum was completed after his assassination by his successor Nerva, whose brief rule of less than two years (AD 96–98) was nevertheless marked by enlightened and humanitarian government. All that remains of the forum itself are a few cracked marble slabs. Ruins of a temple, perhaps dedicated to Minerva, can be seen across Via dei Fori Imperiali. More remnants of the medieval city, recently unearthed, can also be seen here. Beside a length of lovely mottled marble used for a column is a fragment of the perimeter wall of the **Temple of Peace** (later called the Forum of Peace). By another similar column can be seen remains of its pavement. This was built in AD 71–75 by Vespasian, with the spoils of the Jewish War, to commemorate the end of the civil war which followed the death of Nero. Instead of a piazza, it had a large garden decorated with six low brick walls, on the top of which water constantly flowed along little marble channels beside which flower pots apparently contained 'Gallic' roses. The walls have been partly reconstructed and beside them you can see a few fragments of the marble channels. At the end are rows of pots with plants above stacks of column lengths found during the excavations. Towards the Roman Forum can be seen a long base with steps which was part of the surrounding portico which incorporated the temple itself.

A rectangular hall near the temple, used to house the city plans and public property registers, had one of its walls decorated with the *Forma Urbis*, a famous plan of the ancient city carved in some 150 marble blocks. The first fragments were found here in 1562 and another 24 pieces were only unearthed in 1999.

Forum of Augustus

On the other side of Via dei Fori Imperiali you can look down into this forum, dominated by the ruins of the **Temple of Mars Ultor** (Mars the 'Avenger'), built to commemorate the victory of 42 BC when Caesar's assassins Cassius and Brutus were defeated at the Battle of Philippi. Three tall fluted columns with Corinthian capitals supporting an architrave are still standing at the end of the right flank. A broad flight of very high steps ascends to the capacious pronaos where four of the eight Corinthian columns have been partly reconstructed from antique fragments. This was one of the most honoured temples in the Empire. On either side are the three marble steps which led up to the surrounding porticoes. The high wall behind, some 30m high and still partly standing, was built to isolate the forum from the Subura, a crowded and insalubrious residential district.

The 'Colonnacce' of the Temple of Peace

To the right of the Forum of Augustus, very close to the road, are two enormous Corinthian columns in purple and white marble which have survived from the colonnade on the northeast side of the temple in the Forum of Nerva. These have always been known affectionately by the Romans as the *Colonnacce*. In the attic between them is a high relief of a female figure wearing a helmet (usually identified as Minerva/Athena) and in the rich frieze of the entablature women are shown sewing and weaving. After the discovery in 1999 of another female figure, scholars believe the iconographical programme of this temple may have centred on personifications of the provinces symbolising the success of the Roman Empire in bringing peace and unification

The church of Santi Cosma e Damiano

Map p. 223, D3. Open 9–1 & 3–7. Entrance just to the left of the entrance to the Roman Forum.

This large hall, probably once part of the Imperial Fora, was converted into a church in 527 by Pope Felix IV, who also commissioned the beautiful mosaics with fascinating details on the triumphal arch and in the apse (*coin-operated light*). One of the figures is Felix him-

Detail of St Paul from the 6th-century apse mosaic in the church of Santi Cosma e Damiano.

self, holding a model of the church; it is the earliest papal portrait known. In the apse are Sts Cosmas and Damian being presented to Christ at His Second Coming by Sts Peter and Paul. Below them, four rivers symbolising the Gospels flow from the mount on which the Lamb stands, and twelve other lambs represent the Apostles, with townscapes of Bethlehem and Jerusalem on either side. These mosaics clearly inspired other such decoration in the early Christian churches in Rome. The iconography still owes much to the pagan world. Christ, robed in the Imperial purple and gold, holds a scroll like a Classical orator, and St Peter and St Paul, in their white togas, have the appearance of Roman senators.

At the west end a huge window provides a good view into the circular Temple of Romulus in the Roman Forum (see p. 26).

For food and drink suggestions in nearby Via Madonna dei Monti, see p. 35.

THE CORSO

The Corso is Rome's most famous street: it runs in a dead straight line all the way from Piazza Venezia (with the vast white monument to Vittorio Emanuele II; *map p. 222, C2*) to Piazza del Popolo. Lined with grand palaces, Baroque churches and elegant shops, it passes the prime minister's official residence and the Italian parliament building and is always busy with pedestrians and traffic. If you are in a hurry, it is a good idea to keep to the side streets on the left as far as the parliament building (Piazza del Parlamento), and then to the streets off its right side from Via delle Vite north, although it finally becomes much quieter in its last stretch from the church of Santi Ambrogio e Carlo up to Piazza del Popolo.

HISTORY OF THE CORSO

The Corso has been one of the most important thoroughfares in the city since Roman times when it was the urban section of the Via Flaminia, the main road which led north from the capital. At that time it was called Via Lata ('broad way') because it was wider than the other roads of the ancient city. Its present name is derived from the riderless horse races inaugurated here by Pope Paul II in 1466 and which became a celebrated event (*corso* means race). The Corso of Rome subsequently gave its name to the main street in numerous other Italian cities.

Galleria Doria Pamphilj

Near the beginning of the Corso on the left is the huge exterior of Palazzo Doria Pamphilj. Though not particularly easy to appreciate from the street, the façade, built in 1734 is perhaps the finest and most balanced Rococo work in the city. It is by Gabriele Valvassori, an architect who worked in Rome exclusively for the Doria Pamphilj, one of the foremost Roman noble families. They have resided here ever since the 17th century.

Map p. 222, C2. Entrance at Via del Corso 305. Open daily 10–5. Rearrangement was under way at the time of writing. You are lent an audio guide with your ticket. Café on the ground floor.

Above left: Bust of Benedetto Pamphilj by Alessandro Algardi. Algardi was a rival of Bernini, and had it not been for the success of the latter, would have been the foremost sculptor of his day (the mid-17th century) in Rome. The bust on the right is Pope Innocent X, by Bernini.

This is the most important of the patrician art collections to have survived in the city. Period rooms, richly decorated in white, red and gold, and beautifully maintained, provide a sumptuous setting for the fine paintings, and a memorable atmosphere of grand living and elegance prevails. The collection was begun in 1651 by the Pamphilj pope Innocent X. Important additions were made when his nephew Camillo married Olimpia Aldobrandini, widow of Paolo Borghese, and in 1760 when Prince Andrea Doria added his family bequests.

Highlights of the collection

NB: At the time of writing the collection was undergoing extensive rearrangement. The main masterpieces are highlighted below.

From the central courtyard, a grand staircase leads up to the **Salone Aldobrandini**, which is decorated with antique sculptures. Two early masterpieces by Caravaggio (also two of the most famous works in the collection) are to be hung here. They are both of sacred subjects but with extraordinarily innovative iconography. The most striking element in the ***Rest on the Flight into Egypt*** is the elegant figure of a young angel playing the Child to sleep, while the ***Penitent Magdalen*** shows the desolate figure of Mary abandoned in a bare 'room'. Caravaggio evidently used the same model for both Mary Magdalen and the Madonna.

Drinking fountain in the Via Lata.

On the left the **Salone Verde** is to contain the earliest works in the collection, including a lovely *Annunciation* by Filippo Lippi and two predella panels by his less well-known contemporary Pesellino.

Opposite the Salone Verde a few steps lead up into the first of four magnificent galleries arranged around a courtyard, where the paintings decorate the walls in great profusion. Some of the best works are a **double portrait by Raphael** and *Salome with the Head of St John the Baptist* by **Titian**. Paintings by Annibale Carracci, a member of the Bolognese school of painters, who came to work in Rome in 1595, include a *Flight into Egypt*. The leading 17th-century painters of this school, Guido Reni and Guercino, are also well represented. There are landscapes by Claude Lorrain, born in France but who worked all his life in Rome and died here in 1682 (*Mercury stealing the Oxen of Apollo* is one of his finest works).

The **Dutch school** is also very well represented, with a *Deposition* by Hans Memling and genre scenes (including *The Usurers*) by Quinten Massys from the 15th century, as well as works by Pieter Brueghel the Elder, the greatest Netherlandish painter of the 16th century and his son Jan Brueghel the Elder.

The most magnificent of the galleries is the **Galleria degli Specchi**. At one end of it is the little Cabinet, which preserves the gem of the collection, a superb **portrait of Innocent X** commissioned by this Pamphilj pope in 1650 from the great Spanish painter Velázquez when he was staying in Rome. Beside it is a sculpted **bust by Bernini** of the same pope.

The First Gallery leads into a series of **state rooms**, with their creaky parquet floors, once used by the family for receptions and balls, off which can be seen (but not entered) some of the rooms they still use (although the doors into them are kept closed when the family is in residence, usually at weekends). The ballroom was decorated with silk hangings at the end of the 19th century. The family chapel, the dimensions of which give it the appearance of a small church, was designed by Carlo Fontana in 1691. Another room, with late 18th-century red velvet wall-hangings, contains two fine **busts by Alessandro Algardi** of Innocent X and Benedetto Pamphilj (he also carved the bust of Olimpia Aldobrandini Pamphilj at the end of one of the four galleries).

You leave the palace from a room hung with 17th-century landscapes by Gaspard Dughet, brother-in-law of the great French painter Nicolas Poussin, but who was often also confusingly known as 'Il Poussin'. The exit takes you out onto Piazza del Collegio Romano: in Via Lata on the way back to the Corso, don't miss the charming little fountain of a sturdy porter in a beret holding a (leaking) barrel, placed conveniently low down so it is easy to have a drink from it.

Galleria Colonna

Map p. 222, C2. Entrance at Via della Pilotta 17. Open Sat only 9–1. A list of paintings in numerical order is given to visitors at the entrance beyond the charming old turnstile gate.

If it happens to be a Saturday morning, it is well worth crossing over the Corso at this point to visit another splendid Roman *palazzo*. Take Via Santi Apostoli into Piazza Santi Apostoli, one whole side of which is occupied by Palazzo Colonna which incorporates the church of Santi Apostoli (*described below*).

There were numerous cardinals in the venerable Roman Colonna family as well as a pope, Oddone, who lived in a palace on this site as Martin V (*see p. 9*) from 1424 until his death in 1431. The most famous member of the family was Marcantonio, the admiral who commanded the papal contingent at the Battle of Lepanto in 1571, when the Christian armies defeated the Ottomans, whose hopes of becoming a naval power were destroyed.

The very fine collection of paintings, begun in the 17th century with the help of the painter Carlo Maratta, is arranged in magnificent Baroque galleries on the *piano nobile*, sumptuously decorated with frescoes, mirrors and antique sculpture. The setting, with its marble floors and huge columns (to suit the family name), is perhaps even more splendid than the Doria Pamphilj palace. Visitors are provided with plush red seats (and even the old-fashioned bathroom is hidden discreetly behind an ingenious painted door). From the windows you can see the hanging garden with its espaliered orange trees as well as the huge interior courtyard planted with palms and bay trees.

Highlights of the collection include Venetian works by Palma Vecchio, Tintoretto and Veronese, and *A Peasant Eating Beans*, a well-known genre work by Annibale Carracci. In the last room there is an amusing painting of the *Resurrection of Christ* by Pietro da Cortona with no fewer than five members of the Colonna family being helped out of their tombs by angels in order to follow the Saviour to heaven.

Santi Apostoli

Map p. 222, C2. Open 7–12 & 4–7. The chapel of Cardinal Bessarion is only open on Fri and Sat 8.30–11.30.

The church was rebuilt by Carlo Fontana in 1714 and the unusual façade has the appearance of a palace rather than a church. In the portico there is an exquisite bas-relief from Trajan's Forum (2nd century AD) of an eagle with outspread wings inside an oak wreath. The Baroque interior is on a vast scale, with an exceptionally broad nave. The first chapel on the south side has a beautiful late 15th-century *Madonna and Child* by Antoniazzo Romano, the most important Roman artist of his time. It was commissioned by the illustrious Greek scholar Cardinal Bessarion for his chapel just beyond the second south altar (*for opening times see above*). Here a modern walkway above interesting excavations provides a good view of the remains of very unusual frescoes illustrating stories of St Michael Archangel attributed to Antoniazzo and his workshop together with Melozzo da Forlì (the Madonna is an early 17th-century copy of the *Madonna and Child* from the first chapel). Around the door of the sacristy at the end of the north aisle is Canova's first important work in Rome (1787), the Neoclassical monument to Pope Clement XIV.

Sant'Ignazio

Back on the Corso, Via del Caravita leads off the left side into the delightful Rococo **Piazza di Sant'Ignazio** (*map p. 222, C2*), a theatrical masterpiece by Filippo Raguzzini (1728). The buildings in front of the church have curving façades which fit into a careful decorative scheme in relation to the streets between them. The effect is that of a stage set rather than a piazza.

This church (*open 7.30–12.30 & 3–7.15*), begun in 1626 to celebrate the canonisation of St Ignatius Loyola, founder of the Jesuits, rivals the principal Jesuit church, the Gesù (*see p. 76*) in magnificence. The paintings in the vaulting of the nave and apse are the masterpiece of Andrea Pozzo, himself a Jesuit, who was the greatest exponent of the *quadratura* technique, which used painted architectural elements to provide illusionistic decorations on walls and ceilings and which became extremely popular in the Baroque period. The amazing *trompe l'oeil* perspective projects the walls of the church beyond their archi-

Detail of Andrea Pozzo's magnificent *trompe l'oeil* ceiling in Sant'Ignazio (1690s), showing the triumph of St Ignatius surrounded by all the nations of the world.

tectural limits, and Pozzo even provided a cupola, never built because of the lack of funds, in a canvas 17m in diameter. The vaulting and 'dome' are best seen from a small yellow disc set in the pavement about the middle of the nave. Pozzo also designed the sumptuous transept chapels with their marble barely-sugar columns, elaborate reliefs and lapis lazuli urns.

Piazza di Pietra and Piazza Colonna

From Piazza di Sant'Ignazio Via de' Burrò leads into the peaceful square in front of the amazingly high cella wall and huge 15-m columns which belonged to the **Temple of Hadrian** (*map p. 222, C2*), built by Antoninus Pius in 145 and dedicated to his adoptive father. They are today incorporated into the façade of the Chamber of Commerce, a typical example of the ingenious and apparently casual way in which the ancient buildings of Rome often become part of later ones. (The café on the corner of Via di Pietra serves good freshly-brewed tea.)

Just to the north is the spacious **Piazza Colonna** (*map p. 222, C1*), for centuries considered the centre of the city, and important today since the huge 16th-century Palazzo Chigi here is the official residence of the Italian prime minister. In the centre of the square rises the **Column of Marcus Aurelius**, erected in 196 in honour of the philosopher-emperor to commemorate his numerous victories which delayed the barbarian invasions of Italy for several centuries. Inspired by the similar column of Trajan (*see p. 37*), it has worn bas-reliefs illustrating these military exploits, but they are very difficult to see in detail with the naked eye. The graceful fountain has a veined pink and grey basin designed in the late 16th century by the architect Giacomo della Porta.

Adjoining Piazza Colonna is **Piazza di Montecitorio** with the huge Palazzo di Montecitorio, seat of one of the houses of the Italian parliament since 1871. The building was begun for the Ludovisi family in 1650 by Bernini, who gave the façade its convex, slightly polygonal form (the huge red-brick façade on Piazza del Parlamento in Art Nouveau style was added in 1918). The Egyptian obelisk was brought to Rome by Augustus to celebrate his victory over Cleopatra, and he used it as the gnomon of a huge solar calendar near the Ara Pacis (*see opposite*) in the Campus Martius, but it has stood here since 1792.

The quietest stretch of the Corso

The Corso now narrows. Via delle Vite, on the right, is the first of several long, straight streets lined with fashionable shops between the Corso and Piazza di Spagna. Some of these are pedestrianised and the area still has a distinct air of elegance. The central and most famous street is Via dei Condotti, which has a view of the famous Spanish Steps (*see p. 56*) and is home to the Caffè Greco.

Off the left side of the Corso opens the spacious and peaceful piazza, with its cafés and restaurants, in front of the basilica of **San Lorenzo in Lucina** (*map p. 222, C1; open 8am–8pm*). The portico with six delicate Ionic columns and the campanile survive from the 12th-century church. The fourth south chapel, with pretty stuccoes in the dome, was designed by Bernini for Gabriele Fonseca, Innocent X's doctor, and the great sculptor carved Fonseca's expressive portrait bust to the left of the altar. A dramatic Crucifix by Guido Reni dominates the east end of the church. The great classical French painter Nicolas Poussin is buried here (he died in Rome after spending many years in the city).

North of Largo Carlo Goldoni the Corso becomes calmer, from here all the way up to Piazza del Popolo it is in fact closed to traffic for most of the day. The pavements widen out in front of the church of **Santi Ambrogio e Carlo al Corso**, which has a fine dome by Pietra da Cortona recalling Michelangelo's dome of St Peter's and an important feature of the city skyline. In the grand Baroque interior the high altarpiece is a particularly good work by Carlo Maratta. Maratta was the most important painter at work in Rome in the late 17th century and he interpreted the spirit of the Counter-Reformation on a grand scale.

Relief from the 1st-century AD Ara Pacis, celebrating the peace brought to the empire by Augustus.

Mausoleum of Augustus and Ara Pacis

Via dei Pontefici leads left to the conspicuous white modern building which protects the Ara Pacis, the 'altar of peace' (*map p. 220, A3*). It stands at the Tiber side of a square laid out in 1938 in monumental Fascist style around the remains of the circular **Mausoleum of Augustus**, which housed the tomb of Augustus and the principal members of his family and was revered as one of the most sacred monuments of ancient Rome. It is nowadays rather neglected and the interior is at present closed.

The **Ara Pacis** (*open 9–7 except Mon*) is a monumental ancient Roman altar housed in a building of white travertine and glass designed by Richard Meier (2006). Its inauguration, as with any contemporary project, caused quite a stir and not everyone was pleased with it; what is undeniable is that it provides a pleasant, well-lit space in which to view this great work of art, insulated from all traffic noise.

The rectangular altar, consecrated in 13 BC to celebrate the peace that Augustus had established within the Empire, was built of Luni marble and is decorated inside and out with wonderful carvings influenced by Classical Greek and Hellenistic models and representing the supreme achievement of Augustan art. The lower part of the walls have an intricate and beautiful composition of acanthus leaves on which are swans with outstretched wings. Between the jambs of the main (north) entrance are two scenes illustrating the origins of Rome, one with Aeneas, the other with the She-wolf. At the opposite entrance there is a panel with Tellus, the earth goddess, possibly intended as an allegory of Peace. In the interior, where sacrifices took place, there are beautifully carved bucrania. On the altar wall are reliefs of the sacrifice of a boar, a ram and a bull. On the exterior, the side panels illustrate the ceremony that took place during the consecration of the altar itself: the long procession includes Augustus, members of his family, state officials and priests (drawings of the frieze behind the altar explain exactly who is who).

The altar was reconstructed in 1938 from scattered remains unearthed near here from 1568 onwards, although some of the panels found their way into museums (including the Uffizi, the Louvre, and the Vatican). The excellent plans and models here clarify its history and location in the Campus Martius.

Casa di Goethe

On the last stretch of the Corso is the Casa di Goethe (*no. 18; map p. 220, B2; open 10–6 except Mon*) where Goethe stayed with the painter Johann Heinrich Tischbein during his trip to Italy in 1786–88. It contains numerous delightful informal sketches which Tischbein made of Goethe, as well as two paintings by his other painter friend Jakob Philipp Hackert, who accompanied the poet on some of his Italian travels. The little museum gives an important insight into Rome in the days of the Grand Tour.

PIAZZA DEL POPOLO

This wonderful spacious piazza (*map p. 220, A2*) was first laid out in 1538 to provide a scenic entrance to the city from Via Flaminia and the north. At the end of the same century Domenico Fontana erected the splendid obelisk here: made in Heliopolis (the hieroglyphs celebrate the glories of the pharaohs Seti I and his son Ramesses II in the 13th–12th centuries BC), it had originally been brought to Rome by Augustus after his victory over Egypt. The two twin-domed churches were added in the 17th century and the piazza was given its present symmetry by Giuseppe Valadier at the beginning of the 19th century. He added the four charming fountains with lions which spout water at the foot of the obelisk, and the elaborate twin hemicycles with more fountains and heroic Neoclassical statues. Many travellers in past centuries recorded their first arrival in Rome through the monumental Porta del Popolo, the inner face of which was redesigned in 1655 by Bernini.

Santa Maria del Popolo

Map p. 220, A2. Open 7–12 & 4–7; Sun and holidays 8–1.30 & 4.30–7.30. You are asked to make a contribution when you use the green push-button lights in some chapels and in the apse.

Dedicated to the Virgin, the church was apparently built at the expense of the city (the *popolo Romano*), hence its name.

The chapel to the left of the choir has two dramatic paintings by Caravaggio, the *Crucifixion of St Peter* and the *Conversion of St Paul*. These famous masterpieces were executed in 1600–01. The extraordinarily innovative iconography draws our attention to the naturalistic details, such as the strength of the three executioners intent on raising the cross on which St Peter, a frail old man, is already nailed, and the wonderful old cart horse as he steps carefully over the prostrate figure of Saul who has 'seen the light'. Painted in a totally different style is the *Assumption* on the chapel altar, by Annibale Carracci (*illustrated overleaf*), who also decorated the vault above.

In the north aisle, the second chapel (*at the time of writing covered for restoration*) was founded by the great banker Agostino Chigi. It is a fusion of architecture, sculpture, mosaic and painting designed for him by Raphael in 1513. Although there are no works of art here by the famous artist, he provided the design for the statue of the prophet Jonah on the left of the altar, which is the best work of his collaborator Lorenzetto, who also made the pyramidal Chigi tomb which is an integral part of Raphael's architectural scheme (derived from ancient Roman models). The altarpiece of the *Nativity of the Virgin* is by Sebastiano del Piombo (1534). After the death of Raphael and Chigi, work on the chapel was interrupted, and only completed after 1652 for Cardinal Fabio Chigi (Alexander VII) by Bernini, who made some alterations to Raphael's design. He also carved the very fine statue of Habakkuk on the right of the altar and Daniel with the lion by the entrance to the chapel as well as the marble intarsia figure of Death, with the Chigi coat of arms, in the centre of the pavement.

The church also has a number of works by the very skilled Umbrian painter Pinturicchio: the best are high up in the vault in the apse (which has a shell design, an early work by Bramante), illustrating the *Coronation of the Virgin*. In the south aisle he also carried out the fresco of the *Nativity* in the first chapel, and the altarpiece in the third chapel the walls of which are covered with more frescoes now attributed to a collaborator. Monuments to the Mellini family in the third chapel in the north aisle include works by Alessandro Algardi. There is a beautiful bronze effigy of Cardinal Pietro Foscari in the middle of the fourth

Assumption of the Virgin by Annibale Carracci (c. 1600), a superb example of the High Renaissance style, influenced by Titian.

south chapel which is attributed by some scholars (though not *in situ*) to the great Sienese artist Vecchietta (c. 1485).

To return towards Piazza di Spagna, take **Via del Babuino** (*described on p. 57*).

FOOD & DRINK AROUND THE CORSO

The vicinity of the Italian parliament and senate means that there are plenty of good cafés and restaurants in this area. The **Bar Doria** on the ground floor of Palazzo Doria Pamphilj (*map p. 222, C2; open 8–8; entrance from the gallery or from outside on Via della Gatta, off Piazza del Collegio Romano*), in delightful rooms with a fountain, is a very pleasant place to sit and enjoy a snack.

Cafè Giolitti in Via degi Uffici del Vicario (*map p. 222, B1, V.U.D.Vicario; open all day*) has been in business for many decades and now has rather a dated atmosphere but still serves good cakes and ices. It is spacious and has a quiet room inside.

Ciampini and **Vitti** are perhaps the two most pleasant cafés in the delightful Piazza San Lorenzo in Lucina (*map p. 222, C1*). They are next door to each other, and both have tables outside. Vitti looks the smartest and is the one which seems to be favoured by Romans, and it also operates as a restaurant from 10am to 10pm. Ciampini has a restaurant just round the corner in Via del Leoncino where you can have a reasonably-priced plate of pasta. Also in Via del Leoncino is the **Panetteria Cambi**, a grocery store which, unlike many others, is open throughout the day from 8am to 8pm. It bakes its own bread and *schiacciata* as well as simple cakes such as jam tarts. Although it has no seating, it is an excellent place to buy a picnic lunch.

Opposite the church of Santi Ambrogio e Carlo al Corso, the magnificent **Grand Hotel Plaza** (*see p. 171*) has a very elegant old-fashioned cocktail bar on the ground floor. In Piazza del Popolo (*map p. 220, A2*) **Rosati** is a well-known café which seems to have remained unchanged since it was founded in 1922, with its smart uniformed barmen. It is quite spacious with a room upstairs as well as seating outside. It has good cakes, and you can also have a light lunch here. Next door is the equally famous restaurant **Dal Bolognese** (*see p. 183*).

PIAZZA DI SPAGNA

This open space (*map p. 220, B3*), named after the residence of the Spanish ambassador to the Vatican, is still one of the most memorable places in all Rome, where the famous monumental flight of steps which leads up to the church of the Trinità dei Monti on the Pincio Hill provides an extraordinary backdrop. The foot of the steps is a place where Romans and tourists alike tend to come to rest briefly, whether to enjoy the delightful fountain or take a stroll up the steps themselves, or sit on a step and watch the scene. An air of elegance is provided by the peaceful pedestrian streets which converge here from the Corso and Piazza del Popolo, and it is well worth turning down them to see some of Rome's most expensive and fashionable shops.

The Spanish Steps

It was in the early 18th century that Piazza di Spagna was connected to the hillside above by a series of monumental flights of steps designed by the little-known architect Francesco de Sanctis. De Sanctis built little else of note in his lifetime, but this achievement remains a brilliant piece of town planning. The medley of charming houses which line the steps, some with garden terraces, enhance the effect, as do the obelisk and striking façade of the church at the top, whose twin bell-towers add symmetry to the scene.

The fountain (Fontana della Barcaccia), probably by Gian Lorenzo Bernini, in the form of a leaking boat, is well adapted to the low water pressure here. There are almost always people sitting on its rim to refresh themselves.

Piazza di Spagna was for centuries the focus of the artistic and literary life of the city. Foreign travellers usually lodged in the *pensioni* and hotels in the vicinity, and the British colony congregated here. Babington's old-fashioned comfortable 'tea-room' (*see p. 59*) is still open at the foot of the Spanish Steps. In an elegant pink 18th-century house with a little vine-covered terrace (at the foot of the Spanish Steps on the right) is the apartment where the poet John Keats spent the last three months of his life in 1821. It is now the **Keats-Shelley Memorial House** (*entrance at no. 26; open 10–1 & 2–6, Sat 11–2 & 3–6; closed Sun*) and retains the atmosphere of that time, when it functioned as a small *pensione*. Keats booked rooms here for himself and his friend Joseph Severn, having been advised by his doctor to spend the winter in Rome. The poet led what he himself described as a 'posthumous life' here until his death from tuberculosis on 23rd February 1821, aged 25. He is buried in Rome's Protestant Cemetery. The house was purchased in 1906 by the Keats-Shelley Memorial Association and opened to the public as a charming museum and library dedicated not only to Keats and Shelley, but also to Byron and Leigh Hunt, who likewise spent much time in Italy. There are various mementoes, including autograph letters and manuscripts and a painting of Shelley at the Baths of Caracalla by Severn. The death mask of Keats and a sketch by Severn of the poet on his deathbed are preserved in the little room where he actually died.

The fashionable streets around Piazza di Spagna

Rome's most fashionable streets, closed to traffic for most of the day, all lead in to Piazza di Spagna, either from the Corso or from Piazza del Popolo. The most famous is **Via dei Condotti** (*map p. 220, B3*), named from the conduits of one of Rome's great aqueducts, the Acqua Vergine, which ran beneath it. The street is home to the **Caffè Greco**, which for long has been Rome's most distinguished café. Founded in 1760 (and a national monument since 1953), it has a delightful old-fashioned interior with a series of little sitting-rooms with round marble-topped tables. It is decorated with personal mementoes and self-portraits of some of its most famous patrons, who included Goethe, Gogol, Berlioz, Stendhal, Baudelaire, Bertel Thorvaldsen and Wagner.

Via del Babuino, an elegant and relatively peaceful street, filled with antique shops and fashion boutiques, leads to Piazza del Popolo. Turn right up Via Alibert to see **Via Margutta** where many of the houses have vines or wisteria on the façades. Dating from the 16th century, this street was famous as the residence of numerous foreign painters in the 17th century, and it is still a street of artists. Many of the art galleries and studios have interesting courtyards and gardens facing the Pincio Hill. Today it also has a number of antique shops.

Trinità dei Monti and Villa Medici

The obelisk at the top of the Spanish Steps, probably brought to Rome in the 2nd or 3rd century AD, was set up here in 1788. The church of the Trinità dei Monti is reached by another double flight of steps, from the top of which there is a magnificent view of Rome with the dome of St Peter's in the distance. The church (*map p. 220, B3; usually open 10–1 & 4–6.30*) is attached to a convent of French Minims, and the east end (behind a locked grille) is reserved for the nuns. The third south and second north chapels contain the best works by the Tuscan artist

Daniele da Volterra, who was a close friend and follower of Michelangelo: they represent the *Assumption* and *Presentation of the Virgin*, and *Descent from the Cross*.

The Assumption of the Virgin (1548–50) by Daniele da Volterra. The painting contains a portrait of Michelangelo (the apostle with a short white beard and a pink cloak, indicating the Madonna while looking out of the painting on the far right).

From the obelisk there is a good view of the long, straight **Via Sistina** as it descends to Piazza Barberini and then ascends the Quirinal Hill. Named after Sixtus V, it is the first part of a handsome thoroughfare laid out by the pope, which ran up and down four hills of the city for some 3km past Santa Maria Maggiore all the way to Santa Croce in Gerusalemme. It was decorated at certain points by obelisks.

Viale della Trinità dei Monti continues along the side of the hill, past the **Villa Medici** (*map p. 220, B3*), whose two towers make it one of the most conspicuous buildings on the city skyline, almost always visible from a distance. Its gardens are the best preserved in the centre of Rome (*open on Wed, Sat and Sun at 9.45, 11, 12.15 and 3: you are asked to book in advance; T: 06 67611, standard@villamedici.it*). The villa was bought by Napoleon in 1801; it is now home to the Rome branch of the Académie Française.

Continuing up Viale della Trinità dei Monti, take the first path up to the right to reach the **Pincio Gardens** (*map p. 220, B2*), laid out as a Romantic park in 1809–14 by the architect and urban planner Giuseppe Valadier (his greatest achievement is Piazza del Popolo; *see p. 52*). The gardens were the most fashionable Roman *passeggiata* in the 19th century, when the aristocracy and foreign visitors came here in their carriages to hear the band play and admire the sunset over the city. Intersected by broad avenues, they have some magnificent trees and are decorated with busts of famous Italians. They feature prominently in Henry James's novella *Daisy Miller*.

The road continues over a bridge high above a road very busy with fast traffic into the gardens of the **Villa Borghese** (*described on p. 93*).

FOOD & DRINK AROUND PIAZZA DI SPAGNA

Caffè Greco (*Via dei Condotti 86; map p. 220, B3*) is one of Rome's most famous cafés, a little more costly than most other places, but your coffee is freshly ground especially for you. It is worth coming here in any case just to enjoy the slightly rarefied atmosphere. As everywhere else, table service costs a lot more, but the little tables are arranged in very charming rooms beyond the bar. Another old-established place is **Babington's**, at the foot of the Spanish Steps (*map p. 220, B3*). A double door isolates the charming old interior from the bustle of Piazza di Spagna. These English 'tea-rooms' (*open daily 9–8.15*), were founded in 1893 by two English ladies, Anna Maria Babington and Isabel Cargill. It is one of the very few places in Italy where you are not able to have a quick coffee standing up, but sit at a table and wait to be served. Home-made scones and crumpets with strawberry jam for tea, or pancakes and salad for a light luncheon or High Tea.

Ciampini café and restaurant (*Piazza della Trinità dei Monti; T: 06 678 5678; closed winter; map p. 220, B3*) has a few tables outside by the lovely fountain in front of Villa Medici. The large restaurant has tables outside or in glass-walled rooms on terraces with views over Rome.

Caffetteria Museo Atelier Canova Tadolini (*Via del Babuino 160; map p. 220, B3*) is in the former studio of Adamo Tadolini, a pupil of Canova. It remained in his family for three generations. It is still filled to the brim with models and casts, and a tiny space is arranged as a studio. Visitors are welcome to explore, and the whole place retains a very unusual atmosphere. There is a tiny bar and restaurant (with a few tables on the pavement outside).

THE PANTHEON
& PIAZZA NAVONA

The Pantheon

Map p. 222, B2. Open 8.30–7.30, Sun 9–6, holidays 9–1.

Of all the ancient Roman buildings left in the city it is the Pantheon which has survived the best and it is one of its most remarkable buildings not only in Rome but in all the ancient world. The pediment proudly states that 'Marcus Agrippa, son of Lucius, consul for the third time, had [this building] made': Agrippa's third consulate coincided with Augustus' victory over Antony and Cleopatra at Actium (31 BC) where Agrippa had been commander of the fleet (in fact, having married Augustus' only child Julia, he was considered Augustus' obvious successor, until he predeceased him). However, we now know that the entire building was rebuilt by the emperor Hadrian in AD 118–125: it is thought that Hadrian himself was responsible for its extraordinary design, but he generously chose to keep the original inscription.

In the pronaos you can experience what it must have been like to approach an ancient Roman temple: the scale reduces the human fig-

Marcus Agrippa is graciously acknowledged as having built the Pantheon, but it is a later building that survives today, reconstructed by Hadrian in AD 118–125.

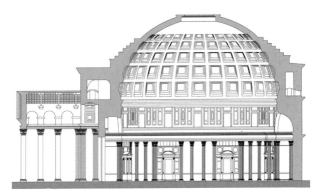

Cross-section of the Pantheon clearly showing its proportions and the vast expanse of the dome, which fills exactly half the interior space.

ure to insignificance. The eight huge monolithic granite columns still stand here as they were built, with the eight others behind disposed in four rows so as to form three aisles leading to the entrance.

The famous dome is totally hidden from the outside, and its impact in the interior is unforgettable. An extraordinarily pleasing sense of proportion prevails, produced by the fact that the height and diameter of the building are the same: 43.3m. The use of light from the opening in the roof displays the genius of the architect, and the intricate design of the coffers is mainly responsible for the effect of space and light (they were probably once ornamented with gilded bronze rosettes). The diameter of the dome, the largest masonry vault ever built, exceeds by more than one metre that of the dome of St Peter's. Its span, which contains no brick arches or vaults, begins at the level of the highest cornice seen on the outside of the building, rather than, as it appears in the interior, at the top of the attic stage. It is supported by a cylindrical wall six metres thick.

More than half of the original coloured marble panels on the walls are still in place and the decoration includes Corinthian columns of yellow marble, porphyry or granite and an entablature with a beautiful cornice. The floor, though restored, retains its original design. The plan of the building was unique since the rectangular pronaos (a feature normally reserved for the entrance to a rectangular temple) precedes a domed rotunda—this was achieved by the addition between the two of an area as wide as the pronaos and as high as the cylindrical wall.

Dedicated to all the gods (*pan theon*), this was conceived as a secular imperial monument as much as a shrine. In 609 it was converted into a church, the first temple in Rome to be Christianised. Its atmosphere is still very much that of a temple with Christian overtones. It is fitting that it was chosen later as the burial place of one of Italy's greatest painters, Raphael, who was also appointed commissioner of antiquities by the pope of his day to ensure that everything possible was done to preserve the ancient buildings of Rome. Also here is the tomb of the first king of Italy, Vittorio Emanuele II, who died in 1878.

Two obelisks

The piazza outside the Pantheon, with numerous cafés and usually full of people, has a typically relaxed Roman atmosphere. There are often a number of horse-carriages waiting for fares here. The lovely 16th-century fountain has an obelisk made for Ramesses the Great which used to decorate an ancient temple of Isis. Anoth-

er, smaller obelisk, also brought from Egypt for the same temple, can be seen close by in front of the church of Santa Maria sopra Minerva. It was Bernini who placed it upon an elephant's back (in 1667), inspired by a woodcut in the famous book, the *Hypnerotomachia Poliphili*, a Renaissance allegory of love. Pope Alexander VII had this woodcut in mind when he commissioned the sculpture, and an inscription underlines its significance, namely that a strong mind nourishes sure-seated hope.

Santa Maria sopra Minerva

Map p. 222, C2. Open 7am–7pm. Coin-operated lights essential.
The church retains its Gothic style from when it was rebuilt in 1280, although its vault and rather too colourful decorations all date from the 19th century. In the south transept is the **Cappella Carafa**, which is covered with celebrated frescoes (1489) by the Florentine master Filippino Lippi. The subject is episodes in the life of St Thomas Aquinas, the great Dominican theologian (this is the Dominican church of Rome, and two other prominent Dominicans are buried here: St Catherine of Siena and Fra' Angelico). On the altar wall is the *As-*

St Thomas Aquinas Confounding the Heretics (1489–91): one of the frescoes by Filippino Lippi in the Cappella Carafa in Santa Maria sopra Minerva.

sumption, with a splendid group of angels, and the altarpeice of the *Annunciation with St Thomas Presenting Cardinal Carafa to the Virgin* is also by Filippino.

Beneath the 19th-century **high altar** is the tomb of the erudite St Catherine of Siena, who died in Via Santa Chiara nearby in 1380 having persuaded the French pope Gregory XI to return to Rome from Avignon a short while before. The precious relic of her head was reclaimed by Siena, her birthplace, three years after her death. She was canonised in 1461 and is one of the most famous Italian saints (in 1999 she was proclaimed a patron saint of Europe). In the **sanctuary** are the tombs of the two Medici popes (Leo X and Clement VII).

At the **foot of the choir steps** on the left is one of the least known (and perhaps least successful) statues by Michelangelo: it portrays the Risen Christ carrying the instruments of the Passion (the bronze drapery is a later addition).

In the **north transept** is the pavement tomb of the great Florentine painter Fra' Angelico, with an effigy taken from his death mask. He died in the convent of the church in 1455 on his third visit to Rome after he had frescoed the little chapel of Pope Nicholas V in the Vatican a few years before. Don't miss the wall tomb here which incorporates a splendid bas-relief of Hercules in a mortal struggle with the Nemean Lion, probably a Roman copy of an original Greek work of the 5th century BC.

On the **corner of the north transept and the nave** is the discreet and exquisitely carved small classical tomb (with his bust) of the sculptor Andrea Bregno, who died in 1506: it is in striking contrast to the showy marble drapery set up in 1643 on the nave pillar by the young Bernini to commemorate a nun named Maria Raggi. The face in the gilt bronze medallion repays a glance, though. There is a sweetness there, and none of the heated agony or ecstasy of Lodovica Albertoni (*see p. 88*) or St Teresa (*see p. 108*).

A marble foot

Via di Santo Stefano in Cacco leads towards Piazza del Collegio Romano and the Corso: it is worth following for a few metres as far as the narrow street on the right (*map p. 222, C2*) which is named **Via del Piè di Marmo** after a colossal marble foot from an ancient Roman statue which, amazingly enough, has survived here for many centuries.

PIAZZA NAVONA

This is Rome's most beautiful and grandest square (*map p. 222, B2*), lined with handsome palaces and numerous cafés, and there is a lovely church by Borromini on one side. The huge raised pavement in the centre is decorated with three magnificent fountains. The piazza is given its spirit through the crowds of Romans and tourists who are always to be seen here enjoying the scene, amongst the pavement artists, street vendors and buskers.

Spectators have in fact been coming here since Roman times, since this was the Stadium of Domitian, inaugurated in AD 86. The square still perfectly retains its stadium shape. It was afterwards used for festivals and jousts and as a market place, and its appearance has remained almost totally unchanged since at least the beginning of the 18th century, as numerous paintings and prints of old Rome attest.

The fountain in the centre, known as the **Fountain of the Four Rivers**, is one of Bernini's most famous and elaborate works. When asked in 1648 to provide a setting for the tall Egyptian obelisk which had been brought to Rome by Domitian, he thought up the idea of

Gian Paolo Pannini's view of the Piazza Navona flooded for use by boats (1756). Crowds throng around the perimeter to watch the spectacle.

supporting it on a huge triangular travertine rocky cave on which are seated four colossal allegorical figures, carved by his assistants, of the four most famous rivers of the world as it was then known: the Danube (Europe; identified by the horse), Ganges (Asia; identified by the figure holding a pole, with flowing locks and a thick beard), Nile (Africa; identified by a lion with this face covered, in reference to its unknown source) and Rio della Plata (America; identified by a figure with his hand raised, and with a pile of coins, beside him, symbolising the riches the river brings to the land). All around sea monsters, exotic vegetation and animals can be seen amidst the gushing water. The dove which crowns the obelisk is the emblem of the Pamphilj pope Innocent X, who commissioned the work. The other two round fountains seem tame in comparison, but they provide a satisfying balance, featuring a Moor and a figure of Neptune.

Sant'Agnese in Agone

Map p. 222, B2. Open 9.30–12.30 & 4–7; closed Mon

Pope Innocent X, who is buried here, ordered Borromini to reconstruct this ancient church which takes its name from the *Agones Capitolini*, the athletic games which were held in the stadium here (a corruption of which led to 'n'agona' and hence the name 'navona'). St Agnes, having refused the advances of a praetor's son, was exposed in the stadium but her nakedness was covered by the miraculous growth of her hair. The great architect here produced a Baroque masterpiece, on an intricate Greek-cross plan. The concave façade adds emphasis to the dome, which dominates the small interior and gives it a remarkable effect of spaciousness. The fresco is by Ciro Ferri, an able pupil of Pietra da Cortona, and the pendentives are by Baciccia, who painted many Baroque ceilings (notably the Gesù; *see p. 76*). The sacristy, also by Borromini, is usually open on weekday afternoons.

Sant'Ivo and San Luigi dei Francesi

Palazzo della Sapienza, a fine Renaissance palace now home to the state archives, stands on the busy Corso del Rinascimento. It was the seat of the University of Rome up until 1935, and the university is still known as *La Sapienza*. The door is always open into the beautiful court designed by Borromini around the charming façade of the little church of **Sant'Ivo** (*map p. 222, B2; only open Sun 9–12*), an unexpected sight and one of the greatest architectural works produced in Rome in the Baroque period. Begun for the Barberini pope Urban VIII, both the courtyard and the church incorporate his device (the bee) into their design, as well as Alexander VII's Chigi device of mounds. The domed church is crowned by an ingenious spiral tower, a unique feature of the city skyline, and it has a remarkable light interior painted in white and entirely devoid of decoration.

Further north, on the peaceful Via della Dogana Vecchia (there is a view of the pronaos of the Pantheon at the end of the Salita de' Crescenzi on the right) is the French national church in Rome, **San Luigi dei Francesi** (*map p. 222, B2; open 10–12.30 & 4–7 except Thur pm. Coin-operated light essential for the Caravaggio paintings*). The church houses three famous and very well-preserved paintings of scenes from the life of St Matthew by Caravaggio, by many considered his masterpiece (in the fifth north chapel). These were Caravaggio's first ever public commissions and are painted in his early luminous period, devoid of the intense, sometimes overpowering, drama of his later works. The angel in the main altarpiece appears to fall right out of the sky above the saint. The colour red, always greatly favoured by the artist, dominates all three paintings. Mathieu Cointrel (who came to be known as Cardinal Contarelli) left specific instructions in his will about how the subject he chose of the calling of his namesake should be portrayed, based closely on the description of the event in the gospels, including the book of St Matthew ('And as Jesus passed forth from thence, he saw a man, named Matthew, sitting at the receipt of custom: and he saith unto him, Follow me. And he arose, and followed him'). The artist shows Christ (with the suggestion of a golden halo) entering the toll-house and pointing straight at Matthew (accompanied by an apostle who has his back to us and repeats the gesture), while Matthew, seated at a table surrounded by a fascinating group of toll-collectors, splendidly painted in contemporary costumes, indicates with his hand his immediate understanding of Christ's gesture. Caravaggio was the most important painter in Italy in the 17th century and made Rome the most influential centre of art in the country during his lifetime. It is interesting to note the totally different style of the late Mannerist frescoes in the vault of the chapel by Cavaliere d'Arpino, who was Caravaggio's master, and who had at first been chosen also to decorate the walls. The high altarpiece of the church, an *Assumption of the Virgin*, is a good work by Francesco Bassano, a painter from the Veneto born some 20 years before Caravaggio.

The Calling of Matthew by Caravaggio (1597–1603), in the church of San Luigi dei Francesi.

A church by Pietro da Cortona and a famous 'talking' statue

Out of the other side of Piazza Navona, reached by the street on the right of the façade of Sant'Agnese, is the church of **Santa Maria della Pace** (*map p. 222, B2; only open Mon, Wed, Sat 9–12*). Tucked away in a quiet corner, it has a delightful 17th-century façade and semicircular porch designed by Pietro da Cortona (who is best remembered in Rome for his Baroque ceiling paintings). The most interesting work in the interior is on the arch above the first south chapel, where the lovely fresco shows the sibyls to whom the future is being revealed by angels, a beautiful work by Raphael dating from around 1511. The adjoining chapel has fine marble decoration dating from later in the 16th century. The first north chapel has frescoes by Baldassare Peruzzi and on either side two exquisite little 16th-century tombs. In the sanctuary, in an altar designed by Carlo Maderno, is the highly venerated 15th-century image of the *Madonna della Pace*, to whom the church is dedicated. The cloisters (*open when exhibitions are in progress*), dating from 1504, are fine works by Donato Bramante, the architect who worked on St Peter's for Pope Julius II.

It is well worthwhile taking a walk in the old narrow streets in the vicinity, including Via dei Coronari and Via del Governo Vecchio, both of which are lined with buildings dating from the Renaissance. A few steps out of the southwest end of Piazza Navona, at the end of Via del Governo Vecchio (*map p. 222, B2*), is a very worn and mutilated Roman statue which may once have decorated Domitian's stadium. It is known as **Pasquino**, named after a tailor who lived near here and who first had the idea of sticking witty or caustic comments on topical subjects to its pedestal. This effective and anonymous way of getting at the city governors persists to this day, and slogans ridiculing contemporary Italian politicians are still often attached to it. A few other outdoor sculptures in Rome were also once used as 'talking' statues.

Palazzo Altemps

Map p. 222, B1. Open 9–7.45 except Mon.

A few steps out of the north end of Piazza Navona, this handsome palace houses part of the archaeological collection of the Museo Nazionale Romano (*see p. 105*) and certainly deserves a visit. The exhibits are beautifully arranged and, in striking contrast with the other museums of ancient sculpture in Rome, the arrangement here is spacious, with just a handful of pieces in each room. The most important sculptures are those collected by Cardinal Ludovico Ludovisi to decorate his villa and garden in Rome (demolished in 1883). Excellent diagrams (also in English) in each room show where the antique statues have been restored or integrated over the centuries, some by Gian Lorenzo Bernini and Alessandro Algardi. The palace belonged to Cardinal Marco Altemps in the 16th century, who was himself a collector, and a few of his pieces remain here, although the finest are now in the Vatican, British Museum and Louvre.

Ground floor

The rooms off the handsome 16th-century courtyard contain many works from the Ludovisi collection. Portraits include the splendid colossal bronze **head of Marcus Aurelius** which was given a porphyry bust made some five centuries earlier, while the bronze cloak and other additions were added in the 17th century. In the corner room part of a medieval tower can be seen beneath the floor as well as fragments of exquisite Roman wall paintings on a bright red ground (2nd century AD) found during the excavations. Two **statues of Athena** are displayed in adjoining rooms: the Roman statue was given its head, hands, feet, and serpent's head in the 17th century by Algardi; the other statue is one of the very few copies (made by an Athenian sculptor) of a renowned statue carved by Pheidias for the Parthenon in Athens (although her arms date from the 17th century). A fine **sarcophagus with Dionysiac scenes** (AD 22), including a procession with a delightful elephant, was unfortunately ruined when used as a fountain.

First floor

In the loggia are some important small **Roman reliefs** which were known and studied in the Renaissance, and were published by the distinguished German scholar Johann Winckelmann, who was considered the greatest expert on Classical works in Rome during the 18th century. Off the loggia are displayed some splendid pieces including a bull (the god Apis) in serpentine porphyry, an Egyptian work dating from 2nd century BC. The bust of a satyr in grey *bigio* marble (displayed on top of an ancient funerary urn and altar) is thought to have been restored by Bernini, and the beautiful figure of Hermes (probably made in the early 2nd century AD) was carefully restored by Algardi. Delightful frescoes survive from the time of Girolamo Riario,

Detail from the *Ludovisi Throne* showing a flute girl.

the first owner of the palace, and they celebrate his marriage to Caterina Sforza in 1477: their wedding presents including plates, ewers and candlesticks are shown displayed on a sideboard in front of a tapestry covered with wild flowers.

The most famous piece in the collection is undoubtedly the **Ludovisi Throne**, one of the most controversial works of art in Rome. It was found at the end of the 19th century in the Villa Ludovisi. It is unique in form and size, and the subjects depicted are difficult to interpret: some scholars suggest it is a forgery, while others believe it to be a Greek original of the 5th century BC. The central relief is thought to represent the birth of Aphrodite as she rises from the sea, supported by two figures representing the Seasons. On one of the sides a naked flute girl is shown sitting on a folded cushion playing a double pipe.

One of the two colossal heads here, called the **Ludovisi Juno**, three times life size, was taken by Winckelmann to be a Greek work, and Goethe had a cast made of it for his residence in Rome (*see p. 52*). In fact it represents Antonia, mother of the emperor Claudius. The other colossal head is, indeed, a Greek original of 470 BC.

Off the loggia, the largest room on this floor displays a splendid huge sarcophagus (3rd century AD) with a battle scene, in excellent condition. Dramatically displayed is the head of a dead Amazon (2nd century AD). The **Galatian committing Suicide** formed part of the same group as the famous *Dying Gaul*, now in the Musei Capitolini (*see p. 16*). This was made at the time of Julius Caesar from an original Greek bronze. In the adjacent room is a two-figure group of a *Satyr and nymph* (Bernini is thought to have carved the head of the satyr). The *Torch-bearer* was created by Algardi using an original antique torso—but here for once he fails to interpret the balanced Classical spirit.

A lovely work by Caravaggio

A few steps from Palazzo Altemps is the church of **Sant'Agostino** (*map. p. 222, B1; open 7.45–12 & 4–7.30*), dedicated to St Augustine, author of the *Confessions*, whose mother, St Monica, is buried here at the east end. In the first north chapel is the *Madonna of Loreto* (1604; *light*), one of Caravaggio's most beautiful paintings. The graceful figure of the Madonna appears at the door of her house to show the blessing Child to two kneeling peasant-pilgrims. Caravaggio's detractors were very critical of the peasants' dirty feet when the painting was first exhibited on this altar, but today it appeals to us perhaps above all because of its extraordinary sense of humanity, and for the poignancy in Mary's burden, suggesting the sorrows she was to endure.

Five prophets on the nave pilasters were painted in 1855 to accompany the splendid *Prophet Isaiah*, frescoed on the third pillar on the north side by Raphael (here clearly influenced by Michelangelo's frescoes on the Sistine ceiling) as part of a funerary monument which included the lovely marble statue of the *Madonna and Child with St Anne* by Andrea Sansovino. Andrea's pupil, Jacopo Sansovino carved the greatly venerated statue of the so-called *Madonna del Parto* (1521) at the west end of the church, the object of innumerable votive offerings from expectant or grateful mothers.

FOOD & DRINK NEAR THE PANTHEON
& PIAZZA NAVONA

This district is particularly well supplied with cafés and restaurants. Both Piazza della Rotonda in front of the Pantheon (*map p. 222, B2*) and Piazza Navona (*map p. ???, B2*) have many cafés with tables outside where you can sit and enjoy these two squares, both closed to motor traffic.

Between the two, in the otherwise undistinguished piazza outside the church of Sant'Eustachio, is **Sant'Eustachio Il Caffè** (*map p. 222, B2; open daily*) which—according to connoisseurs —serves the best coffee in Rome (their coffee is also for sale here). It is very small and has only a handful of tables outside where you can sit (for an extra charge). At no. 55 in the same piazza, closer to the church, next to an attractive little palace with a frescoed façade, is **Caffè Camilloni a Sant'Eustachio** (*closed Sun*). This is much larger and has pastries and snacks, with tables also outside. On another side of the piazza, next to yet another café, at no. 49, is **Zazà**, a tiny bakery which sells pizza a *taglio* (a square piece of pizza as large or small as you wish) and the two most typical Roman snacks: *supplì* (fried rice balls with mozzarella) and *crocchette* (fried potato croquettes). The pizza is excellent, served with numerous different toppings, and the simpler *pizze bianche* provide a welcome change to the ubiquitous tomato sauce. If you are lucky enough to find one of the four tables free on the street outside, you can sit there for no extra charge.

Just off the north side of Piazza della Rotonda is another coffee emporium, **La Casa del Caffè** (at the beginning of Via degli Orfani; *map p. 222, B2*), always crowded with Romans.

Behind the Pantheon, Via di Torre Argentina leads towards Largo Argentina (*map p. 222, B2*) and just before it on the left is **Pascucci**, justly famous for many decades for its fruit milk-shakes (but this is not a place to sit and relax). Opposite is **Il Delfino**, entered from the corner of Corso Vittorio Emanuele, an old-established large self-service restaurant, handy for a quick, very reasonably-priced snack.

For restaurants in the area, see pp. 181–82.

AROUND CAMPO DE' FIORI

This mostly pedestrian area (*map p. 222, B2*) is full of contrasts, from the chaotic bustling life in Campo de' Fiori itself, filled with its street market, to the quieter elegance of the adjoining Piazza Farnese and Via Giulia. It is worth spending time here just to savour the atmosphere, which is typical of Rome at its most appealing.

Campo de' Fiori

As its name ('flowery field') suggests, this was once a meadow, but it has been one of the best known *piazze* in Rome since the 15th century. The grim statue of Giordano Bruno marks the spot where the Neoplatonist thinker and philosopher was burned as a heretic by the Inquisition in 1600. The delightful big 'soup tureen' in pink porphyry and granite was installed as a fountain at one end of the piazza in the late 19th century, and it is here that the flower sellers still gravitate, to make use of its constant supply of water. The square has a hodge-podge of rather undistinguished buildings but it is the bustling activity of Roman shoppers which make it fun to visit. The stalls sell everything from fruit, vegetables and meat to clothing and souvenirs.

At the far end of the square, behind the statue and just to the left, is Piazza del Biscione, where the white, late 16th-century Palazzo Pio (Righetti) was built over part of the ruins of the marble **Theatre of**

Pompey. Impressive remains of its masonry can be seen on request at the restaurant (Pancrazio) on the ground floor. Dating from 55 BC, this was Rome's first stone-built theatre (up to then theatres had been made of wood) and the largest of its time. At the top of the semicircle of seats Pompey built a temple dedicated to Venus, and behind the scena (the backdrop and stage building) there was a huge rectangular portico, off which opened an exedra (the curia). The whole complex was on a huge scale (stretching all the way to the present Largo Argentina; *map p. 222, B2*), and would have dominated the Republican city: Rome was here provided for the first time with a huge cultural covered space outside the heart of the city, and it is known to have been decorated with numerous statues and paintings. Although almost nothing of it now remains above ground, its semicircular form can still be seen close by in the neighbouring streets, one of the most remarkable continuations of urban layout to have survived in the city.

Near the four temples in Largo Argentina there are also a few traces of the curia. It was here that Brutus and Cassius carried out their plot to murder Pompey's famous rival Julius Caesar on the Ides of March 44 BC, an act made even more symbolic since the body apparently fell at the foot of a statue of Pompey himself.

Piazza Farnese

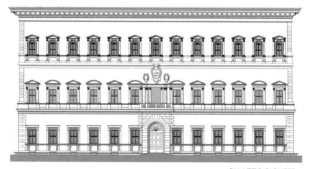

PALAZZO FARNESE

A few metres west of Campo dei Fiori the bustling atmosphere abruptly changes in the elegant and peaceful Piazza Farnese, created by the Farnese in front of their splendid palace. Here are two huge tubs of Egyptian granite, brought from the Baths of Caracalla in the 16th century and used by members of the Farnese family as a type of 'royal box' for the spectacles which were held in the square. They were adapted as fountains (using the Farnese lilies) in 1626 and the sound of water still pervades the square, which is surrounded by a group of distinguished town houses.

Most distinguished of all is **Palazzo Farnese** itself (*map p. 222, A2*), now the French Embassy. This is the most magnificent Renaissance palace in Rome, built in the mid-16th century for Cardinal Alessandro Farnese, afterwards Paul III. It is the most important building by Antonio da Sangallo the Younger, who worked for the same pope on the new basilica of St Peter's. On Antonio's death in 1546 Michelangelo took over work here (as in St Peter's), and provided the upper storeys and superb entablature which crowns the top of the palace. A vestibule with a beautiful colonnade leads into the splendid courtyard (*the courtyard and interior can only be seen by previous appointment on Mon and Thur at 3, 4 and 5. You are asked to send an email or fax at least one month in advance: visitefarnese@france-italia.it; Fax: 06 6880 9791; www.france-italia.it*). The famous *Galleria* has one of the best Baroque ceiling frescoes ever painted, the masterpiece of Annibale Carracci (1603).

The back of the palace and an arch of its courtyard can be seen from its garden gate on Via Giulia (reached by Via dei Farnesi) beside a lovely old wall fountain erected by the Farnese. The porphyry basin is ancient, as is the colossal mask of a girl with long hair, which took on its rather comic expression when the mouth had to be widened to adapt it to the stream of water.

Via Giulia

This very long and dead straight road has remained virtually unchanged since it was laid out parallel to the Tiber by Julius II in the first decade of the 16th century. It is lined with beautiful palaces with fine courtyards, some small churches (most of which are now kept closed), antique shops and art galleries. At the far end is **San Giovanni Battista dei Fiorentini** (*map p. 222, A2; open 7–7*), which was built by the Tuscan architect Jacopo Sansovino for the Florentine community in Rome when Giovanni de' Medici succeeded Julius as Pope Leo X. Many other Tuscan artists were called in to help decorate it with paintings and frescoes, including Filippino Lippi (chapel to the right of the sanctuary) and Santi di Tito (third south chapel). The church is the burial place of the architect Francesco Borromini, the great rival of Bernini and an architect of supreme originality, who committed suicide in 1667. The small museum is worth a visit.

Palazzo della Cancelleria

Map p. 222, B2. Owned by the Vatican, this is not open to the public but the main door into the courtyard is open throughout the day.

Just out of the north side of Campo dei Fiori is another magnificent Renaissance palace, built before Palazzo Farnese around 1486. It appears to have been influenced by Florentine buildings but its architect is unknown, although most scholars believe Donato Bramante was involved at some stage: he probably designed the beautiful courtyard. It has double *logge* with antique columns. On the exterior there is a double order of pilasters and delicate patterned brickwork.

Corso Vittorio Emanuele II

This busy, noisy road, laid out in 1876, is not very pleasurable to walk along, but strung out along its length stand three sumptuous churches, built in the 16th century for the new religious orders founded at the height of the Counter-Reformation and funded by wealthy clerics.

Sant'Andrea della Valle (*map p. 222, B2; open 7.30–12 & 4.30–7.30*) has the highest dome in Rome after that of St Peter's. The interior is magnificently decorated with precious marbles, frescoes and paintings, including a huge high altarpiece of the martrydom of the titular saint (St Andrew), a highly dramatic representation of the subject and typical of much of the sacred art produced in this period.

Further east is the church of the **Gesù** (properly the Church of the Most Holy Name of Jesus; *map p. 222, C2*). This was the main Jesuit church in Rome and its design greatly influenced subsequent Baroque church architecture. Cardinal Alessandro Farnese (nephew of Pope Paul III) paid for its construction. The heavily decorated interior was given its longitudinal plan with an aisleless nave in order to provide as much room as possible for worshippers and to give the high altar even greater prominence during the celebration of the Eucharist. The effect is that of a theatre rather than a place of prayer and private devotion, an effect which was entirely consonant with the aims of the Counter-Reformation, which sought to fight the threat of Protestantism by appealing to people's instincts and emotions. The superb fresco (1683) in the vault, of the *Triumph of the Name of Jesus*, is the masterpiece of the artist known as Baciccia and marks one of the high points of Roman Baroque painting. A mirror on wheels is provided so that you can see the details without cricking your neck. The most elaborate of the altars is in the left transept, where lapis lazuli, gilded bronze, and marble have been used to add splendour to the tomb of the founder of the Jesuit Order, St Ignatius Loyola.

At the other end of the Corso is the **Chiesa Nuova** (*map p. 222, A2*), built under the auspices of St Philip Neri. Next door to the church is an oratory, with a concave façade, designed by Francesco Borromini. It is here that Philip Neri instituted the musical gatherings which became known as 'oratorios', and which have given their name to a form of musical composition. The vault, apse and dome of the church were decorated by Pietro da Cortona (1664) and the whole interior is brilliantly gilded. In the sanctuary are three very fine paintings by the great Flemish painter Rubens, commissioned by the Oratorians before the artist left Rome in 1608 after a stay of eight years.

FOOD & DRINK AROUND CAMPO DE' FIORI

Good food for picnics can be bought in and around Campo dei Fiori, and at the grocery shop called **Vito Ruggeri** (at no. 1–2, on the corner of Via Giubbonari; *map p. 222, B3*), where you can ask for a sandwich to be made up from a 'rosetta' bun filled with a selection of excellent cured meats and cheeses. Founded in 1919, this is a place frequented by local Romans and the service is quick and efficient (NB: it closes between 2 and 5, so if you're planning a sandwich lunch, come and buy it before). Another good choice is **Roscioli** (*Via dei Giubbonari 21; closed Sun*) which is a smart, well-run gourmet wine and cheese shop, as well as a place where you can sit on a stool at the counter to enjoy an excellent meal. It was opened in 1972 a few metres away from the Antico Forno Roscioli, a bakery which claims to have been in business since the beginning of the 19th century, and where you can buy delicious bread and snacks of all kinds.

There is a café (**Caffè Farnese**) on the corner of Piazza Farnese (*map p. 222, A2*) with tables outside.

There are two simple restaurants near Palazzo della Cancelleria (*map p. 222, B2*): **Ditirambo** in the piazza, and **Settimio**, at Via del Pellegrino 117, which skirts its side façade. For descriptions of both, see p. 180.

FROM THE ISOLA TIBERINA TO THE AVENTINE HILL

Isola Tiberina

The picturesque little Isola Tiberina (*map p. 222, B3*) is fun to visit since it is the only island in the city. It is connected to the Tiber's two banks by two pretty little bridges, one leading into Trastevere and the other to the area near the former Jewish ghetto. Ponte Fabricio (only open to pedestrians) is the oldest of all the bridges which still cross the river: it has been here since ancient Roman days when the island was already settled. The inscription records the name of the builder and the date, 62 BC. From here, just downstream, you can see the ruins of the very first stone bridge over the Tiber, built in the 2nd century BC. Known as the Ponte Rotto (broken bridge) since 1598 when most of it collapsed, a single high arch has survived in the bed of the river.

Since ancient times, when there was a temple here dedicated to Aesculapius, the god of medicine, the island has been associated with the work of healing. Today it is almost entirely occupied by a **hospital**, founded in 1548 and modernised in the 1930s, when the lovely palms and pine trees were planted (you can walk around it at water level since there is a wide paving of travertine stone). The little piazza slopes down to the old church of **San Bartolomeo** (*open 9.30–2 & 3.30–7,*

The Tiber in flood, with a view of the Isola Tiberina.

Sun and holidays 9–1). The most memorable thing in the interior is the well-head since it is set into the chancel steps. Traditionally thought to mark the site of a spring connected to the Temple of Aesculapius, this old Roman column was decorated with carvings in the 11th century. In 2000 the church became a shrine to 20th-century martyrs (commemorated at each altar). The remarkable Comunità di Sant'Egidio, which carries out exemplary charitable works all over the world, has had its headquarters here since 1994 (*evening prayers at 8.30*).

The ghetto

Close to Ponte Fabricio on the Tiber bank rises the **synagogue** (*map p. 222, B3*), a huge domed building completed in 1904 in a style which has been termed 'Assyrian Babylonian'. It can be visited from the excellent **Jewish Museum** in the basement (*entrance on Lungotevere dei Cenci; open 10–4.15 or 6.15, Fri 9–1.15; closed Sat; ticket includes admission to the guided tour in English every hour*). With very good labelling, also in English, the museum recounts the history of the Jewish community in Rome, the oldest such community in the world. From 1556 onwards, under Pope Paul IV, the Jews of Rome were segregated and lived in this area subject to various restrictions on their personal freedom. It was not until 1848 that the walls of the ghetto were finally torn down. The museum has a fine collection of textiles, treasures from demolished synagogues, ancient marbles, and documentation recording the deportation of Roman Jews in 1943, following the anti-semitic laws introduced in 1938 (2,091 Roman Jews died in concentration camps in the Second World War). The Span-

Faces of the ghetto: ancient Roman funerary busts above a wall box for donations to help the district's orphans.

ish synagogue, still in use, is shown as well as the magnificent main synagogue above, where services according to the Italian rite are held every day. John Paul II was the first pope recorded setting foot inside a synagogue when he made an official visit here in 1986. The Jewish community in Rome today numbers some 13,500.

Around the old ghetto

Via Portico d'Ottavia traverses the area reconstructed in 1888 after the 'clearance' of the ghetto, when many of the houses were demolished. At the far end of this street, the façade of a house (nos. 1–2), with a long inscription, incorporates some ancient Roman sarcophagi. Opposite is a huge building which is used as a Jewish school. The name of the rather bleak Piazza delle Cinque Scole records the five synagogues which once occupied a building here demolished in 1908 after a fire (although the Jews had been allowed only one synagogue in the ghetto, they got round this restriction by creating five synagogues, one above the other, in this one building). Close by is a group of shops selling articles for Jewish tourists, as well as jewellers and some old-fashioned clothes shops and kosher takeaways and snack bars. The tiny bakery here (*see opposite*) is well worth a visit.

In Via della Reginella, which leads to Piazza Mattei (*map p. 222, B3*), the tall house at no. 27, which has no less than six floors with low-ceilinged rooms, is typical of the crowded housing conditions which used to exist in the old ghetto. The street now has some art galleries, picture framers and antique shops. In the peaceful little Piazza Mattei is the delightful **Fontana delle Tartarughe** (1584, restored, perhaps by Bernini, in 1658, when the tortoises were added). This fountain is one of the loveliest in all Rome. It is worth taking a look at the entrance porticoes and courtyards of the huge Palazzo Mattei here on Via dei Funari and exploring the winding old streets in the quiet residential district typical of old Rome around Piazza Margana (*map p. 222, C3*), tucked away just a few steps from the Capitoline Hill.

Theatre of Marcellus

Via Portico d'Ottavia (*map p. 222, B3–C3*) is named after a huge ancient Roman portico reconstructed by Augustus around 23 BC in honour of his sister Octavia. Beside the church of Sant'Angelo in Pescheria, a few of its 300 columns (and some remains of an entrance) survive. Steps (*open 9–7, winter 9–6*) lead down to a path which passes more Roman ruins and the impressive exterior of the **Theatre of Marcellus**, dedicated by Augustus to the memory of his nephew and son-in-law Marcellus, who died in 23 BC at the age of 19. In the 16th century a palace was constructed in part of the huge cavea and its façade remains. The rest of the building has been partly rebuilt and partly restored.

FOOD & DRINK IN THE GHETTO AREA

There is just one restaurant on the Isola Tiberina, **Sora Lella**, which has good traditional Roman dishes (*see p. 180*).

In the heart of the ghetto, on the corner of Piazza delle Cinque Scole, there is a tiny family-run **Jewish bakery** (*map p. 222, B3; open 8–7.30pm, Fri 8–3.30; closed Sat*), which has been operating here for many years. It is always worth stopping in to see what has just been taken out of the oven (in the morning there are hot doughnuts and buns). Cakes (usually made with ricotta as the main ingredient) are put on show in the window as soon as they are baked, while on the counter there are usually just two types of delicious dry biscuits, the richer ones filled with candied fruit. Many customers also order one or two euro-worth of *brisciole*, roasted pumpkin seeds.

If you want a very simple lunch in a crowded little *trattoria* full of character, try **Sora Margherita** (but it has eccentric opening times; *see p. 181*). Otherwise there are two good restaurants in the Ghetto area, **Piperno** and **Giggetto al Portico d'Ottavia** (*described on pp. 180–81*).

THE VELABRUM

Piazza della Bocca della Verità

This is really just a busy road junction (*map p. 222, C3*), but in a little garden with a fountain there are two ancient Roman temples which have survived so well because they were transformed into churches in the early Middle Ages. They both date from the Republican age (late 2nd century BC), and the charming little round **Temple of Hercules Victor** is particularly striking as it is the oldest marble edifice to survive in Rome. The circular cella of solid marble is surrounded by 20 fluted columns with exquisite capitals (only one of which is missing). It was restored in the Imperial period. Today its roof, added later, gives it a rather quaint appearance and alters the Classical proportions: it would have had an entablature above the columns before the roofline.

Santa Maria in Cosmedin
Map p. 222, C4. Open all day 9.30–5, summer 9.30–5.40; sung Mass according to the Byzantine rite on Sun at 10.30.

Detail of the Cosmatesque pavement of Santa Maria in Cosmedin. The Cosmati were medieval craftsmen who produced decorative pavements and wall cladding from cut fragments of coloured stone.

This medieval church, preceded by a little gabled porch and arcaded narthex, and with a tall campanile of seven storeys, is an ancient foundation, but its location is untranquil and it has lost a lot of its atmosphere. The interior, which incorporates an ancient Roman arcaded colonnade and masonry from earlier buildings, still bears the plan of the first basilica built in the 8th century. Its most interesting feature is the enclosure for the choir (the schola cantorum), with its marble screen, paschal candelabrum, episcopal throne and beautiful pavement, which all survive intact from 1123 and are the work of the Cosmati family. The baldacchino over the high altar (an ancient Roman porphyry bath) is by a later Cosmati (13th century). The former sacristy (now a souvenir shop) contains a precious very early mosaic on a gold ground (706), in a wood frame, poorly lit and easy to miss. You are directed to the exit in order to see the so-called **Bocca della Verità**, a large cracked marble disc, representing a human face, which used to close a drain in ancient times. It was put here in 1632 and the legend grew up that it would bite the hand of any perjurer who dared to come near it. Today tourists queue up to have their photographs taken with their hand in its mouth.

The Bocca della Verità, once a humble drain cover, now a famous photo opportunity.

San Giorgio in Velabro

Map p. 222, C3. Open 10–12.30 & 4–6.30; often used for weddings at weekends.

Seldom visited, this little church stands in an incredibly quiet spot, isolated from the traffic—you can often hear birdsong. It stands just beyond the squat, four-sided Arch of Janus, which formed a covered passage at a crossroads and provided shelter for the cattle-dealers of the Forum Boarium, an important market-place in ancient Rome. To reach the church, take one of the walkways on either side of the arch.

The church is one of the most memorable medieval buildings in Rome. You would never know that the lovely Ionic portico had been totally destroyed in 1993 by a Mafia bomb since it has been superbly reconstructed.

The beautiful plain interior, uncluttered by works of art, has an intimate feel, with 16 ancient columns of granite and pavonazzetto, and lattice-work windows similar to those in Santa Sabina (*see below*). In the apse is a lovely fresco of *Christ with the Madonna and Saints* attributed to Pietro Cavallini (c. 1296), carefully repainted in the 16th century. The beautifully proportioned tabernacle in the form of a canopy dates from the 13th century.

In the altar there is a niche with some exquisite Cosmatesque decoration: through the grille you can still see the supposed skull of St George in a quaint old-fashioned reliquary. This precious relic was brought to Rome by the Greek pope Zacharias in the 8th century and for centuries pilgrims would visit the church when it was displayed (on the first Sunday of Lent) in order to be granted an indulgence. St George, martyred around 300, is one of the most popular of all saints. Since the time of the Crusades he has always been depicted as a knight mounted on a white charger killing a dragon.

On the left of the church is the ornate little Arcus Argentariorum, erected by the money-changers and cattle-dealers of the Forum Boarium market in AD 204 in honour of the emperor Septimius Severus.

In front of the church is an ivy-grown arch where you can see the entrance to a tunnel which is the remains of the huge drain known as the **Cloaca Maxima** (still partly in use). At first a natural watercourse to the Tiber, this was canalised by the kings of Rome around 616–535 BC and arched over in 200 BC. During the Republic it then became part of an extensive hydraulic system, a great engineering feat devised to reclaim the stagnant marshy land in the valleys at the foot of the hills in the centre of Rome around the Roman Forum, and here, just before emptying into the Tiber, it also helped eliminate the marshes of the Forum Boarium. It greatly improved living conditions for the ancient Romans.

THE AVENTINE HILL

This quiet residential area (*map pp. 222, C4 and 221, A1*), without any shops or cafés, boasts one of the most beautiful early Christian basilicas in Rome. Just above Piazza Bocca della Verità, it is best reached from there by following Lungotevere Aventino for about 50m and then taking the pedestrian stepped lane on the left called Clivo di Rocca Savelli (*C.D. Rocca on map p. 222*).

Santa Sabina
Map p. 221, A1. Open 6.30–12.45 & 3–7.
Founded in the 5th century, this lovely church has been carefully restored over the centuries (the last time by Antonio Muñoz in the 20th century). It is entered from a vestibule on the left side of the portico: don't miss the ancient door on the far left of the entrance, which was the original portal, with wooden panels carved with scriptural scenes.

View of the Palatine Hill across the Circus Maximus.

The beautifully proportioned classical interior, with a wide, tall nave, has clean, uncluttered geometric lines. In the spandrels of the lovely fluted Roman Corinthian colonnade the green and purple marble inlay in opus sectile also survives from the 5th century. The mosaic decoration on the entrance wall was made at the same time, and has a long inscription in gold lettering on a blue ground recording the founder's name (Celestine I) and the date 430, and at the sides two female figures who personify the converted Jews and the converted Gentiles. The large windows have transennae with lattice-work all of slightly different designs, which add to the simple beauty. In the centre of the nave is the tomb of a monk who died in 1300, shown asleep in mosaic.

Outside is a lovely old wall-fountain beside a door into a pretty walled garden planted with orange trees, with a parapet from which there are wonderful views over all Rome with St Peter's in the distance.

The Circus Maximus

You can now return along Via di Santa Sabina and take Via di Valle Murcia downhill past a public garden full of roses to the Circus Maximus (*map p. 222, C4 and p. 221, B1*), which today is the largest uninterrupted open space in all Rome. In this unenclosed public park, planted with grass and a row of pines and cypresses, Romans come to stroll, walk their dogs or jog (it is also sometimes used for political demonstrations). It has a magnificent view of the ancient buildings on the lower slopes of the Palatine Hill (*see p. 27*). It was the first circus to be built in ancient Rome, and was used for chariot races and athletic contests throughout the Republican and Imperial periods. The only masonry which survives is at the far east end (fenced off), where some of the curved seats can be seen around a quaint medieval tower.

From the Aventine, it is not far to walk to the Testaccio district, which has some well-regarded restaurants (see p. 186).

TRASTEVERE

Trastevere (*map p. 222, A3–B4*) is a delightful area of old Rome 'across the Tiber', on its right bank. From the Middle Ages onwards it was essentially the popular district of the city, with numerous artisans' houses and workshops. Today it is a sought-after residential area, and it has lots of food shops and numerous restaurants and *trattorie*. It is divided into two distinct parts by the long Viale Trastevere, where the traffic concentrates and the trams and buses run, and which starts at the end of Ponte Garibaldi. The district to the right (as you stand with your back to the river) is always the more crowded, and has the church of Santa Maria in Trastevere. The district to the left, with the church of Santa Cecilia, is in many ways the more attractive and peaceful.

Santa Cecilia in Trastevere
Map p. 222, B4. Open 9.30–1 & 4–7.15. It is well worth coming here when you can also see the splendid Cavallini frescoes in the convent: they are only shown in the mornings 10.15–12.15, Sun and holidays 11.15–12.15. Ring at the door on the left of the portico, or enquire in the church from the nun at the entrance to the underground excavations, which are open 9.30–12.30 & 4–6.30; Sun and holidays 11–12.30 & 4–6.30. The nuns sell delicious marmalade made from the oranges and lemons they cultivate in the convent garden.

This lovely church was built on the house of St Cecilia, a patrician Roman woman martyred here in 230. As the reputed inventor of the organ, she is the patron saint of music. The basilica was erected in 817 by Pope Paschal I. The elaborate early 18th-century façade leads into a courtyard where the huge ancient Roman marble vase (known to have been here since medieval times) was adapted as a delightful fountain in 1929. The portico, with four antique Ionic columns bearing a frieze of 12th-century mosaic medallions, dates from around 1120.

The attractive 18th-century interior has pretty frescoes and an upper gallery reserved for the nuns. In the sanctuary is a very fine **baldacchino** (1293) signed by Arnolfo di Cambio, with lovely marble columns and carvings. Beneath it is the altar and a black marble niche which contains the dramatic **effigy of St Cecilia** in beautiful candid Parian marble. It is considered Stefano Maderno's masterpiece, carved when he was only 23 years old: the sculptor was present when in 1599 a tomb was opened and the saint's body was found, and he depicted her as he saw her, with her face hidden from view. The lu-

Pietro Cavallini: detail of the *Last Judgement* (c. 1293). The subtle range of colours produces an extraordinary effect and the figures come to life as in no other pictorial representation in Rome dating from this time. The angels are particularly striking, with wonderfully colourful wings. Cavallini, a Roman painter and mosaicist, is recognised as one of the most important early masters. He was a contemporary of Giotto, and still today scholars dispute the authorship of certain works between the two great artists. His most important works can be seen here and in Santa Maria in Trastevere (*see overleaf*).

minous 9th-century **apse mosaic** shows Christ blessing by the Greek rite, between saints (including St Paschal, with a square nimbus indicating that he was still living at the time the mosaic was made), and below 12 lambs (the Apostles) emerging from the Holy cities of Bethlehem and Jerusalem, on either side of the Lamb of God in the centre. The long inscription below records the finding of the relics of St Cecilia by Paschal I and the work he did to embellish the church.

Inside the Benedictine convent (*for admission see above*), from the nuns' choir above the west end of the church, you can see the remains of a splendid **fresco of the *Last Judgement*** by Pietro Cavallini. This is a masterpiece of medieval Roman fresco painting (c. 1293) and shows a clear break from Byzantine forms.

The Roman edifices beneath the church can also be visited (*for admission see above*).

A masterpiece by Bernini

Via Madonna dell'Orto and Via Anicia lead past the stables of the mounted police to the church of **San Francesco a Ripa** (*map p. 222, B4; open 7–12 & 4–7.30*). The chapel in the north transept has the famous tomb monument of the Blessed Lodovica Albertoni, a late work by Bernini. She is shown lying on a bed with the luxurious red marble bedcovers spilling onto the ground, splendidly lit from the window on the left. She is in her death throes, but at the moment when physical agony and spiritual ecstasy become one. The erotic charge of the composition is muted by the ten delightful marble cherubs' heads (each a separate portrait) daringly fixed to the frame of the painting above, a work by Baciccia.

NORTHERN TRASTEVERE

San Crisogono

Map p. 222, B3. Open 7.30–11 & 4–7.30.

It is perhaps because this interesting church faces onto the busy Viale di Trastevere that it is little visited by tourists. Founded in the 5th century, and rebuilt in 1129, the plan of the lovely interior is typical of the early Christian basilicas in Rome. Twenty-two ancient Roman columns in the nave were provided with large Ionic capitals in stucco during a reconstruction by Giovanni Battista Soria in the 17th century, when the gilded wood ceiling was installed and most of the altarpieces painted. But the magnificent Cosmatesque pavement, one of the most beautiful and best-preserved in Rome, survives from the 13th century. Soria also designed the baldacchino which rests on four ancient columns of yellow alabaster. The high altar encloses the 12th-century reliquary of St Chrysogonus. The titular saint is shown (with the Madonna and Child and St James) in a lovely mosaic on the wall of the apse, placed here by Soria when it was given its square frame. This may be an early work by Pietro Cavallini, or a follower. Remains of the very interesting early Christian church are entered through the sacristy in the north aisle, and approached down an iron staircase. Part of the masonry of a religious house used by a very early Christian community in the 3rd century can be seen, as well as the ruins of the 5th-century basilica. There are traces of frescoes and marble pavements, and a number of ancient Roman sarcophagi.

Detail of the mosaic on the exterior of Santa Maria in Trastevere.

Santa Maria in Trastevere

Map p. 222, A3. Open all day. At 8.30pm every day the Comunità di Sant'Egidio (see p. 79) holds a service of prayers and organ music when the church, usually full and wonderfully lit, can be seen in all its glory.

The façades of the houses which surround the spacious piazza are in different shades of russet, beige and buff-brown, characteristic of the colours of old Rome. Although the fountain is not particularly attractive, it is said to be one of the oldest in the city and still fills the square with the pleasant sound of water.

The church façade is remarkable for its long mosaic at the top, dating from the 12th-13th centuries and one of the few mosaics in Rome on the exterior of a building. It shows the Madonna flanked by ten saints holding lamps, figures which seem to have no parallel in Christian iconography, although it is thought that this was the first church in Rome dedicated to the Virgin (by Julius I in 337), so they may be there simply to exalt her presence. In the lovely 12th-century interior it is the massive Roman columns which support the nave which first catch the eye. They are particularly splendid with fine capitals and must once have decorated a number of different ancient temples.

The gilded wood ceiling was designed by the Bolognese painter Domenichino in 1617 and he painted the central *Assumption* for it. The east end is heavily decorated with frescoes and sculptures which at first detract from the splendour of the early mosaics on the triumphal arch and in the apse (1140), which are amongst the best preserved in Rome (*coin-operated light at the foot of the sanctuary steps*). In the semi-dome Christ and his Virgin Mother are given equal importance as they sit side by side on the throne beneath the hand of God bearing a wreath and the monogram of Constantine, the first Christian emperor.

They are flanked by saints. Note the exquisite details of fruit and flowers on the soffit of the arch, and Christian symbols and emblems on the arch itself, with Isaiah and Jeremiah at the sides beside two palm trees and a caged bird, representing Christ imprisoned by the sins of man. Between the windows and on the arch is a row of six panels with scenes from the life of the Virgin (from her birth to the Dormition), exquisite and perfectly preserved mosaics by the first great Roman artist Pietro Cavallini (c. 1291; his best work as a painter can be seen close by in Santa Cecilia; *see p. 87*).

In the chapel to the left of the sanctuary there is a very ancient painting of the *Madonna of Clemency*, severely damaged but taken to be an original work of the 8th century or even earlier. You can just discern the regal static figure of the Madonna who holds the Child in front of her, in the Byzantine manner. The two astonished angels, perhaps painted in a different spirit, seem to peer curiously around her shoulders in order to catch a glimpse of the Child. The two cardinals' tombs outside the chapel date from the first years of the 15th century. The Avila Chapel at the end of the aisle here is an intriguing Baroque work.

San Pietro in Montorio

Map p. 222, A3. Church open 8.30–12 & 3–4. Tempietto open 9.30–12.30 & 2–4 except Mon, although always visible from the gate.
The church contains a powerful *Flagellation* by Sebastiano del Piombo (first south altar; *coin-operated light*). Its composition skilfully fits the curved wall of the chapel and the painted columns accentuate the motion of the semi-nude torturers grouped around the central column, against which the twisted figure of Christ is superbly portrayed. Sebastiano trained in Venice and when he moved to Rome in 1511 he worked closely with Michelangelo, who supplied the drawing for this work. In the chapel opposite, Bernini designed the altar in 1647, and the

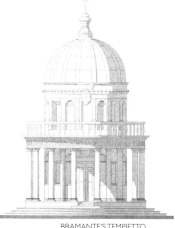

BRAMANTE'S TEMPIETTO

effect, as in so many of his works in churches, is dramatised by hidden lighting.

The door to the right of the church (*for opening times, see above*) gives access to a peaceful little courtyard in the centre of which is the celebrated **Tempietto**, a miniature circular domed building of perfect proportions which combines classical with Mannerist details. It was designed by Donato Bramante in the first years of the 16th century and it is particularly pleasing because of its tiny scale, which allows you to establish an intimate relationship with the building. It marks the spot once thought to have been where St Peter was martyred.

There is a fine view of Rome from the terrace in front of the church. We are here on the edge of the **Janiculum Hill**, which is traversed by a wide avenue with fine pine trees and has several panoramic terraces and the abundant fountain of the Acqua Paola. It also has statues and memorials to Garibaldi and his wife Anita since the hill was a battlefield during the Risorgimento, when Garibaldi came here to rouse the Romans against their papal governors.

Palazzo Corsini

Map p. 222, A3. Via della Lungara 10. Open 8.30–7.30 except Mon.
Palazzo Corsini became the residence of the Corsini family when they moved from Florence to Rome in the 18th century and it still contains part of their collection of paintings formed in the previous century. It has a magnificent entrance staircase and views from the windows of its splendid garden of palm trees. It is particularly rich in 17th- and 18th-century paintings of the Roman, Neapolitan and Bolognese schools. Beyond a room with Corsini portraits, Room 2 has the earliest works including a very unusual small triptych by Fra' Angelico, and a lovely painting of the *Madonna and Child with Scenes from the Life of Christ* by Giovanni da Milano, the only work in Rome by this very skilled Lombard painter (c. 1355). Also here is the *Head of an Old Man* by Rubens. In Room 3 there is a *St John the Baptist* by Caravaggio, one of a number of paintings he made of this subject. In the centre of Room 6 is the marble *Corsini Throne*. Dating from the 2nd or 1st century BC, it is possibly a Roman copy of an Etruscan piece.

Villa Farnesina

Map p. 222, A3. Open 9–1; closed Sun.
Opposite Palazzo Corsini is the entrance to the graceful Renaissance villa which served as the suburban residence of Agostino Chigi 'the Magnificent', the Sienese banker who controlled the markets of the

The Marriage of Alexander the Great and Roxana (detail) by Sodoma (c. 1517).

East and became treasurer of the Papal States in 1510. Here he would entertain Pope Leo X, cardinals, ambassadors, artists and men of letters in grand style, and the villa has somehow retained something of the sumptuous atmosphere it must have had in those days. Baldassare Peruzzi was summoned by Chigi from Siena to build it, and he also painted the ceiling fresco in the **Loggia of Galatea** with the constellations forming Chigi's horoscope. Here also is Raphael's celebrated *Galatea*, a superb composition showing the sea-nymph in a deep red cloak being pulled over the sea on a scallop shell drawn by dolphins. Chigi was a patron of Raphael and also had him provide the innovative decorative programme (and probably also the preparatory cartoons) of the ceiling in the adjoining **Loggia of Cupid and Psyche**, which formerly opened directly on to the garden. In a beautiful painted pergola with festoons of fruit and flowers against a bright blue sky, the story of the young girl Psyche, who incites the jealousy of Venus because of her beauty, is delightfully portrayed by Raphael's pupils, including Giulio Romano. On the upper floor are more painted decorations by Peruzzi and the *Marriage of Alexander the Great and Roxana* by the Sienese painter Sodoma.

FOOD & DRINK IN TRASTEVERE

Trastevere has a great number of restaurants, some of which are described on pp. 183–85. You can picnic on the Janiculum Hill or in the Botanical Gardens (Orto Botanico; *map p. 222, A3*).

Good cakes and biscuits are made at the **Pasticceria Innocenti** (*Via della Luce 21; map p. 222, B4; open weekdays 8–8, 9.30–2 on Sun*), which has retained its splendid old machinery and has a memorable atmosphere.

VILLA BORGHESE

Villa Borghese (*map p. 220*) is the name given to Rome's most extensive and best-known public park right in the centre of the city ('villa' being the name often given to the grounds of grand country residences as well as to the houses themselves). Traversed by numerous roads, most of them closed to traffic, it is the place where many Romans with their children (and dogs!) come to spend their free time and is a lovely place to walk. The main attraction for visitors is the Galleria Borghese, which contains famous works by Bernini, Caravaggio and Titian. On the other side of the park from the Galleria Borghese, on its northwestern border, are two more museums, one dedicated to Italian art of the 19th and early 20th centuries, and the other illustrating the Etruscan civilisation.

The park

This huge green area, first laid out by Cardinal Scipione Borghese in the 17th century, as a garden around his residence, was extended by his descendants in the 18th century. Today it has some magnificent old oaks, giant ilexes and umbrella pines, and is intersected in every direction by avenues and paths decorated with statues, monuments and fountains. There is also a little lake, as well as garden houses, two of which contain small museums. The park is generally well kept and patrolled by mounted police, but as in all other large urban parks it is always best to keep to the main paths.

Approaches

The most direct approach if you are making for the Galleria Borghese is from Via Vittorio Veneto (*map p. 220, C3*); the most pleasant is from the Spanish Steps and the Pincio Gardens (*map p. 220, B2*), which takes you close to the **Museo Carlo Bilotti** (*open 9–7 except Mon*), in a former orangery. Bilotti, an Italian-American who died in 2006, left his collection to the city of Rome. It includes 18 works by Giorgio de Chirico and a portrait of his wife and daughter by Andy Warhol.

MUSEO & GALLERIA BORGHESE

Map p. 220, C1–D1. NB: Open 9–7.30 except Mon, with entrance allowed every two hours, at 9, 11, 1, 3 and 5 and this is the only museum in Rome where it is obligatory to book your visit in advance (T: 06 32810 or www. ticketeria.it; booking service open Mon–Fri 9–6, Sat 9–1). You are asked to get there 30mins before your booked time because you have to buy your ticket and also leave your bag, and there are usually queues.

If the gallery is crowded, it is a good idea to visit the upper floor first (by the spiral stair off Room IV), so moving against the flow. You are allowed to stay in the building for two hours. Labelling is kept to a minimum but there are extremely detailed hand-sheets in each room.

The building was begun for the Borghese family in 1608 but the splendid interior decoration dates from the late 18th century. Cardinal Scipione Borghese, who acquired his collection with the help of his uncle Paul V, was Bernini's first important patron, and the statues he commissioned from the great Baroque sculptor are still preserved here, together with six of his twelve Caravaggios. Much of the antique sculpture was sold by Camillo Borghese to his brother-in-law Napoleon, and is now in the Louvre. However, the museum still contains a splendid collection of sculpture and paintings from all periods. Only the highlights are mentioned below.

Ground floor

Here are exhibited the sculpture collection and the works by Caravaggio. The central **Salone** is magnificently decorated and sets the tone for the surrounding rooms: antique busts and sculptures are arranged side by side with 17th-century statues; the walls are covered with precious marbles and ancient reliefs. The ceiling is frescoed with elaborate scenes dating from the mid-18th century, and ancient Roman mosaics have been set into the floor to add to the effect of grandeur.

Bernini: *Rape of Persephone* (1621–22), showing the impression of fingers on soft flesh, a *tour de force* of sculptural art.

To the right in Room I is one of Canova's most famous works, Napoleon's sister **Pauline Borghese** reclining half-nude on a couch. She lived in Rome as the wife of Camillo Borghese and this portrait dates from 1808 (the great Neoclassical sculptor cleverly put an apple in her hand so that she is depicted in the guise of Venus to lessen the shock of her nudity). In each of the next three rooms are three early masterpieces by Bernini: the **David** in Room II was made when the sculptor was only 25 and the hero's face, with its determined jaw set square, is a self-portrait. Room III contains his famous *Apollo and Daphne* (1624). The dramatic moment when Apollo reaches the nymph and his touch turns her into a laurel tree is portrayed with extraordinary virtuosity with an almost excessive lightness of touch. The group was designed to be displayed against a wall and thus to be viewed from the single (illuminated) viewpoint as you enter the room. The same is true of the **Rape of Persephone** in Room IV, which shows Pluto seizing Persephone in his arms as she struggles to free herself from his embrace.

The last room on the ground floor has no less than six superb **paintings by Caravaggio**, all very different, and illustrating his skills in portraiture, sacred subjects and still lifes. There are two portraits of boys, one of which has a basket of fruit, exquisitely painted. The *Madonna of the Palafrenieri*, painted in 1605, shows St Anne (depicted as an elderly peasant woman) with the Madonna teaching the young Christ Child (totally nude) how to crush a snake, symbolising evil. A brilliant red hue dominates both the *St Jerome* and the *Young St John the Baptist* (the latter is the painter's last known work). *David with the Head of Goliath*, dating from the same period, is one of several paintings Caravaggio made of this subject.

Upper floor

Reached by a staircase (or tiny lift) off Room IV, the upper floor has the gallery of paintings. At the top of the stairs go straight ahead into Room IX, where two beautiful paintings by Raphael are displayed. The **Entombment** (1507) shows the transportation of the dead body of Christ towards the tomb, and was influenced by the works of Michelangelo. The **Lady with a Unicorn** was probably painted the year before (although it has been altered and partly repainted: there may originally have been a dog rather than a miniature unicorn on her lap). The superb head of the blue-eyed lady with golden hair, and the exquisite jewel at her neck are typical of Raphael's greatest works of portraiture. The attribution of the striking **Portrait of a Man** (1502), which shows the influence of northern painters, is disputed between Raphael and his master Perugino. This great Umbrian painter is also represented here with a *Madonna* and a *St Sebastian*.

In the adjoining Room X the painting of **Danaë** by the Emilian painter Correggio shows a subtly erotic scene with the charming young Danaë on her bed beside the winged cupid receiving Jupiter

Raphael: *Lady with a Unicorn* (c. 1506). The work has been altered where the unicorn now sits (hence the lady's rather strangely-shaped right hand). It appears that she once held a dog, symbol of fidelity, where now she clasps the unicorn, symbol of virginity.

transformed into a golden shower. In the largest room (XIV), on a table against the wall opposite the windows, is **Bernini's earliest work**, dating from around 1615, showing the goat Amalthea with Zeus as a child and a small faun at play. It was once taken to be a Hellenistic original, and may even have been made as a deliberate forgery. On the same wall are two painted **self-portraits by Bernini** (and a portrait of a boy). Bernini also carved the two marble portrait busts of his patron, Cardinal Scipione. His famous contemporary Alessandro Algardi is represented in the small room next door (Room XV) with the black marble putto, which is an allegory of Sleep. The last room (XX) contains an early masterpiece by Titian known since the late 18th century as *Sacred and Profane Love*. In fact it was a wedding present and portrays the bride splendidly dressed, beside a nude figure of Venus (apparently an allegory of her eternal happiness in heaven). The two female figures are amongst Titian's greatest achievements. The small *Portrait of a Young Man* is an exquisite work painted around 1475 by the Sicilian artist Antonello da Messina, clearly influenced by the Flemish school.

The Casa del Cinema and Via Veneto

Near the other end of the long Viale del Museo Borghese is the **Casa del Cinema** (*map p. 220, C2*), opened in 2004 in a garden house called the Casina delle Rose (*entrance off Viale San Paolo del Brasile*). Open every day, it has two cinemas, an open-air theatre, exhibition space, a studio where you can consult over 2,500 films on DVD, and a café and restaurant. Just inside the **Porta Pinciana**, an old fortified gateway in the Aurelian walls, begins the broad and tree-lined **Via Vittorio Veneto** (known as Via Veneto), which is still one of the most famous streets in Rome with its luxury hotels and elegant cafés. It was opened in 1886 after the Boncompagni-Ludovisi family sold off the huge park of their villa here as building land, and the grand mansions survive from that period (one of them serves as the US Embassy). It was especially fashionable for its ambience of *la dolce vita* in the 1960s (after the success of Federico Fellini's film of the same name), and its wide pavements still manage to keep an aura of style and grand living.

The Galleria Nazionale d'Arte Moderna and Museo Nazionale Etrusco di Villa Giulia

On the northern side of the park of Villa Borghese there are two important museums, both of which can either be reached on foot across the park, or by tram no. 3 from Trastevere and the Colosseum.

The **Galleria Nazionale d'Arte Moderna** (*map p. 220, B1; open 8.30–7.30 except Mon*), housed in a gallery purpose-built for it in 1911, is the most important collection in existence of Italian 19th- and early 20th-century art. The arrangement is chronological, with works dating from 1780–1883 in the left wing and from 1883–1910 in the right wing. The upper wings have later works up to the 1960s. All the great names of the period are well represented.

The **Museo Nazionale Etrusco di Villa Giulia** (*map p. 220, B1; open 8.30–7.30 except Mon; also accessible by tram no. 2 from Piazzale Flaminio, map p. 220, A2; get off at Belle Arti*) is one of the most important museums in Italy for its Etruscan collections and works from the pre-Roman period found in Lazio, Umbria and southern Etruria. It is housed in a lovely suburban villa built in the 16th century for Pope Julius III.

FOOD & DRINK AROUND VILLA BORGHESE

The **park of Villa Borghese** is the best place in all of central Rome to enjoy a picnic. The **CineCaffè** in the Casina delle Rose, attached to the Casa del Cinema (*off Viale San Paolo del Brasile; map p. 220, C2; open 9–7, later in summer*), also has a restaurant (*closed Mon*). It has become a place where many Romans come to enjoy a snack or a cocktail.

There is a pleasant café, as well as a restaurant, both with tables outside, in the **Galleria Nazionale d'Arte Moderna**. It is a popular lunch spot (with a good buffet), so it is best to book ahead (*T: 06 3229 8223*).

On **Via Vittorio Veneto** (*map p. 220, C3*) there are numerous luxury cafés with tables on the wide pavements, some of them in old-fashioned style and others, such as the Club Doney (at no. 141 next to the Hotel Excelsior) recently refurbished in contemporary style.

THE QUIRINAL HILL

The Trevi Fountain

Tucked at the foot of one of the highest of the seven hills of Rome stands the Trevi Fountain (*map p. 222, C1*), in a crowded little piazza always filled with tourists' voices and the sound of water. This is one of the most famous sights in Rome—and with good reason, for it is undoubtedly the city's most magnificent fountain, made all the more impressive by its confined setting in such a small square. It is the work of the little-known Roman architect and poet Niccolò Salvi, completed in 1732. His theatrical design incorporates, as a background, the entire Neoclassical façade of Palazzo Poli. On the enormous artificial rock, built out of tufa, two giant tritons, one blowing a conch, conduct the winged chariot of Neptune pulled by marine horses which appear to splash and gallop through the water. It is fed by the Acqua Vergine Antica, an aqueduct built by Agrippa in 19 BC to supply his public baths near the Pantheon from a spring some 20km east of the city (the bas-reliefs illustrate its construction). There is still a rooted tradition (it seems to have originated at the end of the 19th century) that if you throw a coin over your shoulder into the fountain before you leave the city it will bring good luck and ensure your return. The coins are collected every Monday morning when the fountain's pump mechanism has to be turned off for cleaning and the money goes to a charity. The fountain has featured in numerous classic Italian films since the 1950s.

Palazzo del Quirinale

To climb the Quirinal Hill from the Trevi Fountain, take Via del Lavatore and then Vicolo Scanderbeg. Via della Dataria then takes you up steps to the top. On the spacious summit stands the huge Palazzo del Quirinale (*map p. 223, D2*), begun in the 16th century as the pope's summer residence and enlarged in the following two centuries. When papal rule of the city ended it was taken over by the kings of Italy and, ever since the monarchy was replaced by the Italian Republic in 1948, the building has been used as the official residence of the President of Italy. The grand interior (*open Sun 8.30–12*) has a good collection of tapestries and a lovely fresco by the innovative 15th-century painter Melozzo da Forlì.

Opposite it are the papal stables (the Scuderie), built in 1722 and restored as an exhibition space in 2000 by Gae Aulenti. The other

The Trevi Fountain (1732), which uses the *palazzo* behind it as a theatrical backdrop.

monumental 18th-century building here is the seat of the Italian constitutional court. There is a lovely fountain with a great antique basin of dark grey granite at the foot of a tall obelisk flanked by a high pedestal with two colossal statue groups of Castor and Pollux, the Dioscuri (sons of Zeus), holding their horses at bay. These have stood somewhere in the city ever since they were carved by a Roman master who lived in the imperial period and who took as his model two Greek originals of the 5th century BC. The pleasant open feel of this space is enhanced by the wide panorama from the balustrade across the rooftops to St Peter's in the distance.

Two Baroque masterpieces

The church of **Sant'Andrea al Quirinale** (*map p. 223, D1–D2; open 8–12 & 4–7; closed Tues*) is often considered the most beautiful of all the churches designed by Bernini. There is a semicircular portico on either side of the façade which is based on the Classical orders, and both have subtle convex and concave designs. The interior remains as the great architect designed it with columns, pilasters and frames in pink and grey marble, and gilded and stuccoed decoration (including numerous cherubim who look down from the lantern and surmount the high altarpiece). The carefully worked-out lighting effect also survives intact, with each chapel lit by windows high up behind the altars.

Only a few hundred metres further on is another lovely little church, this one by Bernini's great contemporary Borromini. **San Carlo alle Quattro Fontane** (*map p. 223, D1; open, together with the cloister and crypt, 10–1 & 3–6, Sat 10–1, Sun 12–1*) has an oval design. It is, however, difficult to study the remarkable façade since it is at a crossroads, very busy with traffic. It was added some 30 years after building of the church began in 1638. Borromini also makes great use of convex and concave surfaces, and triangular shapes which symbolise the Holy Trinity. It is in the little cloister that you can, perhaps, best appreciate his entirely innovative architectural spirit (and don't miss the crypt, kindly opened on request).

Palazzo Barberini (Museo Nazionale d'Arte Antica)

Map p. 223, D1. Entrance on Via delle Quattro Fontane. Open 8.30–7.30 except Mon. The gallery has been undergoing rearrangement for many years. At present only one floor is open.

Palazzo Barberini is one of the grandest palaces in Rome, begun in 1624 for Pope Urban VIII (Maffeo Barberini), and both Bernini and Borromini later worked on it. It houses the Galleria Nazionale d'Arte Antica, which has a good collection of Italian Baroque paintings as well as some foreign works, and it is perhaps particularly memorable for its portraits.

The most important paintings include (to the left, in Room 1) a beautiful portrait of a lady known as *'La Fornarina'* attributed to Raphael or his pupil Giulio Romano. In the next room (2) there is another female likeness, *Ceres* by Baldassare Peruzzi, and in Room 3 *Mary Magdalen* by Piero di Cosimo. A lovely work by the Sienese painter Beccafumi (*Madonna and Child with the Young St John*) can be seen in Room 4. In Room 6 there is Titian's *Venus and Adonis*. The portraits in Room 7 include *Erasmus* by Quentin Massys, and two by Holbein (*Henry VIII* and *Thomas More*). Caravaggio is represented in Room 9 with his evocative *Narcissus*, one of his most celebrated works (*see opposite*), and *Judith with the Head of Holofernes* and *St Francis in Meditation*, both subjects he was clearly intrigued by since be painted several versions of both. One of his followers, Orazio Gentileschi, painted the other *St Francis* (with an angel) exhibited here. Once one of the most famous paintings in all Rome is hung in Room 10: Guido Reni's charming *Portrait of a Lady* (or a Sibyl), traditionally identified with

Beatrice Cenci, whose tragedy fired the imagination of the Romantics (at the age of 22 she was executed for parricide but was for ever afterwards considered to have been innocent). A beautiful oval room designed by Bernini, with Classical statues and busts in niches (the steps lead up to doors into the garden), opens onto the Salone with its magnificent ceiling fresco of *The Triumph of Divine Providence*, glorify-

Caravaggio's *Narcissus* (1597–99) involves the spectator in an extraordinary way. It is also an unusual subject for a painting: the beautiful youth who refused to return the love of those who fell for him and so was punished by Nemesis, who made him become bewitched by his own image when he stopped to drink at a fountain. It is one of the most famous images of the myth ever produced. Caravaggio's typical way of painting 'pools' of light against a dark ground is particularly successful here.

ing the Barberini pope. This is considered the masterpiece of Pietro da Cortona (1639), who painted a number of other palace ceilings in Rome, as well as designing the lovely church of Santa Maria della Pace (*see p. 68*). There are at present just two paintings here: Pietro da Cortona's *Guardian Angel* and Carlo Maratta's *Portrait of Cardinal Antonio Barberini*. The marble busts by Bernini include that of Pope Clement X.

A fountain by Bernini

At the bottom of the street is Piazza Barberini (*map p. 223, D1*), one of the busiest traffic hubs in the city. Isolated in the centre is Bernini's masterpiece, the **Fontana del Tritone** (1643). Four dolphins support a scallop shell on which is seated a triton (or merman) who blows a single jet of water into the sky through a conch shell held up in his hands.

Detail of the Fontana del Tritone showing a honey bee, family emblem of Urban VIII.

FOOD & DRINK NEAR THE QUIRINAL

There are two small pleasant public gardens on Via del Quirinale with benches where you can have a picnic.

A few steps from the Trevi Fountain, **Pizza Piccolo Buco** (*Via del Lavatore 91, opposite the end of Vicolo Scanderbeg; map p. 222, C1; closed Mon*) is a tiny, very simple pizzeria where the wood oven is always kept alight. It has been here for decades and has been run by the same family since the 1970s. It also has four tables outside. With a typically rather laid-back Roman atmosphere, you will usually find some locals who work in the area eating here, and the pizzas are good and reasonably priced.

For a much more sophisticated atmosphere, but still very good value, try the restaurant **Le Colline Emiliane** (*Via degli Avignonesi 22; opposite Palazzo Barberini; described on p. 183*).

MUSEO NAZIONALE ROMANO & THE BATHS OF DIOCLETIAN

This area, very close to the railway station, is a noisy, busy part of the city, but it has the superb national collections of ancient Roman art and the remains of the huge baths built by the emperor Diocletian.

Museo Nazionale Romano (Palazzo Massimo alle Terme)

Map p. 223, E1–F1. Entrance on Via Viminale, just out of Piazza dei Cinquecento in front of the railway station. Open 9–7.45; closed Mon. Excellent labelling, also in English.

This is the most important part of the vast state holdings of ancient Roman art, with numerous Classical masterpieces, which constitute one of the great collections of the world (the epigraph section is displayed across the road and described below, and the Ludovisi collection is kept in Palazzo Altemps; *see p. 68*). At the time of writing, the museum was undergoing rearrangement.

The chronological display starts on the **ground floor** and illustrates Roman Republican sculpture from the time of Sulla (138–78 BC) to Augustus (27 BC–AD 14), including many portraits and some Greek originals. The portraits of Augustus and members of his family are of particular interest and include a celebrated statue of the emperor as *pontifex maximus* or high priest, wearing a toga which also covers his head. Greek originals of the 5th century BC include a *Daughter of Niobe* (the young girl is shown dying as she tries to extract an arrow from her back), the headless statue of a girl in a *peplos*, and the *Pedagogue*. Amongst the bronzes are a *Boxer Resting*, a magnificent work signed by Apollonius, dating from the 1st century BC, and the so-called *Prince*, a Hellenistic bronze of the early 2nd century BC, showing a young man leaning on a lance.

The **first floor** has sculptures of the Imperial period (1st–4th centuries AD), many of them modelled on Classical Greek works. The first rooms have very fine portraits. Sculptures found in the imperial villas outside Rome include the headless *Ephebus of Subiaco*, and the so-called *Maiden from Antium*, a masterpiece of Greek art probably dating from the end of the 4th century BC, which shows a young girl approaching an altar carrying a tray with implements for a sacrifice. There are two marble copies of the famous bronze statue of the *Discobolus* (Discus-thrower) by Myron, one of the most frequently copied

Detail of the wall paintings from the 'Garden Room' of the Villa of Livia (1st century AD) from Prima Porta, just outside Rome.

Greek masterpieces. In another room are bronzes from the huge ships which were built by Caligula to transport visitors across the Lago di Nemi in the Alban Hills south of Rome for the festival of Diana. The last rooms have sarcophagi.

The **second floor** has an excellently displayed collection of exquisite wall-paintings, stuccoes and mosaics which used to decorate Roman buildings from the Republican era onwards. The rectangular room reconstructed from the Villa of Livia at Prima Porta is one of the most memorable spaces in all Rome. The delightful murals, painted for the wife of Augustus, represent an orchard with pomegranates and quinces and a flower garden inhabited by birds. While you stand here you share the spirit of delight felt by the Romans in the natural world and you can fully appreciate their extraordinary artistic skills. Also dating from the Augustan period are the magnificent stuccoes and wall paintings on black, red or white grounds, discovered in the grounds of the Villa Farnesina in Trastevere. There are also superb polychrome marble intarsia panels in opus sectile.

The vaults in the **basement** house the treasury, with valuable gold jewellery and the most important numismatic collection in Italy, covering all periods of its history.

The Baths of Diocletian and the Epigraph Collection

Map p. 223, E1–F1. The rather inconspicuous entrance, through a garden, is at no. 78 directly opposite the railway station. Open 9–7.45; closed Mon. The brick exterior of many of the splendid vaulted rooms of the Baths of Diocletian (*Terme di Diocleziano*) still dominate this area in front of the railway station. Begun in 299, the baths were completed in less than eight years by Diocletian and his co-emperor Maximian. They were the largest of all the ancient Roman baths, and could accommodate over 3,000 people at once. The huge central hall is now occupied by the church of Santa Maria degli Angeli (*see below*). A large collection of ancient epigraphs is beautifully arranged here in modern halls on the site of a 16th-century Carthusian monastery. The collection, which comprises some 10,000 inscriptions in Latin, is one of the most important of its kind in the world. Although less than a tenth of the whole collection is on display, it nevertheless provides a fascinating insight into life in ancient Rome, in all its social, political, administrative, economic and religious aspects (the excellent labelling is also in English).

The round hall displays the earliest pieces: on a simple vase found in Lazio you can see the very first example of the Greek alphabet so far found in Italy, probably dating from the late 9th century. The main hall displays works with inscriptions from the early Republican period (4th–3rd centuries BC). These include ceramics found in the bed of the River Tiber, and a large marble basin with a dedication to Hercules dating from the 3rd century BC, the oldest known example of an inscription with metal lettering. In the room to the left are inscribed statue bases, stone plaques recording public works, and funerary inscriptions all dating from the late Republican period (2nd–1st centuries BC). At the end of the main hall there is a dedication in bronze which was found at the end of the 20th century on the slopes of the Palatine, and which formerly belonged to a bronze statue of Tiberius dating from 7 BC.

A circular stair leads to the second floor and balconies where a very fine display of epigraphs, often with very beautiful lettering, illustrates the social structure of the Roman empire, and other aspects of Roman life. On the wall at the end is displayed the dedicatory inscription, which survives in eight fragments, announcing the completion by Diocletian of the baths on this very site. The third floor has epigraphs relating to the economic life of the city during the Empire and on the balcony are inscriptions from religious sanctuaries. From here there is access to the two upper wings of the large cloister where part of the well-labelled protohistoric collection is displayed.

On the way out through the garden don't miss the huge hall of the old Roman baths (entrance to the right), interesting for its splendid architecture, on a massive scale, with its triple cross-vault partly preserved. Ancient statues are set into the niches and sarcophaghi are displayed around the walls, while in the centre you can see a reconstructed family tomb (known as the Sepulchre of the Platorini and dating from the 1st century AD) with its original sculptures and cinerary urns (found in 1880 on the right bank of the Tiber in the centre of Rome), and two columbaria, one with lovely paintings and the other with a stuccoed vault.

Santa Maria degli Angeli

In the circular Piazza della Repubblica the semicircular porticoed fronts of the *palazzi* built in 1902 by the neo-Renaissance architect Gaetano Koch follow the line of the exedra of Diocletian's baths. In the centre of the piazza is the abundant Fountain of the Naiads (1870) with four groups of faintly erotic reclining water nymphs around a statue of the sea god Glaucus. Here is the huge church of **Santa Maria degli Angeli** (*map p. 223, E1; open 7.30–12.30 & 4–6.30*), built into the great central hall of Diocletian's baths. Even though it was first designed by Michelangelo, its huge scale makes it difficult to appreciate (and the proportions were drastically altered by Luigi Vanvitelli when he moved the high altar to the 'short' arm, and thus converted the nave into a bizarrely long transept). Today it provides Italy with a fitting space for state funerals.

A little further north, on Via XX Settembre, is the church of **Santa Maria della Vittoria** (*map p. 223, E1; open 7–12 & 3.30–7*). It is the work of the Baroque architect Carlo Maderno (1556–1629), and has carefully controlled proportions, with white stuccoes combined with richly coloured marbles. It remains one of the most complete examples of Baroque decoration in all

The Ecstasy of St Teresa (1647–52) by Bernini, in the church of Santa Maria della Vittoria.

Rome. The fourth chapel on the north side is a famous architectural work by Bernini (c. 1650): it contains his marble group of the *Ecstasy of St Teresa*, showing the saint in an almost erotic swoon before an angel beneath golden rays of celestial light (it is ingeniously lit from a hidden side window). Scholars usually agree with the great architect and sculptor himself in considering the chapel and this sculpture his best work.

In 1603 Carlo Maderno also supplied the façade of the church opposite, **Santa Susanna** (*map p. 223, E1; open 9–12 & 4–7*), and this is acknowledged as his best architectural work. The good late Mannerist frescoes and altarpieces in the interior date from the previous decade. If you happen to be here between 9.30 and 11.15 or 4 and 5.30, then ring at the tiny red bell at the door on the left side for one of the 20 Cistercian nuns living here who will show you into a room with a glass floor where you can see the earlier church, and a showcase with a remarkable painted mural of the *Madonna and Child* in Byzantine style, dating from the end of the 8th century (one of the rare works of this period to survive in the city). The shattered pieces were found at the end of the 20th century in the sarcophagus here and it has been painstakingly recomposed from some 7,000 fragments. The nuns sell handmade lace and jam.

FOOD & DRINK NEAR THE BATHS OF DIOCLETIAN

Trimani (*Via Cernaia 37/b; closed Sun; see p. 183*) is a good place to eat (just north of Santa Maria degli Angeli); otherwise you can picnic in the lovely little garden at the entrance to the Baths of Diocletian and the Epigraph Collection at no. 78 (you are allowed free access since the ticket office is inside the building beyond), around a fountain with plenty of benches and shade. Opposite Santa Maria degli Angeli is a covered arcade where the café **Dagnino** (*Galleria Esedra, Via V. Emanuele Orlando 75; map p. 223, E1; open daily*) serves excellent snacks and coffee, as well as cakes and pastries to take away.

SANTA MARIA MAGGIORE & THE ESQUILINE HILL

Santa Maria Maggiore

Map p. 223, E2. Open 7–7 daily. Coin-operated lights essential to see the mosaics at the west end. The Loggia delle Benedizioni, with its mosaics, is only open at 1pm in winter, and twice a day in summer at 9.30 and 1. The church tends to be crowded with tour groups so it is best to come here early. Santa Maria Maggiore is famous as one of the Seven Churches of Rome, the most important places pilgrims were required to visit (*see p. 153*).

It stands today surrounded by busy roads and appears to have two entrances since the east end, rebuilt in the 17th century and approached by steps, has a decorated apse between the two domed papal chapels. Here in Piazza dell'Esquilino is an obelisk, nearly 15m high, set up by Sixtus V in 1587 as part of the design for his Strada Felice, which stretched in a line of straight, carefully planned vistas all the way from the church of Trinità dei Monti (*map p. 220, B3*). The en-

Interior of the basilica of Santa Maria Maggiore, with its 5th-century mosaic panels below the windows.

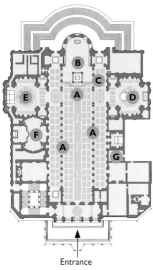

Entrance

A Mosaics
B High altar
C Tomb of Bernini
D Cappella Sistina
E Borghese Chapel
F Sforza Chapel
G Shop and museum entrance

trance to the basilica is in fact from the opposite end, at the highest point of the Esquiline Hill. Outside the entrance rises a very tall, fluted column which Paul V took from the Basilica of Maxentius in the Forum (*see p. 26*) and had his favourite architect Carlo Maderno set up here in 1613, crowning it with a statue of the Virgin and decorating it with a fountain at its base.

The grand west façade, with a loggia from which the pope could bless the people, was designed in 1743 by Ferdinando Fuga, a Florence-born architect whose patron was the Florentine pope Clement XII. The mosaics in the loggia (*for visiting times see above*) date from the 13th century. Behind the entrance façade rises the 14th-century campanile, the highest in Rome.

The interior

The interior retains something of the regal atmosphere of an ancient basilica, partly because the plan of its nave has remained unaltered since it was reconstructed in the 5th century (we know that the first church was built around 358), and it still retains its ancient mosaics.

The basilica is huge but well-proportioned with a longitudinal emphasis, and the nave is divided from the aisles by rows of shining marble columns which support an architrave, copying the architecture of the ancient Roman basilica, or public hall. The lovely Cosmatesque pavement dates from around 1150. The gilded coffered ceiling was added by the Florentine architect Giuliano da Sangallo, who had been summoned to Rome by the notorious Borgia pope Alexander VI (the gilding is said to have been carried out with the first gold brought from the Americas, a gift from Ferdinand and Isabella).

The splendid mosaics **(A)** above the nave columns and over the triumphal arch at the east end date from 440, and are the most important mosaic cycle of this period in Rome. They consist of small rectangular biblical scenes (on the left illustrating the life of Abraham, Jacob and Isaac; and on the right the life of Moses and Joshua), very high up so unfortunately difficult to see with the naked eye. Those on the arch illustrate the early life of Christ. The apse mosaic, the *Coronation of the Virgin*, dates from the late 13th century and is signed by Jacopo Torriti. He also made the mosaics below, between the windows, depicting the life of the Virgin.

The only alterations to the simple grandeur of the central part of the church are the baldacchino over the high altar **(B)**, added by Ferdinando Fuga in the 18th century, and the decoration of the confessio below it: you look down on a huge statue of Pius IX kneeling in prayer: although he reigned for longer than any other pope, he was the last to hold temporal power (*see p. 10*). The large high altarpiece of the *Nativity*, conspicuous since it is permanently lit, is by a little-known 18th-century artist called Francesco Mancini. By the two sanctuary steps **(C)** is the pavement tomb of the Bernini family, including the great architect and sculptor Gian Lorenzo. It is touching that he is commemorated in such a simple way since he spent much of his life designing some of the most elaborate tombs ever produced for his contemporaries.

The side chapels

In the 16th and 17th centuries the popes, besides commissioning many elaborate tombs for the church, added the sumptuous side chapels, some of which are so grand that they are almost churches in themselves. The most interesting are the two huge and magnificent domed chapels opposite each other **(D and E)**. The first was built for Sixtus V by Domenico Fontana in 1585 as the pope's burial place, and it has a profusion of statuary, marble and precious stones. A few years later the Borghese pope Paul V decided to build the chapel opposite as his tomb, making it even more sumptuous. The frescoes in the dome, pendentives, lunettes and arches at the top of the walls are considered the finest work of Cavaliere d'Arpino, master of Caravaggio. Pope Paul is shown kneeling meekly and bare-headed in quite a different spirit from his predecessor Clement VIII, opposite, dressed in his tiara and in the act of blessing his subjects.

In striking contrast is the unadorned Sforza Chapel **(F)**, which is reserved for prayer. It was built by Giacomo della Porta but the very unusual design is by Michelangelo: on an elliptical plan, it has huge arches in the two apsidal side chapels behind columns, and is one of his least-known but most fascinating architectural works.

The museum **(G)** has church silver and liturgical objects mostly from the 17th and 18th centuries. From the open loggia at the west end (*for admission, see above*) you can see the 13th-century mosaics on the earlier façade.

Santa Prassede

Map p. 223, E2–F2. Entrance is in the narrow Via di San Martino ai Monti. Open 7–12 & 4–6.30. Coin-operated lights essential for the mosaics.

Detail from the 9th-century dome fresco of the Chapel of St Zeno.

This church, known to have been in existence on this site by the end of the 5th century, is dedicated to Praxedes, the daughter of a Roman senator called Pudens who is alleged to have given hospitality to St Peter when he first arrived in Rome. Its light interior is particularly welcoming. Pope (and saint) Paschal I built the church in 822 and the mosaic decoration he commissioned still survives. The tiny Chapel of St Zeno (north side), intended as a mausoleum for his mother, Theodora, is perfectly preserved. Even the entrance remains as it was in Paschal's day, with its two ancient columns (one granite and the other a rare porphyry with grey crystals) supporting the carved architrave from a pagan temple, and resting on this, a marble urn dating from the 3rd century. The double row of mosaic heads include the Virgin and Child with St Praxedes and her sister Pudentiana. The interior is one of the most memorable places in all Rome since its walls and vault are entirely covered with delightful mosaics which have a primitive sweetness about them which is unforgettable, and they can be studied with ease since the space is so small. The dome is decorated

The late 4th-century apse mosaic of Santa Pudenziana, showing Christ flanked by St Peter and St Paul, who are each receiving a symbolic crown.

with an image of Christ wearing a toga, in a roundel held up by four bright-eyed angels. The iconography here borrows from the pagan convention of showing a victorious general borne aloft on his shield by winged Victories. The dominant colours on the walls are russet red and emerald green, and numerous saints are shown, including St Paschal himself and his mother (in a square nimbus, denoting that she was still alive when the mosaic was made), along with the two Roman sisters. The pavement is thought to be the oldest known example of opus sectile. The old-fashioned display case exhibits a relic said to come from the column at which Christ was scourged.

The other mosaics from Paschal's time are in the main church: on the choir arch the elect are shown being received into Heaven preceded by angels, and on the apse arch is the Lamb of God with the seven golden candlesticks, the symbols of the Evangelists, and 24 Elders raising their crowns as a sign of glory. The semi-dome has Christ between St Peter, St Pudentiana and St Zeno on the right, and St Paul, St Praxedes and St Paschal on the left. Below them are shown the Lamb, and the flock of the faithful.

In the sanctuary are six Roman columns with a very unusual design incorporating the form of acanthus and laurel leaves. You can visit the crypt with its four early Christian sarcophagi. The light, columned nave (where ancient Roman fragments have been used for the architrave) has pretty 16th-century *trompe l'oeil* frescoes.

Santa Pudenziana

Map p. 223, E2. Open 9–12 & 3–6.

This church, dedicated to Pudentiana, the sister of Praxedes, is one of the oldest in Rome, but today you would only know this because it is so far below the level of the street outside. The interior has lost most of its ancient feel, but still preserves a splendid apse mosaic, the earliest of its kind in all Rome, dating from 390 at the time when Christianity was finally declared the official state religion by the Byzantine emperor Theodosius. It is of extreme interest for its iconography since the figure of Christ recalls representations of Jupiter, and the Apostles, in their togas, resemble so many senators seated in a semicircle around him. This is also one of the first instances in which Paul is shown with the Apostles and he is in pride of place next to Christ, with Peter on the other side.

San Pietro in Vincoli

Map p. 223, E3. Entrance by steep steps up from Via Cavour. Open 8–12.30 & 3–6 or 7 in summer.

The busy traffic artery called Via Cavour, which leads down towards the Roman Forum, dates from 1890 when part of the old city was redeveloped. It has been hailed as the most damaging intervention ever made to the townscape of Rome. But it is worth following for a few hundred metres in order to visit the church of San Pietro in Vincoli, home to Michelangelo's celebrated *Moses*.

The very wide interior of the church has something of an over-restored feel, though the ancient fluted columns are exceptionally fine. Beneath the high altar you can see a reliquary casket which contains the chains of St Peter (in whose honour the church was first built in the 5th century). These are amongst the most revered relics in any church in Rome. The saint is said to have been fettered with these very chains in the Mamertine Prison (*see p. 41*) just outside the Forum. In the north aisle there is a lovely 7th-century mosaic icon of St Sebastian and, at the west end next to the entrance, some small 15th-century tombs including one with the busts of the Pollaiolo brothers, Antonio and Piero, both important artists from Florence.

The church's greatest draw, however, is Michelangelo's famous statue of Moses (south aisle). It is one of the most important sculptures made for the tomb of Pope Julius II, which was famously never completed (the *Slaves* which were also carved for it are now in the Louvre and the Galleria dell'Accademia in Florence). The statue depicts the prophet Moses, shown seated as an old man with a flowing beard

but powerfully built and clearly possessed of an inner strength. The satyr-like horns were supposed to represent the beams of light which radiated from his head after his encounter with God (based on a mistranslation of a Hebrew word, they became a traditional attribute of Moses from the Middle Ages onwards). The two gentle female figures of Rachel and Leah on either side are also by the hand of the great sculptor, but the exact design intended by Michelangelo for the tomb as a whole, which was to have been decorated by some 40 statues, has been lost. Barriers have been installed, but it is still possible to see the lovely painting of *St Margaret* by Guercino in the chapel to the right of the sanctuary.

FOOD & DRINK AROUND THE ESQUILINE

There are plenty of snack bars along Via Cavour where you can get a cold drink and a *panino*. A quieter option is Via Leonina, opposite San Pietro in Vincoli, which has cafés with seating outside. A good choice here is the **Vecchia Roma** (*Via Leonina 10; map p. 223, E2*) which serves tasty pizzas, or bruschetta and house wine for a light lunch. See also p. 35 for places to eat on nearby Via Madonna dei Monti.

Detail of Michelangelo's *Moses* (c. 1515), the supreme example of his 'Terribilità', his ability to evoke inner strength and a sense of awe and majesty.

SAN CLEMENTE &
ST JOHN LATERAN

San Clemente

Map p. 223, E3. Open 9–12.30 & 3–6, holidays 12–6; ticket necessary for the earlier church below ground level. Binoculars are particularly useful to study the mosaics.

San Clemente, dedicated to St Clement, the fourth pope (90–?99), is one of the best-preserved and oldest of Rome's medieval basilicas, with a lovely light interior. It was begun by Pope Paschal II who commissioned the **apse mosaic** in the early 12th century. In the centre is Christ on a Cross charmingly decorated with 12 white doves which represent the Apostles. The semi-dome all around it is filled with circular vine tendrils of the Tree of Life against a gold ground inhabited by birds, stylised flowers, biblical figures, and animals as if in a huge illuminated manuscript (difficult to see in detail without binoculars). Above is the Hand of God and the Dome of Heaven. On the triumphal arch are Christ and the Symbols of the Evangelists and to the right and left, saints and prophets with views of Jerusalem and Bethlehem. Below the row of sheep on either side of the Lamb of God (an iconography typical of numerous other mosaic cycles in Rome) the decoration of the apse was completed in the 14th century with impressive large frescoed figures of Christ, the Virgin and Apostles.

Another feature of this early Christian church is the well-preserved ancient schola cantorum in the centre with its beautifully carved marble enclosure around the two pulpits, candelabrum and reading-desk leading up to the lovely baldacchino over the altar. The ancient marble inlaid pavement of the entire church and its old Roman columns complete the symmetry.

The **chapel of St Catherine** at the west end (on the left as you face the apse) is entirely frescoed by the great painter Masolino (possibly with the help of his famous pupil Masaccio), and is recognised as one of the most important early Renaissance works in all Rome. They were commissioned by the titular cardinal of the church, Branda Castiglione, who particularly admired Masolino's work and had already employed him to paint frescoes in his home town in northern

View of the nave of San Clemente, taken from within the schola cantorum, with the two pulpits visible on either side, and looking towards the magnificent mosaic of the apse.

Italy (Castiglione Olona). The San Clemente frescoes illustrate the life of St Catherine of Alexandria, who spent all her days converting the Romans to Christianity before she was finally martyred. Despite the violence she encountered (attempts to break her on the wheel failed, so she was beheaded instead), the scenes convey a memorable spirit of calm and serenity.

On a lower level (through a door off the right side) you can visit the fascinating remains of the first church, now brightly lit and well labelled, also in English. Mentioned by St Jerome as early as 392, and restored in later centuries, this church was destroyed during the sack of Rome by the Normans in 1084. Remains of it were found during excavations here in 1861 along with fragments of its ancient frescoes illustrating some very unusual legends concerning early saints. Even earlier buildings beneath it, dating from the Roman Republican and Imperial periods (and including a Mithraeum) can also be seen.

There is a lovely little garden court with a fountain outside the west end where you can sit and rest.

Santi Quattro Coronati

Map p. 223, E4. Although the church itself is open for most of the day (except between 12.45 and 3.15), it is best to visit only at 10–11.45 & 4–5.45, Sun 9.30–10.30 & 4–5.45 since the most interesting things to see here, the chapel and cloister, are only open then (the ten nuns who live here are at prayer at other times). The crypt is only sometimes opened on request (since the nun has to close the cloister while she shows it to you).

Set at the top of a steep rise, removed from the busy life of the streets close by, this medieval convent is still surrounded by castellated buildings and entered through a fortified gateway, surmounted by a squat campanile dating from the 9th century (the oldest bell-tower to survive in the city). This is a place to savour the atmosphere of days long past, and it is hardly ever disturbed by more than one or two visitors.

Although of ancient foundation the present church was built by Pope Paschal II (two years after he dedicated San Clemente; *see above*). The most interesting thing to see is the **Chapel of St Sylvester** (*on the right of the second courtyard, ring the old wooden bell to summon a nun: when she answers from behind the grille she will open the chapel door automatically, after requesting a small donation. If there is no reply, wait and try again a little later*). The chapel was built in 1246 and contains a delightful and particularly well-preserved fresco cycle of the same date. It illustrates the conversion of Constantine to Christianity: the story begins on the entrance wall where Constantine is shown enthroned but his spotty face—indicating that he has contracted leprosy—detracts from his dignity, and he is attended by a worried-looking crowd. The subsequent scenes show how, with the help of Pope Sylvester, he comes to be baptised (by total immersion in a font rather too small for him), only after which is he cured. He gratefully presents his imperial tiara to the pope who forthwith places it on his sacred head and, wearing it, is led off by the emperor mounted on horseback. One of the last scenes shows the pope bringing back to life a wild bull (shown bizarrely standing on his head).

The church is entered at the back of the second court. From the north aisle you can visit the tiny cloister (*ring for admission, bell on the right*). This survives from the early 13th century: beneath the pretty little garden a 6th-century baptistery was found. There is another ancient little chapel off it, dating from the 9th century (the crypt of the church, of the same date, can sometimes be seen on request here).

St John Lateran

Map pp. 223, F4 and 221, D1. Open 7–6.30 daily; the cloister (with an entrance fee) is open 9–6. Audio guides are available.

Around the busy Piazza di San Giovanni in Laterano are assembled some of the most important monuments in Christian history. The red granite **obelisk**, the oldest in the city and the tallest in existence, was set up here in 1588 (made in the 15th century BC, it had been brought to Rome from Thebes in 357).

The **basilica of St John Lateran** (San Giovanni in Laterano) is the cathedral of Rome and the mother church of the entire Christian world since it was the first Christian basilica to be constructed (around 314), on land donated for the purpose by the emperor Constantine after he outlawed the persecution of Christians in his dominions. It is named 'in Laterano' because it stands on land once owned by the patrician Laterani family. The popes lived in the Lateran Palace until 1377, when the Holy See was transferred to the Vatican (but the popes were still crowned here up until 1870, when Rome fell to the Italian national army and the pope retreated to the Vatican City).

The basilica has two façades: the principal front, overlooking the vast Piazza di Porta San Giovanni, is a theatrical composition with a two-storeyed portico crowned with 16 colossal statues, added in the early 18th century; the other front dates from 1586 and is by Domenico Fontana. From here you enter directly into the transepts, which were decorated with frescoes in the 17th century.

1 Baldacchino
2 Fresco by ?Giotto
3 Ancient Roman doors
4 Cloister
5 Baptistery

The interior

The huge, light interior somehow lacks atmosphere (and is filled with plastic chairs) but is, of course, much visited because of the basilica's place in the history of Christianity. Although it retains in part its original 4th-century proportions, its appearance is predominantly Mannerist and Baroque: the great architect Borromini was called in to remodel it in 1649, although he was only able to give some sort of conformity to the decoration of the nave pillars and the side aisle altars, the effect of which is largely lost because of the vast scale of the building. As one would expect, there are numerous chapels and funerary monuments from many different periods. The apse mosaics were remade in the 19th century. The lovely Gothic baldacchino (**1**), in the centre of the nave, decorated with frescoes, dates from the 14th century, and behind the grille above are two 19th-century reliquaries, permanently illuminated, said to contain the heads of St Peter and St Paul. In the confessio beneath is the beautiful bronze tomb-slab of Pope Martin V (d. 1431). One of the few other works which has survived from before the 16th century is a fresco fragment on the first nave pillar in the south aisle (**2**) which shows the elderly Boniface VIII proclaiming the Jubilee of 1300 (the first Holy Year; *see p. 141*). The fresco, detached from the loggia of the Lateran Palace, may be by the great artist Giotto. The oldest works of all are the bronze doors of the central door into the nave (**3**), through which the senators of ancient Rome once passed into the Curia building which still stands in the Roman Forum. They were installed here in the 17th century.

The **cloister (4)** (*for admission see above*) is a magnificent example of Cosmatesque art, with colourful marble inlay decorating the little columns as well as the frieze. In the little museum Boniface VIII's cope is preserved, made by English craftsmen in the 13th century.

The baptistery

The **baptistery (5)** (*usually open 7–12.30 & 4–7.30; entrance on Piazza di San Giovanni in Laterano*) is very interesting for its architecture on a central octagonal design (frequently copied in later baptisteries). First built by Constantine c. 315–24, it was remodelled a little over a century later by Sixtus III: the eight columns of porphyry survive from his time and they support an architrave which bears eight smaller white marble columns. The side chapels contain remains of ancient mosaics.

THE CAELIAN HILL

The Caelian Hill is a peaceful district of the city, chiefly residential but with a number of interesting monuments. From Piazza di San Giovanni in Laterano, follow the narrow Via di Santo Stefano Rotondo, which has some Roman remains (but also fast one-way traffic) to reach the church of **Santo Stefano Rotondo** (*map p. 221, C1; open 9.30–12.30 & 2–5; Sun 9.30–12.30*), one of the largest and oldest circular churches in existence (5th century) with a double circular colonnade and two huge columns in the centre supporting three arches. It seems to have been inspired by eastern Byzantine models as well as the buildings of ancient Rome.

Essentially, in terms of its form, Santo Stefano Rotondo is a martyrium, a type of building popular in the early days of Christianity, and related in structure to the masuoleum. Both are centrally planned, that is, their focus is on a central point rather than the layout being a linear progression towards an altar at one end. The style disappeared from Western Christendom until Brunelleschi reintroduced it into Renaissance Florence in the 15th century.

The mausoleum is derived from Classical models, of which two survive in Rome: that of Augustus (*see p. 51*) and that of Hadrian (now Castel Sant'Angelo; *see p. 137*). They are often circular (see Santa Costanza; *p. 154*), sometimes octagonal. The martyrium is an explicitly Christian idea: a temple or shrine built over and around the tomb of a martyr. Santo Stefano Rotondo is a superb example, dedicated to Stephen, the first Christian martyr and constructed in a style deliberately reminiscent of the Church of the Holy Sepulchre in Jerusalem, which rises above the purported burial place of Christ.

Interior of the centrally-planned church of Santo Stefano Rotondo, clearly showing the design of a central shrine surrounded by a colonnade, around which worshippers would have processed.

Also here on the summit of the hill, beside a delightful fountain made from an ancient Roman stone boat, is the church of **Santa Maria in Domnica** (*map p. 221, C1; open 9–12.30 & 4.30–7.30*). It has a graceful portico and lovely interior rebuilt by the Tuscan architect Andrea Sansovino in the 16th century. On the triumphal arch is a beautifully coloured 9th-century mosaic of Christ with two angels and the Apostles, and the larger figures of Moses and Elijah below: in the semi-dome, St Paschal (who restored the church at this time) kisses the foot of the Madonna and Child surrounded by a throng of angels.

Next to the church is an entrance into the public park of the **Villa Celimontana** (*open 7–dusk*), which has some lovely palms and pine trees inhabited by exotic birds. It is a delightful place to stroll or lie on the grass, far from the noise of the city. There is a playground in one corner for children, where they can even have pony rides. There is an exit opposite the church of **Santi Giovanni e Paolo** (*map p. 221, C1; open 8.30–12 & 3.30–6*), in a picturesque corner of the hill where two narrow old roads meet. The church has a lovely 12th-century campanile at the base of which can be seen the huge travertine blocks of a Roman temple. The Ionic portico dates from the same century, but the interior was entirely remodelled in 1718. It is dedicated to two court dignitaries called John and Paul, who were buried here after their martyrdom in the mid-4th century. Beneath the church, and thought to have been on the site of their house, are some remains of **Roman**

houses (*open 10–1 & 3–6 except Tues and Wed; entrance from Clivo di Scauro spanned by the medieval buttresses of the church*), extremely interesting for their lovely wall paintings. Well worth a visit, there is also a little antiquarium here.

Only a short way further downhill is the church of **San Gregorio Magno** (*map p. 221, B1; open 9–12.30 & 3.30–6*), where three oratories which were part of a monastery founded by St Gregory the Great can be visited (*but only open Tues, Thur, Sat and Sun 9.30–12.30*).

FOOD & DRINK NEAR ST JOHN LATERAN

There is a large self-service restaurant with plenty of seating both inside and out at **Caffè l' '800** (*Via San Giovanni in Laterano 278/b; map p. 223, F4; open Mon–Sat*), very close to St John Lateran in a large building built at the angle between Via San Giovanni in Laterano and Via Santo Stefano Rotondo. It is rather old-fashioned but adequate for a quick snack.

The park of Villa Celimontana on the Caelian Hill (*map p. 221, C1*) is an especially nice place to enjoy a picnic.

THE BATHS OF CARACALLA & THE VIA APPIA ANTICA

The monuments described in this chapter are on the outskirts of the historic centre and can be combined in a single day (though you will need the best part of the day to do them justice, especially if travelling by public transport, which is rather infrequent). The Baths of Caracalla are perhaps the grandest and most evocative of all the ancient Roman buildings still standing in Rome because they are isolated and on a huge scale. Parts of the famous Via Appia (now officially protected as a park) still manage to give you the feel of what it must have been like to approach the city from the desolate Roman *campagna* in past centuries.

The Baths of Caracalla

Map p. 221. C2. Open 9–6.30, Mon 9–1. Combined ticket with the Tomb of Cecilia Metella and Villa dei Quintili on the Via Appia. From the Circus Maximus (Circo Massimo on Metro line B, or buses 160 and 628 from Via del Corso) it is a short walk along the wide Viale delle Terme di Caracalla. These baths are so huge that their ruins have always stood above ground. They have never been built over and survive today as one of the most romantic sights of ancient Rome. The huge walls, mighty arches and broken vaults which tower above you against the sky are partly overgrown with vegetation while poppies, marigolds and dai-

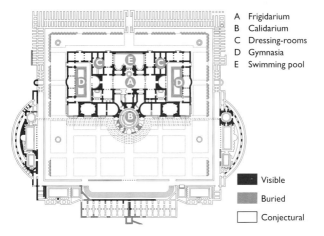

A Frigidarium
B Calidarium
C Dressing-rooms
D Gymnasia
E Swimming pool

■ Visible

■ Buried

□ Conjectural

sies grow in the grass at their feet. They are inhabited, undisturbed, by numerous seagulls, crows and pigeons. In the gardens outside, with their tall pines and cypresses, you can sit in peace on comfortable old benches.

History of the baths

The baths were begun by Caracalla in AD 212 and it has been estimated that it took some 9,000 workers about five years to construct them. As in all the public baths in the city, Roman citizens had free access to them: men and women bathed nude, but separately and at different times of the day.

As you can see from the plan, the baths had a monumental architectural design with various halls symmetrically arranged around a central hall, the frigidarium **(A)**, and the domed circular calidarium **(B)**, which had high windows on two levels designed to admit the sun's rays for many hours of the day (and beneath the floor of which were the furnaces to heat the water). There were dressing rooms **(C)**, open gymnasia for exercises and sports before bathing **(D)**, and domed covered pools with water at various temperatures. You would start with the hottest and end in the frigidarium, and then perhaps take a dip in the outside swimming pool **(E)** before being rubbed down with oil and enjoying a massage. The Romans were the first to give importance to the refreshing combination of exercise and cleanliness for the body and these baths would often have been crowded with up to 1,600 bathers at any one time.

The parts at present open include the two gymnasia which both still have parts of their polychrome paving and mosaic fragments propped against the walls, on either side of the great central hall of the frigidarium. The huge water cisterns, fed by a purpose-built aqueduct, were beneath the exedra on the southern boundary of the garden, where public libraries provided cultural refreshment.

THE VIA APPIA ANTICA

Map p. 3 and overleaf.
Since 1997 this ancient road and the countryside close to it have been officially protected as a regional park—though the project has not been without administrative difficulties and the area is still dogged by through traffic. There are some important catacombs, although these are outside the park jurisdiction. The most important features of the road, and those easiest to visit are mentioned below.

How to get there

However enthusiastic a walker you are, it is sadly not recommended to approach this area on foot since it is seriously disturbed by fast and noisy traffic. Even though the narrow Via di Porta San Sebastiano (just beyond the Baths of Caracalla) has the appearance at first of a charming country lane, as soon as the traffic light changes at its lower end, the cars pound down it at uncontrollable speed. At the point where the Via Appia Antica begins, the traffic intensifies and even on Sundays when the road is officially closed to motor vehicles the stretch of road up to the fork with the Via Ardeatina is particularly unpleasant on foot.

One alternative is to take the **Archeobus**, a distinctive green double-decker with an open top, which leaves from outside Termini Station (*map p. 223, F1*; its terminus is near the metro station) every day at 8.30, 9, 9.30 and 10, and then at 3, 3.30, 4 and 4.30. The ticket is not cheap (there is a discount if you have the Roma Pass card) but you can get on and off at will throughout the day (but remember that it only runs every half hour, and not at all in the middle of the day). There is a guide on board (and audio guides available). At present the stops are as follows: Termini Station, Piazza Venezia, Colosseo (or Circo Massimo on holidays), Baths of Caracalla, Porta di San Sebastiano, Parco Appia Antica, Valle della Caffarella, Catacombs of San Callisto and Domitilla, Catacombs of San Sebastiano, Tomb of Cecilia Metella, Sant'Urbano, Villa Capo di Bove, Stadio delle Terme (near the Baths of Caracalla), Bocca della Verità, Termini Station. The timetable and itinerary are subject to change, however, so check in advance at www. trambusopen.com (T: 06 684 0901 or 800 281 281).

City bus 118 also serves this area (although it is notoriously unreliable; it is not unusual to have to wait for well over 30mins) and runs from outside Piramide metro station, via the Baths of Caracalla and on to Via Appia Antica (with a stop at the park office) as far as the Catacombs of San Callisto, after which it branches off on the narrow but incredibly busy Via Appia Pignatelli. For the return it is often best to use minibus no. 660 which runs every 20mins between the Via Appia Antica (the stop is near the Bar Appia Antica beyond the Tomb of Cecilia Metella on the corner of Via Cecilia Metella) and the Appia Nuova (via Via Cecilia Metella) where it stops at the metro station of Colli Albani on line A (for Termini Station and Piazza di Spagna).

Information

Parco Regionale dell'Appia Antica, Via Appia Antica 42, with an information office at no. 58, T: 06 513 5316. Bicycles can be hired here.

Parco della Caffarella

Entrance about 100m beyond the fork with Via Ardeatina, on the left off Via della Caffarella.

This area of farmland and countryside is probably the area closest to the centre of the city where you can still see a landscape reminiscent of the famous *campagna romana*, the undulating plain around Rome characterised by its wide, open landscape of pastureland, green for most of the year, with a few wooded areas and others covered with typical low vegetation known as the *macchia mediterranea*. The wealthy Athenian Herodes Atticus, patron of the arts and man of letters in the 2nd century AD, famous above all for his numerous buildings in Greece, had a villa here. The area has been used as farmland ever since: some 6,000 sheep still graze here and there are a few tumbledown medieval farmhouses and mills. The tomb of Herodes' Roman wife, Annia Regilla, survives in the form of a temple. Beyond is the romantic Nymphaeum of Egeria, a monumental fountain where one of the early kings of Rome, Numa Pompilius, is said to have come to visit the nymph Egeria. This is a lovely place to take a long country walk.

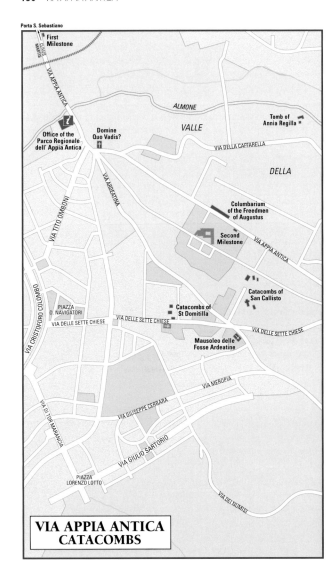

Porta S. Sebastiano

First Milestone

CLIVUS MARTIS

VIA APPIA ANTICA

ALMONE

VALLE

Tomb of Annia Regilla

Office of the Parco Regionale dell' Appia Antica

Domine Quo Vadis?

VIA DELLA CAFFARELLA

DELLA

VIA ARDEATINA

VIA TITO OMBONI

Columbarium of the Freedmen of Augustus

Second Milestone

VIA APPIA ANTICA

VIA CRISTOFORO COLOMBO

PIAZZA D. NAVIGATORI

Catacombs of San Callisto

Catacombs of St Domitilla

VIA DELLE SETTE CHIESE

VIA DELLE SETTE CHIESE

VIA DELLE SETTE CHIESE

Mausoleo delle Fosse Ardeatine

VIA DI TOR MARANCIA

VIA MEROPIA

VIA GIUSEPPE CERBARA

VIA GIULIO SARTORIO

PIAZZA LORENZO LOTTO

VIA DEI NUMISI

VIA APPIA ANTICA CATACOMBS

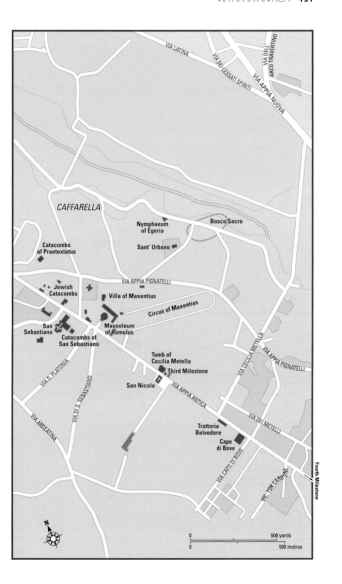

VIA LATINA

VIA DEI CESSATI SPIRITI

VIA DELL' ARCO TRAVERTINO

VIA APPIA NUOVA

CAFFARELLA

Nymphaeum
of Egeria

Bosco Sacro

Sant' Urbano

Catacombs
of Praetextatus

VIA APPIA PIGNATELLI

Jewish
Catacombs

Villa of Maxentius

Circus of Maxentius

San
Sebastiano

Mausoleum
of Romulus

Catacombs of
San Sebastiano

VIA CECILIA METELLA

VIA APPIA PIGNATELLI

VIA D. PLATONIA

VIA DI S. SEBASTIANO

Tomb of
Cecilia Metella

Third Milestone

San Nicola

VIA APPIA ANTICA

VIA DEI METELLI

VIA ARDEATINA

Trattoria
Belvedere

Capo
di Bove

VIA CAPO DI BOVE

WC, TOR CARBONE

Fourth Milestone

N

0   500 yards
0   500 metres

The Catacombs

Two of the most important catacombs in Rome are next to each other off the right side of the Via Appia. Pagan Romans had been cremated and for some 400 years from the early 1st century burial within the city precinct was forbidden, so Christians came here to bury their dead outside the walls. Since space was at a premium, and the soft tufa so easy to quarry, the cemeteries expanded underground. These came to be known as catacombs (or caves) after those of San Sebastiano had been built in an abandoned stone quarry. You can still see many tunnels on different levels, the deepest sometimes over 20m below the ground. In the walls there were tiers of simple rectangular niches (loculi) where the bodies were placed wrapped in a sheet, and then the openings closed with slabs of marble or terracotta on which the names were inscribed. For the wealthier and more distinguished there would be an arched niche with more elaborate decoration or even a small chapel.

When they were first opened to the public in the 19th century the catacombs became one of the most visited sights of Rome and have remained so ever since. They tend to be very crowded with tour groups and have lost much of the atmosphere they must once have had. But it is still exciting to go underground and see one of them (they are all rather similar) with their dark winding corridors which have survived so well for all these centuries. There are sometimes also interesting remains of inscriptions and frescoes. They are usually quite dark with steep steps and uneven ground, so you should take great care.

Catacombs of San Callisto

Open 9–12 & 2.30–5 or 5.30; closed Wed and in Feb. You have to join a guided tour (these are provided about every half hour in English by the well-informed Salesian priests and last around 30mins).

It is best to use the main entrance gate at the fork between Via Appia Antica and Via Ardeatina: the driveway, across open fields, is about 1km long, and passes the Salesian college before reaching a cypress avenue which leads up to the catacombs. There is also a side entrance at Via Appia Antica 110, but since the road is very busy with traffic in this stretch, it is much more pleasant to walk along the drive. NB: After the visit it is best to continue through the estate along the drive (not signposted) to the convenient exit directly onto the Via Appia Antica beside San Sebastiano.

This was the first official cemetery of the early Christian community and so is usually considered the most important. The catacombs were named after St Calixtus, who was appointed to look after the cemetery by the pope before he himself became pope in 217. You are shown an oratory where the dead were brought before burial, and then descend an ancient staircase to the burial corridor on the second level (there were five levels in all). The papal crypt preserves the tombs of popes martyred in the 3rd century, and there are remains of early frescoes.

Catacombs of San Sebastiano

Usually open 9–12 & 2.30–5 or 5.30; closed Sun and from mid Nov–mid Dec. Entrance on Via Appia Antica next to the church of San Sebastiano.
These catacombs have always been known and visited since the bodies of St Peter and St Paul were brought here temporarily for safe-keeping probably in the 3rd century and the church next door, one of the seven pilgrimage churches of Rome, was dedicated to the Apostles. At a later date St Sebastian, who was martyred under Diocletian in 288, was buried here, and the catacombs still bear his name.

A very steep stair leads down to the first level below ground. Beyond a chapel and the crypt of St Sebastian steps then continue down to where the so-called Piazzola has three tombs, extremely interesting for their architecture with beautiful, well preserved stucco decoration and frescoes in their vaults. They date from the early 2nd century and it is believed that they were used for both pagan and Christian burials. From the room known as the Triclia, where funerary banquets were held (and with graffiti invoking the Apostles inscribed on the walls) you go up through a chapel with a huge 14th-century wood Crucifix into the church, which now has a pleasant 17th-century interior.

Beyond the catacombs, after Via San Sebastiano branches to the right, the Via Appia becomes suddenly much more peaceful and the traffic diminishes noticeably. The most interesting stretch of the ancient road begins here.

The Circus of Maxentius

Open 9–1, closed Mon. Entrance at Via Appia Antica 153.
This is the best preserved of the Roman circuses and has been left in its grass-grown state so that you can walk all around it. It was a huge stadium built in AD 309 to hold some 10,000 spectators. As you approach it you can see the two square towers with curved façades at its main entrance where there were stalls for the contestants. Along the top of the walls on the left long side which supported the tiers of seats, you can see broken amphorae in the masonry: these were used to lighten the vaults. In the centre is the round *meta* (turning post) and low wall which marked the course for the chariot and quadriga races

View along the further reaches of the Via Appia Antica.

(usually of seven laps). Other buildings here, including the palace of Maxentius and the mausoleum of his son Romulus are at present fenced off for restoration. From this romantic spot, only disturbed by the sight of the cars on the busy Via Appia Pignatelli in the far distance beyond the ruins of a triumphal arch, there is a good view of the tomb of Cecilia Metella.

The Tomb of Cecilia Metella

Open 9–1 hour before sunset; closed Mon.

The ancient Appia, here paved in small square cobbles, called *san-pietrini*, rises to this tomb, the most famous landmark on the entire road, a massive circular tower still faced in marble on a square base and very well preserved. In many ways it is most interesting from the exterior rather than inside. Around the upper part there is an elegant frieze with garlands of fruit and bucrania. The inscription in handsome large letters records Cecilia, who was married to Crassus, elder son of the triumvir and one of Caesar's generals in Gaul. Inside you can see the sepulchral chamber, now open to the sky, the end of a lava flow from the Alban Hills (the volcanic formation that rises just to the south of Rome), and a small collection of antique sculpture. The tomb was later incorporated into a castle by the Caetani, remains of which can be seen nearby (beneath a two-light window the very worn third milestone of the Via Appia survives).

The outer Via Appia and Capo di Bove

About 100m beyond the Tomb of Cecilia Metella a stretch of the wonderful old *basolato*, with its massive polygonal blocks of grey basaltic lava from the Alban hills, was carefully restored in 2000 (and the road is, at last, officially closed to traffic). The Appia was 4.2m wide to allow two carts to pass each other and on either side were pavements for pedestrians, still partly preserved. You soon come to a group of houses with a *trattoria* opposite a bar on the corner of Via Appia Pignatelli (and the bus stop for minibus 660; *see above*). A little way further on, where there is an interruption in the old paving stones, is a simple grocery shop. Beyond on the right, at no. 222, is the entrance gate to **Capo di Bove** (*open 10–4, Sun 10–6*), a garden where some Roman baths of the 2nd century AD with mosaic floors have been excavated. A villa here now houses a study centre with the archives of the great conservationist Antonio Cederna (d. 1996), who did so much towards creating the park to preserve this ancient road. Visitors are welcome and you can sit and enjoy the peaceful little garden.

The road, now surfaced with *sanpietrini*, continues past some villas with very grand entrances, and luxurious gardens, most of them built in the 1950s and 1960s. When Goethe walked out along this road in 1786, he commented: 'These people built for eternity; they omitted nothing from their calculations except the insane fury of the destroyers to whom nothing was sacred.' (*Italian Journey*, Tr. W.H. Auden and Elizabeth Mayer). At the Vicolo di Tor Carbone begins the most beautiful stretch of the road, still with its massive old paving stones and lined with pine trees and numerous ancient tombs. The tombs, some of which were reconstructed here in the 19th century by Antonio Canova (and others replaced by casts, easily identified by their yellow tint) include sepulchres in the form of temples, or simple funerary monuments, and line the road for many miles. Beyond the 11th milestone the road becomes more and more deserted.

The very interesting ruins of the huge **Villa dei Quintili** include a museum (*open Tues–Sun 9–6*), but can at present only be visited from the Via Appia Nuova. Nearby there is a park in which you can see long stretches of a number of magnificent old aqueducts. It can at present only usually be visited from the Via Appia Nuova.

FOOD & DRINK ON THE VIA APPIA

There are a number of restaurants and a few cafés along the Via Appia Antica. They are given in the order in which you will pass them on your way out of Rome: **La Botticella da Franca** (*no. 28, T: 06 513 6792; closed weekends*), inside an ancient Roman building, is a very simple place where you will usually also find Romans enjoying a meal. **Priscilla** (*no. 68, T: 06 513 6379; closed Sun*) is a very small, typical *trattoria*. Nearby, is the **Bar l'Incontro** (*no. 64, closed Sun*) where you can have a simple snack. **Hostaria Antica Roma** (*no. 87, T: 06 513 2888; closed Mon*) serves not particularly exciting food, but is worth visiting since it is inside an ancient columbarium, still with its rows of niches which contained urns for ashes. **Cecilia Metella** (*no. 125; T: 511 0213; closed Mon*) is one of the best places to have a reasonably priced good meal on the road. **Hostaria dell'Archeologia** (or **L'Archeologia**; *no. 139; T: 06 788 0494; closed Tues*), with a large garden but on a busy crossroads, has for long been one of the best-known places to eat here. It is also one of the most expensive, with a very good wine list. **Alessandrini** (*no. 198, T: 06 780 3922; closed Sun and Mon*) is a pleasant *trattoria*, a sound choice and in a convenient position on Via Cecilia Metella, just beyond which the most interesting part of the old road can be explored. It is opposite the **Bar Appia Antica** (*no. 175; open daily*) which has a few tables outside and which also serves snacks. A little further, on the right at no. 204, there is a simple **grocery shop** (just about the only one on the whole road) where you can have a good sandwich (*panino*) freshly made for you (*open daily 9–1*). You can have a **picnic** a little further on in the garden of Capo di Bove (*no. 222*) or in the peaceful stretch of the road beyond Vicolo di Tor Carbone. Other lovely places to picnic include the Baths of Caracalla, the Parco della Caffarella, the estate of the Catacombs of Priscilla, and the Circus of Maxentius (but for these, you should buy your picnic before leaving the centre of Rome).

ST PETER'S & THE VATICAN MUSEUMS

The finest approach to the Vatican City is to cross the Tiber over **Ponte Sant'Angelo** (*map p. 219, D2*), a pedestrian bridge upon whose parapets stand ten famous angel sculptures, designed by Bernini and executed by his pupils in 1688. Each angel holds one of the Instruments of the Passion: the scourge, column of the Flagellation, Cross, nails, crown of thorns, titulus (name board bearing the letters INRI), vinegar sponge, garments and dice, lance, sudarium (the cloth with which Christ's face was covered at the Deposition). The bridge itself is ancient, built by Hadrian in AD 134 as a grand approach to his circular mausoleum, which still stands on the other side, and is known today as **Castel Sant'Angelo**. The lower part of the building, up to the first string course, is ancient. The upper section and the battlements date from the Middle Ages, when it became a fortress. It saw service in 1527 during the Sack of Rome by the troops of the emperor Charles V (*see p. 9*). Pope Clement VII and his cardinals and bishops took refuge here.

From Castel Sant'Angelo it is a short walk to the head of the long, broad, ceremonious Via della Conciliazione, completed in 1937 and named in honour of the 'conciliatory' Lateran Treaty of 1929, by which the papacy acknowledged that it would never regain temporal sovereignty in Italy and the Italian state in turn recognised that the Vatican was independent and exempt from Fascist law. At the end of the street you cross the busy Piazza Pio XII to enter St Peter's Square.

This land is hallowed by the fact that it was here that St Peter was buried after his martyrdom nearby (in AD 67). Peter was the Apostle whom Christ had singled out: 'Thou art Peter, and upon this rock I will build my church; and I will give unto thee the keys of the kingdom of heaven'. Peter is often referred to as the first pope, and today his successors live here, in the independent Vatican State, most of which is closed to the general public with the exception of the magnificent Vatican Museums and Sistine Chapel and St Peter's basilica itself.

Information office
On the left side of St Peter's Square, T: 06 6988 1662 or 06 6988 2019, www.vaticanstate.va.
You are not allowed inside St Peter's or the Vatican City wearing shorts, mini skirts or with bare shoulders.

St Peter's Square

Map p. 219, C2 (Piazza San Pietro).

It was Bernini who provided the magnificent setting for the basilica: a huge, circular piazza formed by a quadruple row of Doric columns. This welcoming space is often filled with people who come to see the pope or attend the celebrations which accompany the Christian calendar (papal audiences are sometimes held here, and on Sundays at midday the pope recites the *Angelus* from a window in the Vatican buildings which can be seen towering up above the piazza to the right). Bernini found the obelisk already here (it came from Alexandria, but used to decorate a Roman circus), and he adapted the two lovely fountains to complete the symmetry of the central space.

ST PETER'S BASILICA

Map p. 219, B2. Open April–Sept 7–7; Oct–March 7–6. Entrance on the right side of St Peter's Square, where there is a security check so there can be queues (it is usually possible to enter the basilica directly from the Vatican Museums so that you avoid this queue; see p. 151).

St Peter's basilica is the most important Roman Catholic church in the world, and the one that all visitors to Rome feel they should visit, following in the steps of pilgrims of past centuries. The first church was begun by Constantine and consecrated in 326: although it was a magnificent huge building it was only half the size of the present St Peter's. It survived right up until the middle of the 15th century when it was decided that it should be rebuilt, though this proved a long and complicated task which progressed slowly over the following centuries, and with many alterations to its plan, while the dilapidated old basilica was left standing. Important architects who became involved at one time or another included Leon Battista Alberti, Donato Bramante, Raphael, Antonio da Sangallo the Younger, Michelangelo, Carlo Maderno, and Bernini.

The present appearance of the basilica dates from the 17th century although its most splendid feature, its dome, was designed by Michelangelo in the previous century. Even if this is not visible from the façade, it is one of the most conspicuous features of Rome's skyline, and can be seen from many miles outside the city.

Detail of one of Bernini's two celebrated semicircular travertine colonnades in St Peter's Square, topped by statues of saints and martyrs.

Treasury

To the dome and grottoes

I	Michelangelo's *Pietà*	7	Alexander VII
2	Dome	8	John XXIII
3	Throne of St Peter	9	Clement XIII
4	Statue of St Peter	10	Tomb of the last
5	Innocent VIII		Stuarts
6	Urban VIII	11	Treasury entrance

The interior

This is on a vast scale but the proportions are so measured that you never feel completely overwhelmed. It was soon decided that ordinary painted altarpieces would be lost in such a space, so all but one were made in miniature mosaic. Don't miss the first chapel on the right (**1**) where Michelangelo's lovely marble *Pietà* is displayed. Made in 1499 when the sculptor was just 24, this is the only sculpture he ever signed. It looks touchingly small and fragile amongst all the magnificence in the church, and the beautiful Madonna appears to be younger than her Son.

The most interesting part of the basilica is the centre, beneath Michelangelo's great dome (**2**), where you can see the huge Baroque baldacchino built by Bernini with its magnificent gilt-bronze twisted columns supporting an elaborate canopy (made from bronze melted down from the ceiling of the Pantheon's porch). At the east end is the enormous throne of St Peter (**3**), supported by statues which the great architect designed, beneath a gilded stained glass window showing the glory of the Holy Dove which becomes the focal point of the whole church.

Against a nave pillar the elegant seated bronze statue of St Peter (**4**) stands out not only for its relatively small scale compared to the other works of art in the church but also for its extended foot which has been worn away by the touch of worshippers. It is thought to have been made around 1296 by the Tuscan sculptor and architect Arnolfo di Cambio.

As you would expect, the basilica is filled with a great many papal monuments. The only one to survive from the old basilica is that of

Innocent VIII, who died in 1492 **(5)**. Made of bronze, it is the work of the great Florentine sculptor Antonio Pollaiolo. Of the magnificent monuments from later centuries, those commemorating Urban VIII **(6)** and Alexander VII **(7)** by Bernini are the most elaborately impressive. However, the simple tomb of John XXIII **(8)**, with its fully robed wax effigy, is the one where you are most likely to find a group of people gathered in prayer, since 'Papa Giovanni', who was beatified in 2000, is still remembered for his profound humanity. There are also a number of Neoclassical tombs by Antonio Canova, including that of Clement XIII **(9)** and the last Stuarts **(10)** who, exiled from England because of their Roman Catholicism, were naturally welcomed in Rome in the 18th century.

The **treasury** (*open April–Sept 8–6.50, Oct–March 8–5.508*) has some works of art from the old basilica as well as precious ecclesiastical objects (the earliest piece is a Cross from the 6th century). Also here is exhibited the huge tomb of Sixtus IV, the pope who gave his name to the Sistine Chapel, a masterpiece in bronze by Antonio Pollaiolo, which fills one whole room.

The Vatican Grottoes (Tombe dei Papi)

Open April–Sept 7–6, Oct–March 7–5; entrance from the portico on the extreme right of the façade.

This underground area beneath the basilica, really a huge crypt, contains more papal tombs. The present entrance is near the tomb of Boniface VIII who died in 1303. He is remembered as the pope who instituted the custom of the Holy Year or Jubilee, when all those who made the pilgrimage to Rome were promised temporal forgiveness of their sins. The result was a surge in pilgrim numbers. Around the corner, at the west end, can be seen a very fine kneeling statue of Pius VI by Canova. The last chapel on the right has the simple tomb slab of John Paul II, who died in 2005. At the end, behind glass and flanked by two lions and two angels, a mosaic marks the site of the tomb of St Peter himself. The exit is from the other aisle, through rooms with architectural fragments, and you emerge just inside the Vatican City which you leave through the Arco della Campana gate on the extreme left-hand side of the façade of St Peter's.

On a lower level still are **the tomb of St Peter and the necropolis**, dating from the 1st century AD (a mausoleum here has the most ancient mosaics yet discovered on a Christian subject). They can only be seen on a guided tour by previous appointment (*T: 06 6988 5318; scavi@fsp.va*).

Detail of the ceiling of St Peter's basilica.

The dome

Open April–Sept 8–6, Oct–March 8–5; entrance from the portico on the extreme right of the façade.

A lift or staircase ascends to the roof beside the spring of the dome. Two stairways lead on up to a curving corridor from which you can enter the first circular gallery around the interior of the dome, which provides a splendid view of the basilica. You can continue up between the two shells of the dome to the lantern from which there is a wonderful panorama of the city.

THE VATICAN MUSEUMS

Map p. 219, C1. Open 9–6 (last entry 4pm). Closed Sun except the last of each month when there is free entry 8.30–2 (last entry 12.30). The museums are also closed on a number of Church holidays throughout the year, so always check the website before your visit. Entrance on Viale Vaticano, a longish walk around the walls of the Vatican City along Via di Porta Angelica to the north of Bernini's colonnade in Piazza San Pietro. The entrance is a short walk from Ottaviana on Metro line A, or bus 81 from Piazza Venezia (returning along Via del Corso) to Piazza del Risorgimento.

Visiting the museums

You can book a visit online (www.vatican.va), and in this case you are given an entry time so you avoid queueing. For this service you pay a booking fee (added to the cost of admission). Otherwise there are almost always long queues outside the entrance, especially in the early morning. It is often best to come here around 3.30, just before closing time; this leaves you 2$^{1}/_{2}$ hours to see the museums. Sometimes staff shortages mean that the less frequented museums are closed. The best way to see everything is to make more than one visit, but given the cost and the crowds this may not be practicable.

The museums are arranged in a group of buildings which centre on two extremely long corridors (on two levels) built by Donato Bramante for Julius II. Be prepared for a lot of walking. Because of their vast extent and the sheer number of visitors, the first impression is overwhelming. If you arrive at a busy time, you can find yourself caught up in a chaotic mass of people surging forward towards the Sistine Chapel.

The routes imposed by the Vatican authorities must be adhered to, and the description below follows one of them, taking you out of the Sistine Chapel and on to St Peter's at the end. Doing this means that you go straight into St Peter's, avoiding the queue at the security check. However, if the Scala Regia staircase is closed, you will need to walk back to the museums exit.

BEFORE STARTING THE SISTINE ROUTE

Vatican Picture Gallery

This is in a building on its own, reached by turning right at the top of the winding entrance ramp. It was opened in the present building in 1932 and today has a slightly dated feel (the labelling is not particularly good). Nevertheless, it is usually blissfully uncrowded. It has mostly Italian paintings and is arranged chronologically and by schools. In Room II is one of Giotto's best works, the *Stefaneschi Altarpiece*, and in Room III there are two beautiful panels by Fra' Angelico. The largest room (VIII) in the gallery is devoted to Raphael: the lovely *Coronation of the Virgin* was his first large composition, painted in Perugia in 1503 when he was just 20 years old; the magnificent *Madonna of Foligno* is a mature work. The *Transfiguration* is his last work (the lower part was probably completed by his pupils, including Giulio Romano). Raphael also supplied the cartoons for the ten celebrated tapestries here illustrating the Acts of the Apostles, which were woven in Brussels for the Sistine Chapel. One of the least famous but most memorable works by Leonardo da Vinci—his *St Jerome*—is hung in

Leonardo da Vinci: St Jerome (c. 1480).

Room IX. Another remarkable work is Giovanni Bellini's *Pietà*. There are also good 16th-century works by Federico Barocci, Guido Reni, Domenichino and Guercino.

Gregorian Museum of Pagan Antiquities and Pio Christian Museum

Both these museums are in a building dating from 1970. The excellent modern display of the **Gregorian Museum of Pagan Antiquities** has stood the test of time, and the atmosphere is peaceful. It is well worth saving time to come here (it is the closest museum to the entrance and exit). Arrows indicate the itinerary around the well-labelled collection, which has some very fine sculptures including Greek originals and large Roman statues and reliefs. In the open gallery above, the **Pio Christian Museum** has a magnificent collection of sarcophagi, arranged by subject matter. Below, a **Philatelic and Numismatic Museum** was opened in 2007 which documents the postal history of the Papal States and the stamps and coins issued since the founding of the Vatican State in 1929. On the floor below is the very fine **Ethnological Missionary Museum**, founded in 1927 (hardly ever visited) which has a remarkable collection of works from all over the world, and the primitive and more recent cultures of each country are arranged according to subject matter. In 2008 the sections devoted to China, Japan, Korea, Tibet and Mongolia were opened, and there is excellent labelling, also in English.

THE MAJOR MUSEUMS

At present the marked 'Sistine Route' takes you up the Neoclassical Simonetti Staircase from Quattro Cancelli **(A)** (the square hallway to the left of the entrance ramp) and traverses the long galleries of candelabra, tapestries and maps. The route is often unbearably crowded and you can have the feeling of being in a railway station at a peak rush-hour rather than amongst some of the greatest works of art ever produced. If you have more time, the route described below works well (though on wet days, the door into the Cortile della Pigna might be closed).

VATICAN MUSEUMS

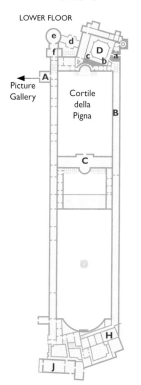

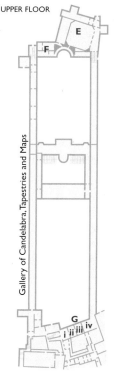

A Quattro Cancelli	e Circular Hall
B Chiaramonti Museum	f Hall of the Greek Cross
C New Wing	E Etruscan Museum
D Pio-Clementino Museum	F Egyptian Museum
a *Apoxyomenos*	G Raphael Rooms (i–iv)
b *Apollo Belvedere*	H Borgia Rooms
c *Laocoön*	J Sistine Chapel
d *Belvedere Torso*	

From the Quattro Cancelli a door leads into the vast Cortile della Pigna (Courtyard of the Fir Cone), named after the colossal bronze fir cone in the semicircular niche, made in the 1st century AD, which used to decorate the portico of Old St Peter's (where it was described by Dante). In ancient Roman times it was part of a fountain (there were water spouts under its scales).

Cross the courtyard to the doorway directly opposite where you came in. This takes you to the Chiaramonti Museum.

Chiaramonti Museum and New Wing

Extending for some 300m along Bramante's east corridor, the **Chiaramonti Museum (B)** is a superb collection of ancient sculpture, with an old-fashioned and crowded display, typical of how a museum of antiquities was arranged in the past, and lending the whole a romantic, rather neglected feel, with the dusty pieces, poorly labelled, all staring sightlessly into space. It includes numerous fine Roman works, including some good portraits. At the end on the right a door leads into the **New Wing (C)**, a magnificent hall 70m long, which crosses the courtyard. This is definitely a place to seek out, for its wonderful ancient sculpture and for its peace and quiet (the tour groups rarely have the time or energy to visit). The sculptures include the *Augustus of Prima Porta*, one of the most famous portraits of the emperor, shown as a general dressed in an intricately carved cuirass about to address his troops. There are numerous other portraits, and replicas of famous Greek works such as the *Wounded Amazon*, *Resting Satyr* and the *Doryphorus* (*Spear-bearer*) of Polyclitus, which illustrates the great sculptor's famous canon of proportions for the human form.

Pio-Clementino Museum

Reached by the stairs by the entrance to the Chiaramonti Museum (you retrace your steps), the **Pio-Clementino Museum (D)** is another wonderful collection of Greek and Roman sculptures. Just to the left of a room with a statue of the *Apoxyomenos* **(a)**, an athlete scraping the oil from his body with a strigil, is the **Octagonal Courtyard of the Belvedere**, which has always displayed some of the most precious pieces in the Vatican collections, and is one of the most pleasant spots in the museums. Here you can truly enjoy some masterpieces in a congenial atmosphere. The courtyard is airy and open to the sky, and is filled with the soothing sound of water from its trickling fountain. It is also provided with comfortable old stone bench-

The *Apollo Belvedere*, a 2nd-century Roman copy of a Greek bronze original.

es. In the recesses at the four short corners are the most famous sculptures. The ***Apollo Belvedere* (b)** entered the Vatican collections in 1503 and was one of the most admired statues in the entire city in the days of the Grand Tour. It shows the slender and elegant figure of the young god stepping forward to see the effect of the arrow he has just shot. The famous ***Laocoön* (c)** is an expressive sculptural group of the priest of Troy with his two sons caught in the coils of the serpents sent by Apollo to crush them to death. The violent, a 2nd-century Roman copy of a Greek bronze original, realism of the conception as well as the extreme skill and accurate detail with which the agonised contortions of the bodies are rendered are typical of late Hellenistic sculpture (this is thought to be an original work of the 1st century BC). The statue of Hermes is a copy of an original by Praxiteles. In the fourth corner are three Neoclassical statues by Antonio Canova, in a very different spirit—though clearly inspired by antique originals.

Beyond a room charmingly filled with numerous statues of animals, you enter an 18th-century hall named after the statues of the Nine Muses displayed around the walls. In the centre is the famous ***Belvedere Torso* (d)** which has the signature of Apollonius, an Athenian sculptor of the 1st century BC. The figure is sitting on a hide laid over the ground and it is not known who it represented—possibly Ajax meditating suicide. When it was found in the Campo dei Fiori at the time of Julius II it was greatly admired by Michelangelo and Raphael, and was subsequently frequently copied by Renaissance artists. The domed **Circular Hall (e)** is another 18th-century addition, clearly

Exquisite small Roman mosaic of a basket of flowers in the Hall of the Greek Cross.

modelled on the Pantheon. There is a splendid Roman mosaic in the centre and a huge monolithic porphyry basin found in the Domus Aurea. Around the walls are displayed important statues and busts of colossal dimensions, including a fine head of Jupiter. The last of these Neoclassical rooms is the **Hall of the Greek Cross (f)** which is dominated by two magnificent porphyry sarcophagi, the tomb chests of St Helen, the mother of Constantine, and Constantia, his daughter.

From here, go up the Neoclassical Simonetti Staircase to the upper floor. The Sistine Route takes you along the long Gallery of Candelabra, Gallery of Tapestries and Gallery of Maps to reach the Raphael Rooms. One floor further up is the **Etruscan Museum (E)**, with an outstanding collection. The **Egyptian Museum (F)** is also very fine.

Raphael Rooms

These are a series of four rooms **(G)** decorated with frescoes by Raphael and are the masterpiece of the young artist who was called to Rome from Urbino by the pope in 1508 (he died only twelve years later, at the age of 37). The two to spend the most time in are those in the centre, the Stanza d'Eliodoro and the Stanza della Segnatura, but before entering them you have to pass through the **Sala di Costantino (iv)**, which was painted almost entirely after Raphael's death by his pupil Giulio Romano and shows episodes from the life of the emperor Constantine. Off it is the Room of the Chiaroscuri (from the windows of which you can usually get a glimpse of the Loggia with its vault decorated with *grottesche* by Raphael but which is closed to the public), and here you can look into a charming little chapel entirely frescoed by Fra' Angelico in 1448–50 with scenes from the lives of St Stephen and St Lawrence.

In the Raphael Rooms much of the complicated and unusual iconographical scheme was worked out by Julius II together with the artist in order to demonstrate parallels between his pontificate and glorious episodes in history. Raphael demonstrates his enormous skill as an illustrator in these magnificent works. The **Stanza d'Eliodoro (iii)**, shows (on the principal wall to the right) the *Expulsion of Heliodorus from the Temple at Jerusalem*, illustrating a story from the Book of Maccabees about a man sent from Asia Minor to steal the temple treasure. Julius II is portrayed sitting in the papal chair, and Raphael portrays himself as one of the chair-bearers. To the left is the *Mass of Bolsena*, recording a miracle of 1263 when a priest who doubted the truth of transubstantiation had all uncertainty banished when he saw real blood dripping from the altarcloth at Bolsena. Once again the scene includes a portrait of Julius II, who visited Bolsena in 1506. It is painted in exceptionally warm colours in a harmony of reds. The works on the other two walls glorify the pontificate of Julius' successor Leo X. On the long wall is *Leo I Repulsing Attila*, and on the fourth wall the *Liberation of St Peter* (alluding to Leo X's own imprisonment by the French in 1512): this is divided into three night scenes, with remarkable light effects (the interior of the prison is seen through a high barred window in the centre). The adjoining **Stanza della Segnatura (ii)** is the most famous of the rooms. On the long wall opposite the entrance is the *Disputation on the Holy Sacrament*, with a monstrance with the Host on an altar below surrounded by famous theologians and saints, while in the celestial zone above Christ appears between the Virgin and St John the Baptist. In the celebrated *Parnassus* scene Apollo is playing the violin in the shade of laurels, surrounded by the nine Muses and the great poets. On the wall facing the *Disputa* is the splendid *School of Athens*, symbolising the triumph of Philosophy. On the steps of the magnificently vaulted Palace of Science the greatest philosophers and scholars of all ages are gathered around the two supreme masters, Plato and Aristotle (the bearded Plato is said to be a portrait of Leonardo da Vinci).

The last room, the **Stanza dell'Incendio (i)** was painted in 1517 from Raphael's design and glorifies events in the lives of two earlier popes named Leo (III and IV) which glorify by association the reign of Raphael's contemporary Leo X.

Outside the chapel of Urban VIII a stairway leads down to the six **Borgia Rooms (G)** which have very beautiful ceilings painted by Pinturicchio in 1492–95. Here begins the Museum of Modern Religious Art, opened in 1973 with over 50 rooms of works

The Sistine Chapel

This is the goal of all the tourist groups which enter the Vatican Museums and it can be very crowded and noisy, with announcements over the loudspeaker making the atmosphere even less appropriate. Try, if you can, to im-

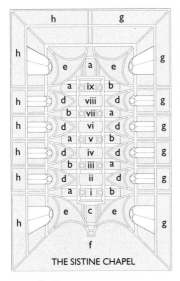

THE SISTINE CHAPEL

a   Prophets
b   Sibyls
c   Jonah
    Scenes from Genesis
    i   *Separation of Light from Darkness*
    ii   *Creation of Sun and Moon*
    iii *Separation of Land from Water*
    iv   *Creation of Adam*
    v   *Creation of Eve*
    vi   *Expulsion from Paradise*
    vii *Sacrifice of Noah*
    viii *The Flood*
    ix   *Drunkenness of Noah*
d   Forerunners of Christ
e   Old Testament scenes
f   *Last Judgement*
g   Scenes from the life of Moses
h   Scenes from the life of Christ

agine this as a holy place, dedicated to prayer and penitence.

This large chapel is named after Pope Sixtus IV who ordered its construction in 1475 and ever since it has been used during the conclaves to elect a new pope. It was Julius II who persuaded Michelangelo to fresco the barrel vault in 1508. This is perhaps the greatest pictorial decoration in Western art, carried out in just four years. Its complicated iconography, an exaltation of Christian theology, combines Old and New Testament figures, as well as themes from pagan prophecy and Church history. The powerful figures and scenes are painted against an architectural background, with an effect of high relief and rich colour on a huge scale. Using a small scaffolding platform which spanned the width of the chapel (and with very little light to see by), Michelangelo began work in the area furthest from the altar. During cleaning operations on the lunettes in the lower curved part of the vault, it was discovered that it took him just three days to paint each of the Hebrew prophets (**a**) and pagan sibyls (**b**) on their thrones directly onto the fresh plaster (without the help of a cartoon or sketch). These include the splendid large figure of Jonah (**c**) issuing from the whale—given pride of place above the altar since his 'resurrection' prefigured that of Christ. Along the centre of the vault are nine large scenes from Genesis (**i–ix**), from the Creation to events in the life of Noah. These are framed by decorative pairs of beautiful nudes, Michelangelo's famous *ignudi*, the most idiosyncratic elements in the ceiling (thought to have been inspired by his studies of the *Belvedere Torso*). In the lunettes over the windows are figures representing the forerunners of Christ **(d)** and in the spandrels at either end are scenes of salvation from the Old Testament **(e)**.

It was only 20 years later, in 1535–41, that Paul III commissioned Michelangelo to paint the huge fresco of the *Last Judgement* **(f)** on the altar wall. Against a brilliant blue background this is filled with a crowd of nude figures around the powerful figure of Christ in the upper centre, which seems to be derived from Classical models. This great work incorporates numerous wonderfully painted figures. In the slack, flayed skin of St Bartholomew can be seen Michelangelo's own self-portrait.

The very fine frescoes on the long walls were originally the only decoration in the chapel: Sixtus IV commissioned them in 1481–83 from the most important artists of his day including Perugino, Botticelli, Signorelli, Pinturicchio and Domenico Ghirlandaio. They illustrate the life of Moses **(g)**, and the Life of Christ **(h)** and are well worth studying, even though one's attention is inevitably taken up by the works of Michelangelo, which are on such a different scale.

You can often leave the museums now by the Scala Regia, which takes you down to St Peter's basilica.

FOOD & DRINK IN THE VATICAN

The Vatican is not an easy place to find a good-value, simple place to eat. But off the left side of St Peter's Square, the **Bar Gastronomia 'De' Penitenzieri'** (*Via Penitenzieri 16, opposite the church of Santo Spirito in Sassia; map p. 219, C3*) is a peaceful and pleasant café where you can sit and have a snack. Otherwise, there are a few places where you can find a pizza in Borgo Pio (off the other side of St Peter's Square; *map p. 219, C2*). A few blocks north of Borgo Pio, **Il Matriciano** (*Via dei Gracchi 55; map p. 219, C1*) serves a good, reasonably-priced light lunch. There is a café and self-service restaurant inside the Vatican Museums or you can bring a (discreet) picnic with you and sit and eat it on one of the benches in the courtyard outside the Picture Gallery or in the huge Cortile della Pigna.

Ostia Antica: view of the lower decumanus maximus.

OUTSIDE THE ANCIENT WALLS & OSTIA ANTICA

Basilicas outside the ancient walls

Of Rome's famous 'Seven churches' (St Peter's, St John Lateran, Santa Maria Maggiore, San Paolo fuori le Mura, San Lorenzo fuori le Mura, Santa Croce in Gerusalemme, and San Sebastiano), which were always the most important places pilgrims were required to visit, the four last were outside the walls. San Sebastiano stands near the Via Appia (*map p. 131*). San Paolo fuori le Mura, San Lorenzo fuori le Mura, and Santa Croce in Gerusalemme are still popular pilgrimage sites today, and can all be reached by public transport.

All the basilicas described below are marked on the overview map on p. 3. For San Paolo, Underground line B from Termini and Colosseo; for San Lorenzo, bus 71 from Piazza San Silvestro off the Corso (map p. 222, C1), and for Santa Croce, bus 571 from Largo Argentina and Piazza Venezia (map p. 222, B2 and C2; or on foot in c. 10mins from St John Lateran; map p. 223, F4). For Sant'Agnese, express bus no. 60 along Via Nomentana from Piazza Venezia (map p. 222, C2).

San Paolo fuori le Mura is the largest church in Rome after St Peter's. It had to be completely rebuilt after a fire in 1823 and it has entirely lost its ancient feel. In spiritual terms, however, it is still of the first importance, built over the site where St Paul was buried after his martyrdom in c. 64. In 2009 the Pope announced that his remains had been identified in the sarcophagus beneath the high altar, and in the same year a 4th-century wall painting of the head of a middle-aged man with a pointed black beard was found in some nearby catacombs on Via Ostiense. St Paul is traditionally depicted with a black beard, and the image is the oldest known representation of the great apostle and martyr.

San Lorenzo fuori le Mura suffered serious damage from bombs in the last War, but nevertheless retains its venerable character with a magnificent ancient presbytery and fine Cosmati work. It is dedicated to St Lawrence, a Roman deacon and the city's most celebrated martyr after the apostles Peter and Paul. He was put to death here in 258, apocryphally by roasting over a gridiron. The basilica rises over his burial site.

Harvesting and crushing grapes, from the 4th-century church of Santa Costanza, a pagan-seeming scene with an overtone of Christian meaning.

Santa Croce in Gerusalemme, near St John Lateran, is dedicated to the Holy Cross. It was built on land owned by Helen, the mother of Constantine, who had discovered what she believed to be the True Cross on a pilgrimage to Jerusalem. The most precious relic in the basilica is the so-called Titulus Crucis, a fragment of wood said to be a piece of the signboard that was nailed to the Cross of Christ, bearing the words 'Jesus of Nazareth, King of the Jews'. The building preserves its interesting architecture from a reconstruction in 1744.

Sant'Agnese fuori le Mura is another important basilica in early Christian history. St Agnes, a virgin martyr exposed naked in the Stadium of Domitian (today's Piazza Navona) before being put to death by the sword, was buried here in 304. Much of the church still dates from the 7th century, including the lovely mosaic of the saint in the apse. Beneath can be visited interesting catacombs which were in use in St Agnes's day. In the garden is a round mausoleum, now the church of **Santa Costanza**, built by Constantine's elder daughter Constantia on her estate here around 354. It is her burial place and that of her sister Helena, and is remarkably well preserved, annular in plan with 24 granite columns in pairs around the central shrine. The original porphyry tomb chest is now in the Vatican (*see p. 148*); a copy is preserved *in situ* here. The barrel vaulting of the encircling ambulatory still has its fascinating early Christian (4th century) mosaics against a white ground. Interestingly, many are still pagan in character, though with an overlay of Christian meaning. The scene of

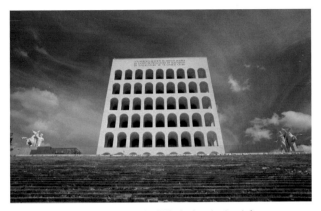

The famous 'Square Colosseum' in the EUR district, a landmark for anyone travelling to and from Fiumicino airport. It was built in 1938–43, and is officially the Palazzo della Civiltà Italiana, the 'Palace of Italian Civilisation'.

the grape harvest illustrated here seems secular in character but for the fact that grapes and vines had been adopted by Christians as an important symbol of the sacrifice of Christ, of the death of the body and the release of the spirit. In one of the semi-domes is the oldest known representation of Christ as Pantocrator, the Almighty, seated on the orb of the earth. In this version he is shown giving the keys of heaven to St Peter.

1930s architecture in Rome: the district of EUR

Map p. 3. Underground line B from Termini and Colosseo.

Anyone interested in Fascist town planning should make time to visit the monumental white marble buildings of the Esposizione Universale di Roma, now always abbreviated to EUR, a district laid out for the 1942 World Expo which was, in fact, cancelled because of the Second World War. The buildings were designed in a monumental and triumphalistic style to symbolise the achievements of Fascism: the most famous is the 'Square Colosseum' (*illustrated above*). Approached by a ten-lane highway, EUR is still a very distinctive district of Rome (some of the buildings are used for government offices or museums arranged for educational purposes). The wide avenues, spacious *piazze* and gardens and lakes between them have always had an empty, show-town sort of feel, although today this is an upmarket residential district.

A day out of Rome at Ostia Antica

Excavations and museum open Tues–Sun 8.30–dusk; closed Mon. Train from Stazione Ostiense beside Porta San Paolo (map p. 221, A3) every 15mins for Ostia Antica (journey time 30mins). The station is only a few minutes' walk from the site entrance. There is a self-service restaurant and café on the site, as well as a good bookshop.

Ostia Antica was the port of ancient Rome at the mouth of the Tiber and its ruins survive in a beautiful park of umbrella pines and cypresses. So much of it is left that you can gain here a fascinating glimpse of the city life of the ancient Romans and in particular an idea of their apartment houses and the streets with their shops, workshops and taverns. Ostia is as important as Pompeii and Herculaneum in this respect, and excavations have been carried out here over the course of the last two centuries.

The city, which was probably Rome's first colony, was founded around 335 BC and flourished up until the time of Constantine. At the height of its prosperity it had up to 80,000 inhabitants. All of Rome's overseas imports and exports passed through Ostia, and it ensured a constant supply of produce to the capital.

The entrance is by a stretch of the ancient Via Ostiense which led straight to Rome, some 20km inland. You still enter the city through the Porta Romana in the Republican walls, and the main street or decumanus maximus (over one kilometre long) begins just inside the gate. It is still paved with its old, irregular basalt blocks.

The buildings which survive in ruins all over the vast site include numerous apartment blocks where the middle- and lower-class inhabitants lived. These usually had four storeys and reached a height of 15m, the maximum permitted by Roman law. They were built of brick and had little ornamentation, but each room had its own window and wall paintings and many had balconies (some of the best preserved include the Casa di Diana and the Casa dei Dipinti). There are also a few grander houses designed on just one floor around an atrium with columns and loggias and sometimes a nymphaeum (one of the most representative is the House of Cupid and Psyche).

The warehouses (some with as many as 60 separate rooms) are arranged around arcaded courtyards for the loading and unloading of

Street view in ancient Ostia, a typical scene of brick-built ruins amid the umbrella pines. An apartment house here survives in its lower storeys, with the remains of what would have been a balcony above the second-floor windows.

merchandise, and there are also market places. The most impressive of the bath houses to have survived is that of Neptune, named after its fine mosaic of the sea god (the Baths of the Seven Sages also has good mosaics). One of the best preserved streets is Via della Fontana. Near the theatre built by Agrippa, the spacious Piazzale delle Corporazioni is particularly interesting: the mosaic trademarks of the 70 guilds and commercial associations from all over the known world who had their offices here are well preserved in the paving of the arcade.

No fewer than 15 Mithraic sanctuaries have been found at Ostia: the Persian cult of Mithras became very popular in the Imperial period. There are also many temples dedicated to traditional Roman deities, the most important of which is the Capitolium which still faces onto the Forum. Evidently different religious cults flourished here without disharmony, and one of the most interesting sacred areas is the Campo della Magna Mater, south of the Forum towards the southern gate in the walls. On the outskirts of the town a Synagogue was found (in use from the 1st to the 5th centuries) and a small Christian basilica. A museum houses some of the very fine sculptures found amidst the ruins.

PRACTICAL INFORMATION

PLANNING YOUR TRIP

When to go

The climate of Rome is usually very pleasant except in the height of summer and periodically in the winter. The best months to visit are November or March: the most crowded periods are Easter, May and June, September, October and Christmas. July and August have become less crowded in the last few years (in August many Romans themselves are away), but the summer is usually uncomfortably hot.

Websites on Rome

The most useful website is that of the municipality: www.060608.it
Information for the disabled: www.romapertutti.it
Information on the Roma Pass card: www.romapass.it
Public transport: www.atac.roma.it
Airports: www.adr.it
Vatican www.vatican.va

Disabled travellers

All new public buildings now obliged to provide access and facilities for the disabled. In the annual list of hotels published by the APT tourist association, hotels which provide hospitality for the disabled are indicated. Airports and railway stations provide assistance and certain trains are equipped to transport wheelchairs. The seats at the front of city buses are reserved for disabled passengers, as is ATAC bus no 590. There are free parking spaces for disabled drivers. In the list of opening times of museums and galleries available from the APT, those which are accessible to wheelchairs are indicated. The historic centre of Rome, however, remains a difficult.

Local tourist offices

The municipal tourist office website is www.060608.it, and their telephone number is the same: 06 0608.

They run a number of tourist information points in green kiosks which should supply you with all the up-to-date information you need (known as PIT, *Punti di Informazione Turistica*). In the centre of the city, these are open daily 9–6: Via del Corso (Largo Goldoni, near Via Tomacelli; *map p. 222, B1–C1*), the Fori Imperiali (*map p. 223, D3*),

Castel Sant'Angelo (*map p. 219, D2*), Piazza San Giovanni in Laterano (*map p. 221, D1*), Trastevere (Piazza Sonnino, north of San Crisogono; *map p. 222, B3*), Via Marco Minghetti, which leads out of the Corso on the opposite side from Via Caravita; *map p. 222, C2*), Via Nazionale (Palazzo delle Esposizioni; *map p. 223, D2*), and Via dell'Olmata (Santa Maria Maggiore; *map p. 223, E2*).

The Roma Pass

This is worth buying. It gives you free entrance to two museums and considerable reductions at many others, as well as three days' free transport in Rome. It can be purchased directly at the museums, at tourist information points, and at airports and railway stations.

GETTING AROUND

To and from the airport

Fiumicino: (also called Leonardo da Vinci; T: 06 65951, www.adr. it; 26km southwest of the centre). Non-stop trains run from Stazione Termini (*map p. 223, F1*) every half hour from about 7am to 9.15pm (in 30mins) and the metro runs there every 15mins from Stazione Roma Tiburtina (*map p. 3*), via Ostiense and Trastevere, from about 5am to 11pm (in 40mins). There are also night bus services between Stazione Tiburtina and the airport. **Ciampino** airport (T: 06 794941, www.adr.it; 13km southeast) can be reached by underground Line A from Stazione Termini to Anagnina station, and from there by CO-TRAL airport bus from 6am to 10pm (every 30mins). If you arrive late at night it is best to take a taxi. Taxis cost standard meter charges plus an airport supplement, or a price by agreement in advance.

By train

Stazione Termini (Piazza dei Cinquecento; *map p. 223, F1*), is Rome's main station. It has left-luggage facilities and a supermarket open 24hrs. **Stazione Roma Tiburtina** (*map p. 3*) is used by some trains. Both stations are on the metro. The railway stations of Ostiense and Trastevere are on the line to Fiumicino airport.

By bus and tram

Rome is well served by a fairly efficient bus and tram service. The service of orange buses is run by ATAC (Azienda Tramvie e Autobus del Comune di Roma. www.atac.roma.it). The ATAC information kiosk is on Piazza dei Cinquecento in front of Stazione Termini (*map p. 223, F1*). Tickets are not sold on board; you buy them in advance, either at tobacconists, bars and newspaper kiosks, or at ATAC booths and from automatic machines at many bus stops and metro stations. They are valid for 75mins on any number of lines and for one journey on the metro. They have to be stamped on board the vehicle. Those found travelling without a valid ticket are liable to a heavy fine.

It is usually well worthwhile purchasing a one-day ticket, a BIG (*biglietto giornaliero*) which expires at midnight of the day it was purchased, a three-day ticket, or a seven-day ticket. Available from the usual outlets, it must be stamped just once on board.

Two blue electric mini-bus services (nos. 116 and 117) operate a circular route through some of the most beautiful districts of the centre of town on weekdays from 7.40am–10pm.

Express (*espressi*) bus no. 60 provides a fast service between Piazza della Repubblica (*map p. 223, E1*), Piazza Venezia (*map p. 222, C2*), the Colosseum (*map p. 223, E3*) and Porta San Paolo (Piramide; *map p. 221, A3*). A good bus for St Peter's and the Vatican (*map p. 219*) is no. 64 from Stazione Termini (*map p. 223, F1*) via Piazza Venezia.

There are usually no bus or underground services in Rome on 1 May or on the afternoon of Christmas Day, and services are limited on other holidays. Night bus services operate from ten past midnight to 5.30am; the numbers on these routes are followed by 'N'. Because of one-way streets, return journeys do not always follow the same route as the outward journey

The few tramlines which survive are slow but in some cases charmingly old-fashioned. A new line (with modern tramcars) runs to Trastevere from Largo Argentina (*map p. 222, B2*).

By underground

There are two lines on Rome's underground (*metropolitana*). There are no stops in the historic centre. Useful stops on the fringes are, on Line A: Via Ottaviano (near the Vatican; *map p. 219, C1*), Piazzale Flaminio (Piazza del Popolo; *map p. 220, A2*), Piazza di Spagna (*map p. 220, B3*), Piazza Barberini (*map p. 223, D1*), Piazza della Repubblica (*map p. 223, E1*), Stazione Termini (*map p. 223, F1*), San Giovanni in Laterano (*map p. 223, F4*). Useful stops on line B are Stazione Termini (*map p. 223, F1*), Colosseo (*map p. 223, D3*), Circo Massimo (*map p. 221, B1*), Piramide (*map p. 221, A3*). Line B also serves San Paolo fuori le Mura (*map p. 3*) and EUR (*map p. 3*). Services run from 5.30am to 11.30pm; on Sat the last train is at half past midnight.

By taxi

Taxis (white or yellow in colour) are provided with an identification name and number, the emblem of the municipality of Rome, and a meter; you should always make sure the latter is operational before hiring a taxi. The fare includes service, so tipping is not necessary. Licensed taxis are hired from ranks; there are no cruising taxis. It is never advisable to accept rides from non-authorised taxis at the airports or train stations. There are additional charges for travel at night (10pm–7am), travel from railway stations, on Sundays and for each piece of luggage.

To call a taxi dial 06 06 09.

By bicycle

A system of bike sharing has been introduced by the municipality of Rome, called roma-n-bike. This includes the first half hour free and subsequently just a Euro or so up to a maximum of 4 hours a day. Information from the information kiosks, or www.roma-n-bike.com or T: 060608. The most useful stands are in Largo Argentina (*map p. 222, B2*), Campo de' Fiori (*map p. 222, B2*), Trevi Fountain (*map p. 222, C1*), Piazza Navona (*map p. 222, B2*), the Pantheon (*map p. 222, B2*), Piazza del Popolo (*map p. 220, A2*), Piazza di Spagna (*map p. 220, B3*) and Piazza Venezia (*map p. 222, C2*).

MUSEUMS, GALLERIES & MONUMENTS

Opening times for museums, collections and monuments are given in the text (though opening times vary and often change without warning). An up-to-date list of opening times is always available at the tourist information kiosks. All museums are usually closed on the main public holidays in Rome: Easter Sunday, 29 June and 15 Aug. The closing times given in the text indicate when the ticket office closes, which is usually 30–60mins before the actual closing time. **Admission costs**. British citizens under 18 and over 65 are entitled to free admission to state- and municipality-owned museums and monuments, and all EU citizens between the ages of 18 and 25 are entitled to a half-price ticket for them (you must show proof of nationality). There is a student discount for the Vatican museums.

Reductions can be had if you buy the Roma Pass (*see p. 160 above*). An inclusive ticket, called the Roma Archeologia Card, valid for 7 days, allows entrance to the main state-owned archaeological sites and museums in Rome. There is also a 7-day inclusive ticket for the four museums run by the Museo Nazionale Romano.

La Settimana dei Musei Italiani (Museum Week) has now become established as an annual event, usually held in March or April. Entrance to most museums is free during the week, and some have longer opening hours. Some private collections and monuments not generally accessible are opened at this time.

CHURCHES

Catholic basilicas and churches

The four great patriarchal basilicas are San Giovanni in Laterano (St John Lateran), the cathedral and mother church of the world; San Pietro in Vaticano (St Peter's); San Paolo fuori le Mura and Santa Maria Maggiore. These, with the three basilicas of San Lorenzo fuori le Mura, Santa Croce in Gerusalemme and San Sebastiano, comprise the Seven Churches of Rome.

Some churches, including several of importance, are open only for a short time in the morning and evening (opening times have been given where possible in the text below, but might vary). Most churches now ask that sightseers do not visit the church during a service.

Many pictures and frescoes are difficult to see without lights, which often have to be operated with coins. When visiting churches it is always useful to carry a torch and a pair of binoculars. Churches in Rome are very often not orientated. In the text the terms north and south refer to the liturgical north (left) and south (right), taking the high altar as being at the east end.

Dress

If you are wearing shorts or have bare shoulders you can be stopped from entering some churches, including St Peter's.

Roman Catholic services

The ringing of the evening Ave Maria or Angelus bell at sunset is an important event in Rome, where it signifies the end of the day and the beginning of night. The hour varies according to the season. On Sunday and, in the principal churches, often on weekdays, Mass is celebrated until 1 and from 5–8. High Mass, with music, is celebrated in the basilicas on Sunday at 9.30 or 10.30 (the latter in St Peter's).

The choir of St Peter's sings on Sunday at High Mass and at vespers at 5. The Sistine Chapel choir sings in St Peter's on 29 June and whenever the Pope celebrates Mass.

Roman Catholic services in English take place in San Silvestro in Capite (*map p. 222, C1*); San Clemente (*map p. 223, E3*); and Santa Susanna (*map p. 223, E1*). San Clemente also offers services in Irish.

Church festivals

On saints' days Mass and vespers with music are celebrated in the churches dedicated to the saints concerned. On the evening of 6 January there is a procession with the *Santo Bambino* (the statue is a copy of the one stolen in 1994) at Santa Maria in Aracoeli (*map p. 222, C3*). The Octave of the Epiphany (13 Jan) is held at Sant'Andrea della Valle (*map p. 222, B2*). The Blessing of the Lambs takes place at Sant'Agnese fuori le Mura (*map p. 3*) on 21 Jan around 10.30. In St John Lateran (*map p. 223, F4*) a choral Mass is held on 24 June, in commemoration of the service held here in 1929 by Pius XI after the Lateran Treaty was agreed. The Pope attends the Maundy Thursday celebrations here, when he gives his benediction from the loggia. Holy Week liturgy takes place on Wednesday, Thursday and Friday at St Peter's, St John Lateran, Santa Croce in Gerusalemme (*map p. 3*) and other churches. On 5 Aug the legend of the miraculous fall of snow is commemorated at Santa Maria Maggiore (*map p. 223, E2*) in a pontifical Mass in the Borghese Chapel. On Christmas morning in this basilica a procession is held in honour of the sacred relic of the Holy Crib. The church of Sant'Anselmo on the Aventine Hill (*map p. 221, A1*) is noted for its Gregorian chant at 9.30 on Sun. The singing of the *Te Deum* on 31 Dec in the church of the Gesù (*map p. 222, C2*) is a magnificent traditional ceremony.

Papal audiences

General audiences usually take place at 10 or 10.30 on Wed mornings, either in the New Audience Hall inside Vatican City or in St Peter's Square (when the pope is driven by jeep). Audiences are now also sometimes held in St Peter's. To attend you are required to apply in writing to the Prefettura della Casa Pontificia, 00120 Città del Vaticano. T: 06 6988 3114. Or you can apply in person at the Office of the Prefecture, entered through the Portone di Bronzo in St Peter's Square (*open Mon to Fri 9–1*).

Non-Catholic churches and places of worship

American Episcopal   St Paul's Within the Walls, Via Napoli 58,

	T: 06 488 3339 (*map p. 223, E1*)
Anglican	All Saints, Via del Babuino 153, T: 06 3600 1881 (*map p. 220, B3*)
Baptist	Piazza San Lorenzo in Lucina 35, T: 06 687 6652 (*map p. 222, C1*)
Jewish	Synagogue, Lungotevere dei Cenci, T: 06 684 0061 (*map p. 222, B3*)
Methodist	Piazza Ponte Sant'Angelo, T: 06 686 8314 (*map p. 222, A1*)
Muslim	Centro di Cultura Islamica, Via della Moschea (Parioli; west of Villa Ada), T: 06 808 2167 (*map p. 3*)
Scottish Presbyterian	St Andrew's, Via XX Settembre 7, T: 06 482 7627 (*map p. 223, E1*)

ENTERTAINMENT

Listings information

Free up-to-date information in English is available from the APT, and in the excellent little leaflet *L'Evento* published in Italian and English every two months by the municipality of Rome and available from their information kiosks. For up-to-date information: www.060608. it or T: 06 0608.

Un *Ospite a Roma*—a magazine in Italian and English with information on current events in the city—comes out once every fortnight and is given away free at hotels and information offices. There is also a monthly publication called *Romavision* (also in English) which provides much useful information. The most comprehensive source of information used by the Romans themselves is *Roma c'è*, which is published every Thursday. It can be bought at newsstands. The Italian listings are decipherable and there is a brief section in English at the back.

SHOPPING

The smartest shops are in Via Frattina and Via Condotti, which lead out of Piazza di Spagna (*map p. 220, B3*). A good and less expensive shopping area is in the area of the Pantheon and Campo Marzio (*map p. 222, B2*). Another important shopping street in the city (if in a less attractive area than the above) is Via Cola di Rienzo (*map p. 219, D1*) in the Prati district, between Piazza del Risorgimento and the Tiber.

The supermarket at Termini Station is open 24hrs a day, and there are supermarkets with good deli counters and fresh bread at Via Giustiniani 18/b (*map p. 222, B2*) near the Pantheon; and Via Cola di Rienzo 173, inside the Coin department store, close to the Vatican (*map p. 219, D1*).

Opening hours

More and more shops in the historic centre are staying open all day now, although food shops still usually close between 1 and 5.

English books are stocked at the following shops:

The Lion Bookshop, Via dei Greci 33 (just off Via del Corso; *map p. 220, B3*), T: 06 3265 0437. Open 10–7.30; Mon 3.30–7.30. The shop also has a reading room and tea and coffee.

The Anglo-American Book Co., Via della Vite 102 (near Piazza di Spagna; *map p. 222. C1*), T: 06 679 5222. Open 9–1 & 2–6; Sat 9–1. Closed Sun.

The Almost Corner Bookshop, Via del Moro 45 (*map. 222, A3*), T: 06 583 6942. Closed Mon morning.

The Economy Book and Video Center, Via Torino 136 (*map p. 223, E2*), T: 06 474 6877. Closed Sun.

Feltrinelli International, Via Vittorio Emanuele Orlando 84 (*map p. 223, E1*), T: 06 482 7878. Open daily 9–8.

ADDITIONAL INFORMATION

Banking services

Banks are usually open Mon–Fri 8.30–1.30, and for one hour in the afternoon, usually 2.30 or 3–3.30 or 4; closed Sat, Sun and holidays. A few banks are now open on Sat mornings, including the Banca di Roma in Piazza di Spagna (*map p. 220, B3*), and the Banca Nazionale del Lavoro at Via del Corso 266 (*map p. 222, C2*). All banks close early (about 11) on days preceding national holidays.

Crime and personal security

For all emergencies, dial 113 or 112.

As in large towns all over the world, pickpocketing is a widespread problem in Rome; it is always advisable not to carry valuables in handbags, and to be particularly careful on public transport.

Cash, documents and valuables can be left in hotel safes. It is a good idea to make photocopies of all important documents in case of loss. Particular care should be taken when using a credit card to draw cash from an ATM.

Crime should be reported at once, theft to either the Polizia di Stato or the Carabinieri. A detailed statement has to be given in order to get an official document confirming loss or damage (*denunzia di smarrimento*), which is essential for insurance claims. Interpreters are usually provided.

Polizia di Stato foreigners' office, T 06 4686 2102.

Carabinieri	T: 112
Municipal police	T: 06 67691
Traffic police	T: 55441
Railway police	T: 06 481 9561

To report the loss or theft of a credit card, call:

Visa	T: 800 822056
Mastercard	T: 800 872 050
American Express	T: 06 7228 0371

Emergency services

For all emergencies, T: 113: the switchboard will coordinate the help you need.

First aid services (*pronto soccorso*) are available at all hospitals, railway stations and airports. San Giovanni, in Piazza San Giovanni in Laterano (*map p. 223, F4*), is the central hospital for emergencies: for first aid, T: 06 7705 5297. The American Hospital in Rome, in the eastern outskirts at Via Emilio Longoni 69 (T: 06 225 5290), is a private English-speaking hospital which accepts most American insurance plans. The International Medical Centre will refer callers to English-speaking doctors, T: 06 488 2371, nights and weekends T: 06 488 4051.

First-aid and ambulance service	T: 118
Red Cross ambulance service	T: 5510
Fire brigade	T: 115
Road assistance	T: 116

For all other emergencies, see 'Crime' above.

Pharmacies

Pharmacies or chemists (*farmacie*) are identified by their street signs, which show a luminous green cross. They are usually open Mon–Sat

9–1 and 4–7.30 or 8. Some are open 24hrs a day, including the one outside Stazione Termini on Piazza dei Cinquecento (*map p. 223, F1*). A few are open on Sundays and holidays, and at night: these are listed on the door of every chemist, and in the daily newspapers.

Public holidays and annual festivals

The main holidays in Rome, when offices and shops are closed, are as follows:

1 January (New Year's Day)	1 November (All Saints' Day)
25 April (Liberation Day)	8 December (Immaculate Conception)
Easter Monday	25 December (Christmas Day)
1 May (Labour Day)	26 December (St Stephen)
15 August (Assumption)	

In addition, the festival of the patron saints of Rome, Peter and Paul, is celebrated on 29 June as a local holiday in the city.

Museums are usually closed on 29 June, Easter Sunday and 15 August, and there is usually no public transport on 1 May and the afternoon of Christmas Day.

Annual festivals

5–6 January: Epiphany (Befana), celebrated at night in Piazza Navona

Shrove Tuesday: Carnival is celebrated in the streets and *piazze*

21 April: Anniversary of the birth of Rome, celebrated on the Capitoline Hill

23–24 June: Festa di San Giovanni, at night, near the Porta San Giovanni, near St John Lateran

First Sunday in June: Festa della Repubblica, a military parade in the Via dei Fori Imperiali

July: Festa di Noantri, celebrations in Trastevere for several weeks

Telephones and postal services

Telephone numbers in Italy can have from seven to eleven numbers. All now require the area code, whether you are making a local call or a call from outside Rome.

Directory assistance (in Italian) is available by dialling 1288. The telephone exchange at Termini station is open until midnight.

Rome area code	06
dialling UK from Italy	(00 44) + number
dialling US from Italy	(00 1) + number
dialling Rome from UK	(00 39) 06 + number
dialling Rome from US	(00 39) 06 + number

The head post office in Rome is in Piazza San Silvestro (*map p. 222, C1*), open daily 9–6. Stamps are sold at tobacconists displaying a blue 'T' sign as well as post offices. Letters and postcards for outside Rome should always be posted into red boxes, or the blue boxes in the centre of town. The Vatican postal service—which has its own stamps which are not valid for the Italian state postal service—is usually thought to be more efficient: it costs the same and there are post offices in Piazza San Pietro and the Vatican Museums, as well as in Trastevere in the courtyard of Palazzo San Calisto, Piazza San Calisto 16 (*map p. 222, A3*; blue letterbox).

Tipping

Most prices in hotels and restaurants include a service charge, and so tipping is far less widespread in Italy than in North America. Even taxi-drivers rarely expect more than a Euro added to the charge (which officially includes service). In restaurants prices are almost always inclusive of service, so always check whether or not the service charge has been added to the bill before leaving a tip. In hotels, porters who show you to your room and help with your luggage, or find you a taxi, usually expect a couple of Euro.

ACCOMMODATION

Rome offers a wide range of accommodation from well-known luxurious hotels to family-run B&Bs, and monasteries and convents. The following is a selection, listed by area.

Prices are as follows, for a double room per night in high season:

€€€€ (over €400)   €€ (€100– €200)
€€€ (€200– €400)   € (around €100)

BLUE GUIDES RECOMMENDED

Hotels, restaurants and cafés that are particularly good choices in their category—in terms of excellence, location, charm, value for money or the quality of the experience they provide—carry the Blue Guides Recommended sign: ■. All these establishments have been visited and selected by our authors, editors or contributors as places they have particularly enjoyed and would be happy to recommend to others. To keep our entries up-to-date reader feedback is essential: please do not hesitate to contact us (www.blueguides.com) with any views, corrections or suggestions, or join our online discussion forum.

Around Campo de' Fiori

€€ **Campo de' Fiori**. The rooms are small, some quieter than others. The best are the three with parquet floors on the top (sixth floor), where two of them have their own terrace. All the guests can use the lovely little roof terrace, which has a superb view of all Rome's greatest monuments. However, the staff could be friendlier. *Via del Biscione 6, T: 06* *6880 6865, www.hotelcampodefiori. com. 23 rooms. Map p. 222, B2.*

€€ **Teatro di Pompeo**. ■ Located in a quiet, small square, this tranquil hotel sits on the remains of an ancient Roman theatre built by Pompey (its original 55 BC circular structure is still partly visible in the lounge and breakfast room in the basement). All the rooms feature old wood-beamed ceilings and tiled floors. All rooms are very quiet. Cordial staff. *Largo del Pallaro 8, T: 06 687 2812, www.hotelteatrodipompeo.it. 13 rooms. Map p. 222, B2.*

€ **Albergo del Sole**. Reputed to be on the site of the oldest hotel in the city and still something of an institution (it is one of the rare hotels in the city which still has some rooms without bathrooms and where breakfast is not served). There is a labyrinth of corridors and back stairs, with no less than four little terraces and gardens connected with iron steps. The rooms on the top floor with a terrace are the most pleasant, while others (considerably cheaper) are pretty basic. If you coincide with a group booking, the hotel can be noisy. It has its own garage. *Via del Biscione 76, T: 06 6880 6873, www.solealbiscione.it. 60 rooms. Map p. 222, B2.*

On the Corso

€€€€ **Grand Hotel Plaza**. Opposite the church of Santi Ambrogio e Carlo, on the part of the Corso which is closed to traffic. First opened around 1865, this is a magnificent and delightfully old-fashioned hotel. You cross the spacious ground floor reception rooms, including a huge ballroom, to get to the comfortable bar and restaurant. There is a huge marble lion clambering down the splendid Art Nouveau staircase with its stained glass windows (even the lift is worth notice). Pleasant rooms with parquet floors. There are two terraces open in the warmer months: the one with lovely old lemon trees in tubs has views of the Villa Medici and Trinità dei Monti and comfortable places to sit in peace. *Via del Corso 126, T: 06 674952, www.grandhotelplaza.com. 200 rooms. Map p. 222, C1.*

Near the Forum

€€€€ **Forum**. Old-established hotel in an area otherwise lacking in good accommodation. It overlooks the Imperial Fora and is just a few steps from the entrance to the Roman Forum, yet is surprisingly peaceful. Many of the rooms, and the rooftop garden terrace (with restaurant and bar service), offer some of the city's best views onto the ruins of ancient Rome. Although the décor is slightly dated, it has a quiet and distinguished atmosphere with cordial staff. Parking available. *Via Tor de' Conti 25, T: 06 679 2446, www.hotelforumrome.com. 78 rooms. Map p. 223, D3.*

Near the Pantheon and Piazza Navona

€€€€ **Grand Hotel de la Minerve**. In a lovely position by Santa Maria Sopra Minerva. The building has served as a hotel since the late 18th century, and its old-fashioned feel was retained by Paolo Portoghesi when he was called in to make some renovations in 1990. Quiet interior courtyard and comfortable rooms. Restaurant indoors in winter, and on the roof terrace in summer. Professional service. *Piazza della Minerva 69, T: 06 695201, www.grandhoteldelaminerve.it. 135 rooms. Map p. 222, B2.*

€€€ **Raphael**. An independent hotel run by the son of the founder, and for many a favourite place to stay. It is tucked away, completely covered with a vine, wisteria and bougainvillea just out of Piazza Navona. Some of the rooms are a bit small but the more expensive ones have their own terraces. Those on the third floor have recently been re-designed by Richard Meier. The rooms at the front can be noisy at weekends, when the restaurant on the piazza below is full. The hotel has its own restaurant on a charming roof terrace, right beside the dome of Santa Maria della Pace and with views of the tower of Sant'Ivo and the dome of the Pantheon. *Largo Febo 2, T: 06 682831, www.raphaelhotel.com. 55 rooms. Map p. 222, B2.*

€€€ **Santa Chiara**. ■ Excellently staffed family-run hotel with a devoted clientèle. It is just two steps away from the Pantheon. During recent renovations the rooms on three floors of one wing, overlooking Piazza Minerva, have been modernised and given parquet floors. It is well worth asking for a room on the 4th floor since some of these (such as 407) have their own delightful little terraces. There are also a number of pleasant single rooms (408 has its own terrace). If you require total silence, you can chose a room on the inner courtyard. There is now a little patio on the street towards the Minerva where you can sit and enjoy the scene. *Via Santa Chiara 21, T: 06 687 2979, www.albergosantachiara.com. 90 rooms. Map p. 222, B2.*

€€–€€€ **Del Senato**. Delightful, old-established hotel in an attractive 19th-century building overlooking the Pantheon. You need to book well in advance. The rooms mostly have parquet floors and are handsomely furnished. Some have views of the Pantheon although those at the back are quieter. One has a frescoed ceiling and four-poster bed. Lovely roof terrace in summer. *Piazza della Rotonda 73, T: 06 678 4343, www.albergodelsenato.it. 57 rooms. Map p. 222, B2.*

Around Piazza di Spagna

€€€€ **Hassler Roma**. ◾ In a wonderful position at the top of the Spanish Steps, this has been one of the most famous independent luxury hotels in Rome for many years. Huge reception rooms on the ground floor; palm court at the back where breakfast is served in good weather; terrace on the 7th floor. Many of the rooms have private terraces or balconies. The magnificent penthouse suite has its own huge private roof terrace, totally secluded, with a view from the Quirinal to the Villa Medici. The panoramic restaurant (Imàgo; *open evenings only*) has views over all Rome. Professional service in great style. For the hotel's annexe, Il Palazzetto, see below. *Piazza Trinità dei Monti 6, T: 06 699340, www.hotelhassler.com. 95 rooms. Map p. 220, B3.*

€€€€ **D'Inghilterra**. ◾ In a quiet cul-de-sac surrounded by Rome's most fashionable shopping streets a few steps from Piazza di Spagna and a brisk seven-minute walk from Piazza Venezia, this is one of the best-known old-established hotels in the city, with a long-standing returning clientèle as well as a distinguished historic guest list. The rooms overlook Via Borgognone or an interior court, and those on the fourth floor have been modernised. Some can be rather small (specify if you want space); only one room (suite no. 676) has a terrace. The Caffè Romano restaurant, where breakfast is served (also open to the public for lunch and dinner) has a few tables outside. The English-style bar, low-ceilinged and snug, is famous for its Bloody Marys. *Via Bocca di Leone 14, T: 06 699811, www. royaldemeure.com. 97 rooms. Map p. 222, C1.*

€€€ **Intercontinental De La Ville Roma**. Next door to the Hassler Roma, in a good position at the top of the Spanish Steps. Some of the rooms are rather small. There is a restaurant, and the very pleasant roof terrace has fine views. It has a quiet atmosphere although it does take groups. There is a small garage nearby (you should book a space ahead of arrival). *Via Sistina 69, T: 06 67331, www.rome.intercontinental.com. 192 rooms. Map p. 220, B3.*

€€ **Gregoriana**. A small hotel on one of the quieter streets in this very central area. The rooms are smallish, with modern furnishings and wood floors. The top floor has very comfortable suites (including no. 3 with a large terrace). Good bathrooms. Breakfast room in the basement. No groups. The staff could be more friendly. *Via Gregoriana 18,*

T: 06 679 4269, www.hotelgregoriana.it. 16 rooms. Map p. 222, D1.

€€€ **Il Palazzetto**. On a tiny street running parallel to the Spanish Steps, this is a delightful annexe of the Hassler Roma with just four elegant rooms overlooking the Steps. It is considerably cheaper, and has its own restaurant (closed Mon) and wine bar. *Vicolo del Bottino 8, T: 06 6993 41000, www.ilpalazzettoroma.com. 4 rooms. Map p. 220, B3.*

€€ **Scalinata di Spagna**. In a perfect position beside the Spanish Steps. The rooms are on two floors and some are a bit small, but all are pleasantly furnished. The three rooms on the first floor have their own terraces; the largest room is no. 6. Breakfast is served on the first floor next to a charming terrace where you can sit in warm weather. The hotel is quiet (no groups taken) and has a particularly friendly atmosphere with very cordial young staff. *Piazza Trinità dei Monti 17, T: 06 6994 0896, www.hotelscalinata.com. 16 rooms. Map p. 220, B3.*

€€ **Internazionale**. Pleasant hotel at the top of the Spanish Steps. The rooms are particularly spacious—those at the back are very quiet, and some have balconies. The breakfast room has delightful, old-fashioned décor, and the pretty terrace has a view across to the Vatican and St Peter's. Well run, with very helpful staff. Garage. No groups. *Via Sistina 79, T: 06 6994 1823, www.hotelinternazionale.com. 40 rooms. Map p. 220, B3.*

Trastevere

€€€ **Buonanotte Garibaldi**. ■ From the raised pavement near the bottom of Via Garibaldi you enter a beautiful garden court with orange trees and magnolia, reminiscent of Spain or Morocco, which provides the special feature of this delightful B&B, owned by an artist, Luisa Longo, who lives here. There are just three rooms: the blue room on the first floor has a lovely large terrace, and one of the other rooms is also available as a single room. They are all well furnished in a crisp, modern style with delightful fabrics hand-painted by Luisa, who has her atelier off the courtyard. She offers guests tea and home-made biscuits in her spacious living room, as well as a superb breakfast with home-made jam (and even bacon and eggs if you so wish) in the elegant dining room. *Via Garibaldi 83, T: 06 5833 0733, www.buonanottegaribaldi.com. 3 rooms. Map p. 222, A3.*

€€€ **Donna Camilla Savelli**. Lovely, peaceful hotel occupying three floors of the former convent of Santa Maria dei Sette Dolori. It doesn't at present take groups and has no restaurant. There is a large garden in the old cloister and plenty of places to sit and relax. Rooms are adequately furnished. *Via Garibaldi 27, T 06 588861, www.hotelsavelli. com. 77 rooms. Map p. 222, A3.*

€€ Guesthouse Arco de' Tolomei. ■ Lovely B&B (you are given your own key) in the wing of the delightful house where the owners live. It is in a very short backstreet, rarely used by cars, just north of Via dei Salumi, entered through the arch from which the street is named. The rooms are delightfully furnished and the three on the upper floor have their own terraces. Guests are encouraged to use the books and guides as well as the computer, although the owners (together with their very friendly staff) are always available to help plan your day. The simple sounds of life in the street below is exceptional in any city today. Breakfast is served in the family dining room. On the less busy side of Trastevere, and close to some excellent and reasonably-priced restaurants. If you should need it, there is a garage nearby in Via Anicia. *Via Arco de' Tolomei 27, T: 06 5832 0819, www. bbarcodeitolomei.com. 6 rooms. Map p. 222, B3.*

€€ Hotel Santa Maria. ■ This is a very unusual hotel, recently built in an area which once housed a convent (the porticoes recall the convent cloister) and later a repair yard for carriages. In the heart of Trastevere, just a few metres from Piazza Santa Maria in Trastevere. The rooms, plainly furnished with tiled floors, are built on just one storey around two large garden courts planted with orange trees. It is totally removed from the noise and confusion of the surrounding streets, although you can of course hear the other guests if they are sitting out in the gardens. Bicycles can be borrowed, free of charge. Suitable for families as some rooms can sleep four or more. Breakfast is served across the courtyard in a pleasant room, beyond a bar where a free evening buffet is prepared with snacks between 5.30 and 7 (you buy your own drinks). Very pleasant staff. If you give advance warning you can park inside (just two places) or at the garage next door. The Residenza Santa Maria (*see below*) is under the same management. *Vicolo del Piede 2 (on the corner of Via della Pelliccia), T: 06 589 4626, www.hotelsantamaria. info. 18 rooms. Map p. 222, A3.*

€€ Residenza Santa Maria. ■ A sister establishment of the Hotel Santa Maria. In a charming building on a quiet street, with a tiny inner courtyard with comfortable chairs. Rooms (some of which can sleep families) have wood ceilings and are tastefully furnished (the paintings are copies of works by the artist Antonio Donghi, grandfather of the manager). Breakfast is served downstairs in a remarkable barrel-vaulted room which was once a Roman cistern, appropriately decorated with ancient marbles. *Via dell'Arco di San Calisto 20, T: 06 5833 5103, www. residenzasantamaria.com. 6 rooms. Map p. 222, A3.*

€ **Casa di Santa Francesca Romana a Ponte Rotto**. Simple hotel in the house where St Francesca Romana lived and died in 1440, in one of the quietest parts of Trastevere. Although a religious institution, there is no curfew. Just opposite, in the same street, is the excellent *trattoria* Da Enzo (*see p. 185*), and there are numerous other good restaurants in the vicinity. Rooms are basically furnished with tiled floors, and some of them can sleep families of three or four. *Via dei Vascellari 61, T 06 581 2125, www.sfromana. it. 37 rooms. Map p. 222, B4.*

Around the Vatican

€€ **Hotel Bramante**. In an old building just off Borgo Pio, this is a beautifully decorated hotel with a welcoming atmosphere. Tiled floors and beamed ceilings in the rooms. Very convenient for St Peter's and the Vatican but well away from the crowds. *Vicolo delle Palline 24, T: 06 6880 6426, www.hotelbramante.com. 16 rooms. Map p. 219, C2.*

€€ **Sant'Anna**. In a delightful, quiet pedestrian street with local shops, very close to St Peter's, this has perhaps the most pleasant location of all the hotels near the Vatican. A small hotel decorated in Art Deco style, the rooms have frescoed walls which gives them a pleasant, spacious feel. The ample rooms on the top floor have small terraces. You can sit out in the charming tiny garden court in good weather. Parking. *Borgo Pio 133, T: 06 6880 1602, www. hotelsantanna.com. 20 rooms. Map p. 219, C2.*

Near Termini Station and Santa Maria Maggiore

€€€€ **St Regis Grand**. When it opened in 1894, this was the first hotel in Rome to have electric light and a bathroom for every room. In winter, afternoon tea is still served in the magnificent Salone, which retains its Art Nouveau decoration. Even though the rest of the hotel has been discreetly modernised, a delightful, elegant atmosphere remains, with a magnificent staircase and very spacious corridors. With its marble baths and Murano chandeliers it still recalls a day when no expense was spared. Rooms are heavily furnished and have close carpeting. Professional service, cordial staff. Restaurant. Owned by the Starwood group, it is very convenient for the station but otherwise the position is not very attractive. *Via Vittorio Emanuele Orlando 3, T: 06 47091, www.stregis.com. 161 rooms. Map p. 223, E1.*

€ **Antica Locanda**. ■ A delightful family-run hotel in an excellent location in the Monti district (close to the Colosseum), well supplied with restaurants and very peaceful. Rooms have nice wooden floors and beamed ceilings. The quietest rooms are those on Via del Boschetto. *Via del Boschetto 84, T: 06 484894, www.antica-locanda.com. 12 rooms. Map p. 223, D2.*

€ **Hotel Giuliana**. Run by an English lady and her daughter, this hotel is on the first floor of a large *palazzo* with a spacious staircase and old-fashioned lift. It is on the busy main road which leads north from the basilica of Santa Maria Maggiore, and is extremely handy if you need to be close to the railway station. Ask for a room on the quieter Via Cesare Balbo, which overlooks a street market (held in the mornings). Rooms are simply furnished and have cool tiled floors. There is a tiny bar and breakfast area. *Via Agostino Depretis 70, T: 06 488 0795, www.hotelgiuliana.com. 11 rooms. Map p. 223, E2.*

On the Aventine Hill

€€ **Aventino San Anselmo Hotels**. A group of three hotels, all in early 20th-century villas surrounded by gardens, very close to each other in the exceptionally peaceful residential district of the Aventine. You can park on the quiet roads outside. **Hotel Sant'Anselmo** (*Piazza Sant'Anselmo; 34 rooms*), **Villa San Pio** (*Via Santa Melania 19; 78 rooms*), **Aventino Hotel** (*Via San Domenico 10; 21 rooms*). *Piazza Sant'Anselmo 2, T: 06 570057, www.aventinohotels.com. Map p. 221, A1.*

€€ **Domus Aventina**. Housed in an ex-convent, entirely modernised. Spacious rooms, some with balconies, which face onto a courtyard and the wall of Santa Prisca. The terrace on the ground floor overlooks a garden filled with palms, shrubs and a magnolia tree. *Via di Santa Prisca 11/b, T: 06 574 6135, www.hoteldomusaventina.com. 26 rooms. Map p. 221, B2.*

Via Veneto

€€€€ **Eden**. Owned by Starwood hotels this is one of Rome's famous luxury-class hotels, just off the Via Veneto. Very elegant with all the comforts and services you would expect. Its roof restaurant, La Terrazza (*open daily*), with a panoramic view of the city, is still considered by many to be one of the best in Rome. *Via Ludovisi 49, T: 06 478121, www.hotel-eden.it. 121 rooms. Map p. 220, C2.*

€€€€ **Excelsior**. One of Rome's most famous hotels, opened in 1906 (now owned by the Westin group). It has the grand and luxurious atmosphere you would expect, an indoor swimming pool and fitness centre. The Doney restaurant is on the ground floor. *Via Veneto 125, T 06 47081, www.excelsior. hotelinroma.com. 287 rooms. Map p. 220, C3.*

€€€ **Victoria**. Just off the top end of Via Veneto, set back from the noisy road which skirts the park of Villa Borghese, this is a Swiss-run hotel which offers excellent value. Spacious, spotless rooms mostly with parquet floors, and good bathrooms. Friendly and efficient staff. In good weather a restaurant operates on the small roof terrace (there is a view over the Borghese gardens, although you do hear the traffic up here). There is another restaurant on the ground floor, and both have reasonably-priced set menus. *Via Campania 41, T: 06 423701, www. hotelvictoriaroma.com. 111 rooms. Map p. 220, C2.*

Monastery accommodation

Monasteries and convents in Rome are an excellent option for good-value accommodation in the city, particularly as some of the buildings are located in central positions that rival many hotels. Each property is individually run, and all offer clean, basic accommodation, many with private bathrooms. Monastery Stays offer an online booking service (for Rome and the rest of Italy). Using their website (www.monastery-stays.com) you can choose the location of your accommodation and view its facilities before making a booking. It is best to book well in advance, particularly during Easter and the summer season. Note that most of the institutions have a curfew, around 10.30 or 11pm.

RESTAURANTS

You can eat extremely well in Rome in the simplest places as well as the most sophisticated. There are still many professionally run *trattorie* and restaurants where you can get a very good, reasonably-priced meal made with fresh seasonal ingredients.

Basic Roman cuisine has surprisingly few typical dishes: short pasta is often served in a spicy sauce (*alla matriciana* or *amatriciana*) made from bacon, tomato, *pecorino* cheese and chilli; spaghetti *alla carbonara* has beaten egg, bacon, *pecorino* and black pepper. Other home-made types of fresh spaghetti include *bucatini* and *tonnarelli*, often served with *cacio* cheese and black pepper, or with walnuts. *Fettuccine* are ribbon noodles usually served with a meat sauce or porcini mushrooms. Another typical first course is *gnocchi di patate*, small potato dumplings served in a meat and tomato sauce. A traditional Roman soup is *stracciatella*, a meat broth with parmesan and a beaten egg.

Second courses include *abbacchio arrosto* or *al forno* (roast suckling lamb), *saltimbocca alla romana* (veal escalope with ham and sage), *coda alla vaccinara* (oxtail stewed in a tomato and celery sauce), and *ossobuco al tegame* (stewed shin of veal).

Vegetables are usually very good. Artichokes (*carciofi*) are an important part of the Roman cuisine and cooked in a great variety of ways. They are always young and small so they can be eaten whole. If served *alla giudia* they are deep fried, whereas *alla Romana* means they will be stuffed with wild mint and garlic and then stewed in olive oil and water. Courgettes (*zucchini*) are sometimes served *ripieni* (stuffed) or grilled or fried. Their flowers (*fiori di zucca*) can be stuffed with mozzarella cheese and salted anchovies, dipped in batter and fried. Particularly good green vegetables such as *cicoria* (chicory) and *broccoletti* or *broccoletti di rapa* (broccoli and rape) are served lightly cooked, sometimes with garlic, and dressed just with olive oil. *Misticanza* is a rich green salad with a great variety of wild lettuce and herbs.

Rome is well supplied with good fresh fish. You can also eat very good pizza here: Rome is considered second only to Naples for this national dish. Wines from all over Italy are freely available.

Even in the simplest places it is always wise to reserve a table. The Romans themselves particularly enjoy eating out and restaurants can get very crowded. Nearly everywhere has seating outside (especially since the ban on smoking indoors was introduced), even if this means only one or two tables on the street. It is quite acceptable to order just one course. Prices include service, unless otherwise stated on the menu (if in doubt, check with the waiter).

Below is a selection of restaurants grouped according to location and divided according to price per person for dinner, with wine. For Blue Guides Recommended ■, see p. 170.

€€€€	over €125	€€	€30–€80)
€€€	€80–€1250	€	under €30

Additional places to eat have been indicated at the end of each chapter. These are restaurants, cafés and wine bars close to the monuments described where you can stop and have anything from a snack to a full meal during a day of sightseeing.

Around Campo de' Fiori

€€ **Ditirambo**. In the piazza just north of Campo de' Fiori, a simple, cosy place with two small main rooms, but also with seating outside. It serves rather unusual dishes such as *polipo con ceci* (octopus with chickpeas) and *maialino al mirto* (suckling pig with myrtle) so is a welcome change from normal Roman fare. The desserts are also excellent and there is a good wine list. A sound choice. Closed Mon lunch. *Piazza della Cancelleria 74, T: 06 687 1626. Map p. 222, B2.*

€€ **Settimio**. With an unassuming entrance, this is a simple, small restaurant with a limited menu of typical Roman dishes including *stracciatella* (meat broth with beaten egg) and *involtini* (thin rolled slices of meat cooked in a sauce) but remains in the very best tradition of serious cuisine served in a basic but very pleasant setting. The Cesanese del Piglio is an excellent wine from Lazio. Closed Wed. *Via del Pellegrino 117, T: 06 6880 1978. Map p. 222, A2.*

Isola Tiberina and the Ghetto

€€ **Piperno**. ■ Traditional Roman cooking (much use is made of offal), and Roman Jewish dishes too, including the delicious fried artichokes. Refreshing house Frascati. Beside the church south of Piazza delle

Cinque Scole. Closed Mon, and Sun evening. *Monte dei Cenci 9, T: 06 6880 6629. Map p. 222, B3.*
€€ **Sora Lella**. A small, neat, family-run *trattoria* in a charming location on the Tiber island, close to Ponte Fabricio. It has

been run by the same family since 1940. Traditional Roman cooking, such as *amatriciana* (pasta in a tomato sauce with chunks of cured pork) and *coda alla vaccinara* (oxtail stew). Home-made desserts. Closed Tues lunch and Sun. *Via di Ponte dei Quattro Capi 16, T: 06 686 1601. Map p. 222, B3.*

€ **Giggetto al Portico d'Ottavia**. Beside the church of Sant'Angelo in Pescheria (one of the stumps from the columns of the ancient Roman portico after which the street is named survives amongst the tables on the pavement). It uses fresh produce including excellent artichokes and has good pasta dishes, and traditional Roman fare such as *abbacchio* (lamb). Extensive wine list. Closed Mon. *Via del Portico d'Ottavia 21, T: 06 686 1105. Map p. 222, C3.*

€ **Sora Margherita**. This is a tiny *trattoria* behind a door which is firmly closed outside hours. It is one of the cheapest places to eat in all Rome. Officially a 'cultural association' or club run by Lucia, but if you manage to have a meal here it will certainly be a memorable experience. Booking essential for an evening meal. Open in winter Tues–Sun 12.30–3, dinner only Fri and Sat with just two sittings, one at 8 and the other at 9.30. Open in summer Mon–Fri 12.30–3, dinner only Fri at 8 and 9.30, closed Sat and Sun. *Piazza delle Cinque Scole 30, T: 06 687 4216. Map p. 222, B3.*

Near the Pantheon

€€€€ **La Rosetta.** ■ A famous place a few steps from the Pantheon, held to be the top fish restaurant in Rome. The menu is very short but each dish is prepared with great care to accentuate the flavour of wonderfully fresh fish and seafood. Oysters are often available as an *hors d'oeuvre*, and clams feature in the pasta dishes. Excellent list of wines and champagne. Set menu available. It has a few tables outside on the street. Closed Sun. *Via della Rosetta 8 (Ros. on map), T: 06 686 1002. Map p. 222, B2.*

€€€–€€ **Da Fortunato al Pantheon**. From the tables outside there is a good view of the Pantheon. An efficiently-run, traditional Roman restaurant with particularly high-quality food. Frequented by politicians and businessmen. Seasonal fare and good fish. Closed Sun. *Via del Pantheon 55 (Pan. on map), T: 06 679 2788. Map p. 222, B2.*

€€ **L'Eau Vive**. In a 15th-century palace this has become a well-known restaurant over the last few decades. It is run by French nuns (for charity) so you will find only traditional French cuisine here—and you will not be disappointed. Closed Sun. *Via Monterone 85, T: 06 6880 1095. Map p. 222, B2.*

€ **La Sagrestia**. On the street running east out of Piazza della Rotonda towards Sant'Ignazio, is a rather anonymous place, with a very extensive menu, but the cooking is sound and the pizzas excellent. Frequented by Romans who want a good but not grand meal. Closed Wed. *Via del Seminario 89, T: 06 679 7581. Map p. 222, B2.*

Near Piazza Navona

€€€€ **Il Convivio Troiani**. ■ Hidden away in a very narrow lane (only wide enough to be used as a park for motorbikes) you would never come upon this small restaurant by chance (just behind Palazzo Altemps, to the right of the entrance to the museum, take Via de' Giglio d'Oro and then turn left into Vicolo dei Soldati). Professionally run by a delightful proprietor, it serves extremely imaginative dishes in an intimate atmosphere. *Hors d'oeuvres* include prawns with goat cheese strudel and smoked aubergine purée. The pasta is home-made and served with fish, game and duck sauces. Meat or fish dishes provide the main courses which usually include lamb, pigeon and rabbit. The desserts are magnificent, with chocolate or fruit as the main ingredient and featuring sorbets, mousses, and water ices. There is an excellent 'menù degustazione'—a many-course set menu. Open evenings only, closed Sun. *Vicolo dei Soldati 31, T: 06 6880 5950. Map p. 222, B1.*

€ **Cul de Sac 1**. Out of the southwest corner of Piazza Navona, this claims to have been the very first wine bar to open in Rome. Long and narrow, warm and friendly, it makes a pleasant change from pizza whenever an informal or frugal meal is required. Cheeses, cold meat, vegetable quiches are on offer, but also hearty lentil soup in winter. There are over 700 wines to choose from. Closed Mon lunch. *Piazza Pasquino 73, T: 06 6880 1094. Map p. 222, B2.*

€ **Montecarlo**. A good place for a simple meal, with crowded old-fashioned tables, in a narrow lane off Corso Vittorio Emanuele II. It has a bustling atmosphere without any pretension, typical of Rome, and it can be difficult to find a free table. Good simple local dishes (including the desserts). No credit cards. Closed Mon. *Vicolo Savelli 12, T: 06 686 1877. Map p. 222, A2.*

Piazza del Popolo

€€€–€€ **Dal Bolognese.** ■
In a wonderful position on
Piazza del Popolo, with elegant
clientèle and professional service. As the name suggests, the
cuisine is from Bologna, with
excellent fresh pasta. Closed
Mon. *1/2 Piazza del Popolo, T: 06
361 1426. Map p. 220, A2.*

Near the Quirinal Hill, Santa Maria Maggiore, and Termini Station

€€€€ **Agata e Romeo.** Situ-
ated on the busy road which
runs from Santa Maria Maggiore
to Piazza Vittorio Emanuele, this
restaurant is considered by many
to be the best in Rome for fish.
Closed Sat and Sun. *Via Carlo
Alberto 45, T: 06 446 6115. Map
p. 223, F2.*
€€ **Le Colline Emiliane.**
■ This restaurant is very
convenient for the Quirinal
and Galleria Nazionale in
Palazzo Barberini. A pleasant,
old-fashioned place where it is
unusual to find a non-Italian. It
has a discreetly simple interior
which seems to have survived
from the days when there were
far fewer restaurants in the
city. The service is impeccable
and you are treated with great
respect whether you choose to
have a long drawn-out culinary
experience, or just a quick plate
of pasta with salad. If you order
the excellent pumpkin ravioli
(*ravioli di zucca*) you are even
asked how sweet you would like
them. Closed Sun evening and
Mon. *Via degli Avignonesi 22, T:
06 481 7538. Map p. 223, D1.*
€€–€ **Trimani.** Located quite
near the station (north of Santa
Maria degli Angeli), this is one of
the oldest wine shops in Rome,
with a friendly wine bar round
the corner. Excellent wine list.
The menu includes a few hot
dishes, such as soups, quiches,
grilled beef and seasonal vegetables, as well as a tempting
selection of cheeses, smoked fish
and cured pork. Good desserts.
Closed Sun. *Via Cernaia 37/b, T:
06 446 9630. Map p. 223, F1.*

Trastevere

€€€€ **Alberto Ciarla.** Well-
run, old-established restaurant, which still gets into the
restaurant guides particularly for
its fish, and has a good selection
of wines. There are a number
of (slightly cheaper) set menus.
Open evenings only; closed Sun.

Piazza San Cosimato 40, T: 06 581 8668. Map p. 222, A4.

€€€ **L'Archetto**. Run by a husband and wife team—she is a sommelier and he worked at the White House during the Clinton administration. Today it is popular with Russians. Open Tues–Sun, evening only. Closed Mon. *Via Goffredo Mameli 23, T: 06 581 5275. Map p. 222, A4.*

€€€–€ **Checco er Carettiere**. This has been one of the best-known restaurants in Trastevere for many years, although some Romans now feel it has rather had its day. It offers traditional Roman dishes, such as *coda alla vaccinara* (oxtail stewed in a tomato and celery sauce), but you can also order a simple grilled fish. Home-made desserts. Closed Sun evening. *Via Benedetta 10, T: 06 581 7018 or 580 0985. Map p. 222, A3.*

€€€ **La Gensola**. On the corner of Via della Gensola (north of Via Salumi), two steps out of Piazza in Piscinula. Run by Irene and Claudio it serves excellent fish. *Piazza della Gensola 15, T: 06 581 6312 or 06 5833 2758. Map p. 222, B3.*

€€ **Il Ciak**. Good Tuscan food, recommended by locals as the best place in the city to eat steak. Open evenings only. *Vicolo de' Cinque 21 (west of Via del Moro), T: 06 584801 or 06 589 4774. Map p. 222, A3.*

€€ **Le Mani in Pasta**. In a peaceful area of Trastevere, this is a well-run restaurant with good food, particularly strong on meat dishes (but also fish when available). Closed Mon. *Via dei Genovesi 37, T: 06 581 6017. Map p. 222, B4.*

€€ **Paris**. A comfortable restaurant near Piazza Santa Maria in Trastevere, Paris offers traditional Italian cooking with many good Roman dishes such as fried courgette flowers stuffed with mozzarella and anchovies and *zuppa di arzilla* (fish soup with broccoli). Excellent wine list. Closed Sun evening, and Mon. *Piazza San Calisto 7/a, T: 06 581 5378. Map p. 222, A3.*

€€ **La Tana de Noantri**. On one of the little streets leading out of Piazza Santa Maria in Trastevere, always busy with pedestrians, this typical Roman *trattoria* has tables outside on the pavement, and also across the street occupying a little piazza against the side wall of the church. The restaurant is very large, with many customers, but the ingredients are fresh and the dishes not too rich, so you can also enjoy a light lunch here. *Via della Paglia 1, T: 06 580 6404. Map p. 222, A3.*

€ **Antico Carlone** (also called Antica Trattoria 'da Carlone'). In a quiet back street of Trastevere (off Via della Lungaretta, near Piazza in Piscinula), this is a good place to come for a filling pasta dish: *gnocchi* (potato dumplings); *pappardelle a fiori di zucca* (pasta ribbons with courgette flowers; *fettuccine asparagi e funghi* (home-made pasta with asparagus and mushrooms); *tonnarelli alle noci* or *al cacio e pepe* (fresh pasta similar to spaghetti with a walnut or cheese and black pepper sauce). If you still have room for a second course, these usually include roast lamb (*abbacchio arrosto*) and veal (*saltimbocca alla romana*), but you get the impression that the chef's attention is mainly concentrated on the first courses. Very pleasant staff and relaxed atmosphere with some seats outside. Good value. Closed Mon. *Via della Luce 5, T: 06 580 0039. Map p. 222, B3.*

€ **Trattoria da Enzo**. Tucked away in a lovely old street in a quiet corner of Trastevere (off Via dei Genovesi in front of Via Santa Cecilia), this is a very small place which serves excellent-value, good food, and so has become very popular (you are unlikely to find a table if you haven't booked). It also has one or two tables outside. Well worth a visit. Closed Sun. *Via dei Vascellari 29, T: 06 581 8355. Map p. 222, B4.*

Via Veneto

€€€€ **La Terrazza dell'Hotel Eden**. Having the best view in the city tends to distract attention from the food, but the modern interpretations of Italian classics are expertly prepared and beautifully presented. Open daily. *Via Ludovisi 49, T: 06 478121. Map p. 220, C3.*

€€€ **Papà Baccus**. A fairly-priced restaurant not far from Via Veneto, serving light food, mostly Tuscan in origin. Professional yet friendly service. Very good desserts and wines. Closed Sat lunch, and Sun. *Via Toscana 36, T: 06 4274 2808. Map p. 220, C3.*

Outside the historic centre

Garbatella

€ **Moschino**. This is some way outside the centre in a delightful position, cool in summer, near S. Paolo fuori le Mura and the Garbatella metro stop on Line B (*map p. 3*). It has very good food and extremely reasonable prices, but the 'take it or leave it' atmosphere might put many people off. Despite the off-hand service it is always full of Romans and well worth a visit if you decide to take a day off sightseeing. Closed Sun. *Piazzetta Benedetto Brin, T: 06 513 9473.*

Monte Mario

€€€€ **La Pergola, Hotel Cavalieri Hilton**. In the last few years this restaurant in the Hilton Hotel, west of Via Trionfale (*map p. 3*) has become famous. It has three Michelin stars and is classified among the top ten restaurants in the country. Imaginative cuisine, impeccable service and elegant décor. Open evenings only; closed Sun and Mon. *Via A. Cadlolo 101, T: 06 3509 2152.*

The Parioli

€€€–€€ **Al Ceppo**. A long-standing favourite with locals in the quiet Parioli quarter, on the road that skirts the south perimeter of Villa Ada (*map p. 3*). The menu always features specialities from the Marche region, and the grilled meats are especially good. Closed Mon. *Via Panama 2, T: 06 841 9696.*

Piramide

€€ **La Sella del Diavolo**. If you are visiting the splendid museum of ancient Roman sculpture in the Centrale Montemartini, La Sella del Diavolo is right beside its entrance. Spacious rooms frequented by Italians who work nearby. Particularly good for fish and Sardinian specialities. Efficient, professional service. Open daily, lunch only. *Via Ostiense 102, T: 06 578 1260. Map p. 3.*

Portuense

€€ **Wine Bar Gambero Rosso**. Attached to a cooking school, self-service restaurant with a few excellent dishes, popular with young people. It is run by an association which publishes the Gambero Rosso ('red crayfish') guide to the best places to eat in Rome. South of Trastevere (*map p. 3*). Closed Sun and Mon evening. *Via Enrico Fermi 161 (off Viale Marconi near Ostiense), T: 06 551 1221.*

Testaccio

€€€ **Checchino dal 1887**. Close to the old city slaughter house, in an area known for its honest, typical cuisine (*map p. 3*), and run by the same family for over a hundred years, Checchino serves the most traditional Roman fare. Simple décor and good wine list (also available by the glass). Closed Sun and Mon. *Via di Monte Testaccio 30 (parallel to Via N. Zabaglia), T: 06 574 3816. Just beyond (west of) map p. 221, A3.*

€ **Da Oio a Casa Mia**. ■ A simple Roman *trattoria* run by a family who once owned a successful butcher's shop, with excellent traditional dishes including *coda alla vaccinara* (oxtail) and an unusual version of *spaghetti alla carbonara* made with 'glicia' (salt pork), pecorino cheese and black pepper (but without egg). Closed Sun. *Via N. Galvani 43, T: 06 578 2680. Map p. 221, A2.*

For the Via Appia Antica, see p. 136.

GLOSSARY

Acrolith, statue where the head and undraped (visible) extremities are of stone, while the remainder is of wood

Aedicule, small opening framed by two side columns and a pediment, originally used in Classical architecture; a niche of this shape

Ambo (pl. *ambones*), pulpit in a Christian basilica; two pulpits on opposite sides of a church from which the Gospel and Epistle are read

Amphora (pl. *amphorae*), antique vase, usually of large dimensions, for oil and other liquids

Antefix, ornament placed at the lower corners of the tiled roof of a temple to conceal the space between the tiles and the cornice

Antiphonal, choir-book containing a collection of antiphons—verses sung in response by two choirs

Antis, in antis describes the portico of a temple where the side walls are prolonged to end in a pilaster flush with the columns of the portico

Apodyterium (pl. *apodyteria*) dressing-room in a Roman bath

Apse, vaulted semi-circular end wall of the chancel of a church or chapel

Archaic, period in Greek civilization preceding the classical era: from about 750 BC–480 BC

Architrave, the horizontal beam placed above supporting columns; the lowest part of an entablature; the horizontal lintel above a door.

Archivolt, moulded architrave carried round an arch

Atlantis (pl. *atlantes*), male figure used as a supporting column; a Telamon

Atrium, forecourt, usually of a Byzantine church or a classical Roman house

Attic, topmost storey of a Classical building, hiding the spring of the roof; of pottery, describing an ancient Greek style from Attica (c. 650 BC–400 BC)

Baldacchino, canopy supported by columns, for example over an altar

Basilica, originally a Roman hall used for public administration; in Christian architecture, an aisled church with a clerestory and apse, and no transepts

Biga, a two-horse chariot

Borgo, a suburb; a district of town; a street leading away from the centre of a town

Bottega, the studio of an artist; the pupils who worked under his direction

Bozzetto (pl. *bozzetti*), sketch, often used to describe a small model for a piece of sculpture

Bucchero, Etruscan black terracotta

Bucrania, a form of Classical decoration—skulls of oxen between flower garlands

Calidarium (or *caldarium*), room for hot or vapour baths in a Roman bath complex

Campanile, bell-tower, often detached from the building to which it belongs

Camposanto, cemetery

Canopic vase, Egyptian or Etruscan vase enclosing the entrails of the dead

Carceres, openings in the barriers through which the competing chariots entered the circus

Cardo, the main street of a Roman town, at right-angles to the decumanus

Cartoon, from *cartone*, meaning large sheet of paper—a full-size preparatory drawing for a painting or fresco

Caryatid, sculpted female figure used as a supporting column

Cavea, the part of a theatre or amphitheatre occupied by the row of seats

Cella, sanctuary of a temple, usually in the centre of the building

Chiaroscuro, distribution of light and shade in a painting

Ciborium, casket or tabernacle containing the Host (Communion bread)

Cipollino, onion-marble; a greyish marble with streaks of white or green

Cippus (pl. *cippi*), sepulchral monument in the form of an altar

Clerestory, upper part of the nave wall of a church, above the side aisles, with windows; usually a feature of Gothic architecture

Cloisonné, from the French *cloison*, partition; a type of enamel decoration divided by narrow metal strips, typical of Byzantine craftsmanship

Columbarium, a building (usually subterranean) with niches to hold urns containing the ashes of the dead

Confessio, crypt beneath the high altar and raised choir of a church, usually containing the relics of a saint

Corbel, a projecting block, usually of stone, to support an arch or beam

Cornice, topmost part of a temple entablature; any projecting ornamental moulding at the top of a building beneath the roof

Cosmatesque, **Cosmati**, medieval style of mosaic decoration or cladding consisting of geometric patterns made up of (often) ancient marble fragments

Cryptoporticus, vaulted underground corridor

Cuneus, wedge-shaped block of seats in an antique theatre

Cyclopean, unmortared masonry blocks attributed by the ancients to the giant Cyclopes

Decumanus, main street of a Roman town, running parallel to its longer axis

Diaconia, early Christian charitable institution

Dipteral, temple surrounded by a double peristyle

Diptych, painting or ivory tablet in two sections

Engaged column, a column (or pilaster) which is not freestanding but is partially embedded into the wall

Entablature, upper part of a temple above the columns, made up of an architrave, frieze and cornice

Ephebus, Greek youth under training (military or university)

Exedra, semicircular recess

Ex-voto, tablet or small painting expressing gratitude to a saint

Flavian, of the emperors Vespasian, Titus, Domitian, Nerva and Trajan; or the period of their rule

Forum, open space in a town serving as a market or meeting-place

Fresco, (in Italian, *affresco*), painting executed on wet plaster (*intonaco*), beneath which the artist had usually made a working sketch (*sinopia*).

Frieze, strip of decoration usually along the upper part of a wall; in a temple, the horizontal feature above the columns between the architrave and the cornice

Frigidarium, room for cold baths in a Roman bath complex

Gens, Roman clan or group of families linked by a common name

Giallo antico, red-veined yellow marble from Numidia, present-day Algeria and part of Tunisia

Gigantomachia, contest between giants

Gonfalone, banner of a medieval Italian Republic

Graffiti, design on a wall made with an iron tool on a prepared surface, the design showing in white. Also used loosely to describe scratched designs or words on walls

Greek-cross, church plan based on a cross with arms of equal length

Grisaille, painting in various tones of grey

Grottesche (or grotesques), delicate ornamental decoration characterised by fantastical motifs, patterns of volutes, festoons and garlands, and borders of vegetation, flowers and animals or birds. This type decoration, first discovered in Nero's Domus Aurea, became very fashionable and was widely copied during the late Renaissance.

Herm (pl. *hermae*), quadrangular pillar decreasing in girth towards the ground surmounted by a head

Hexastyle, temple with a portico of six columns at the end

Hydria, a vessel for water

Hypogeum, underground chamber, typically of a tomb (usually Etruscan)

Impasto, early Etruscan ware made of inferior clay

Imperial period, span of ancient Roman history under the Roman emperors (27 BC–476 AD)

Impluvium, rainwater pool or cistern in the centre of an atrium in a Roman house

Insula (pl. *insulae*), tenement house

Intarsia (or *tarsia*), a decorative inlay of wood, marble or metal

Intercolumniations, the space between the columns in a colonnade

Intonaco, plaster

Krater, a large, open bowl used for mixing wines, especially in ancient Greece

Kylix (pl. *kylices*), a wide, shallow vessel with two handles and a short stem

Laconicum, room for vapour baths in a Roman bath complex

Latin-cross, a cross where the vertical arm is longer than the transverse arm

Loggia (pl. *logge*), covered gallery or balcony, usually preceding a larger building

Lunette, semicircular space in a vault or ceiling, or above a door or window, often decorated with a painting or relief

Maenad, female participant in the orgiastic rites of Dionysus (Bacchus)

Matroneum, gallery reserved for women in early Christian churches

Meta, conical turning-post for chariot races in a circus or stadium

Metope, panel carved with decorative relief between two triglyphs (three vertical bands) on the frieze of a Doric temple

Mithraeum, temple of the god Mithras, a sun deity originating in Persia

Monolith, single stone (usually a column)

Narthex, vestibule of a church or basilica, before the west door

Naumachia, mock naval combat for which the arena of an amphitheatre was flooded

Niello, black substance (usually a compound of sulphur and silver) used in an engraved design, or an object so decorated

Nimbus, luminous ring surrounding the heads of saints in paintings; a square nimbus denoted that the person was living at that time

Nymphaeum, a summer house in the gardens of baths and palaces, originally a temple of the Nymphs, decorated with statues of those goddesses, and often containing a fountain

Octastyle, a portico with eight columns

Oinochoë, wine-jug, usually of elongated shape, for dipping wine out of a krater

Opus alexandrinum, mosaic design of black and red geometric figures on a white ground

Opus etruscum, type of *opus quadratum* where the blocks are placed alternately lengthwise and endwise

Opus incertum; masonry of small irregular stones set in mortar (a type of concrete)

Opus quadratum, masonry of large rectangular blocks without mortar

Opus reticulatum, masonry arranged in squares or diamonds so that the mortar joints make a network pattern

Opus sectile, mosaic or paving of thin slabs of coloured marble cut in geometrical shapes

Opus spicatum, masonry or paving of small bricks arranged in a herring-bone pattern

Opus tessellatum, mosaic formed entirely of square *tesserae* (pieces of marble, stone or glass)

Opus vermiculatum, mosaic with *tesserae* arranged in lines following the design contours

Palazzo, any dignified and important building

Palombino, fine-grained white marble

Paschal, pertaining to Easter

Patera (pl. *paterae*), small, circular ornamental disc, usually carved; Greek or Roman dish for libations to the gods

Pavonazzetto, yellow marble blotched with blue

Pendentive, concave spandrel descending from the four 'corners' of a dome

Peperino, earthy, granulated tufa, much used in Rome

Peplos, draped women's woollen mantle made from a single piece of cloth usually open at the side

Peripteral, of a temple, surrounded on all sides by a colonnade

Peristyle, court or garden surrounded by a columned portico

Piano nobile, main floor of a palace

Pietà, representation of the Virgin mourning the dead Christ

Piscina, Roman tank; a pool for ablutions; a basin for an officiating priest to wash his hands before Mass

Pluteus (pl. *plutei*), marble panel, usually decorated; a series of them used to form a parapet to precede the altar of a church

Podium, a continuous base or plinth supporting columns, and the lowest row of seats in the cavea of a theatre or amphitheatre

Polyptych, painting or panel in more than three sections

Pozzolana, reddish volcanic earth (mostly from Pozzuoli, near Naples) largely used for cement

Predella, small painting or panel, usually in sections, attached below a large altarpiece, illustrating scenes of a story such as the life of a saint

Presepio, literally, crib or manger. A group of statuary of which the central subject is the Infant Jesus in the manger

Pronaos, porch in front of a temple cella

Propylaea, columned vestibule or gateway approaching a temple

Prostyle, temple with columns on the front only

Pulvin, cushion stone between the capital and the impost block

Putto (pl. *putti*), figure sculpted or

painted, usually nude, of a child

Quadriga, a two-wheeled chariot drawn by four horses abreast

Repoussé, relief-work in metal that has been achieved by hammering from the back, thus punching out the design

Republican period, span of ancient Roman history dating from c. 509 BC to 31 BC (preceding the Imperial period)

Rhyton, drinking-horn usually ending in an animal's head

Rosso antico, red marble from the Peloponnese

Rostra, orator's platform named from ships' prows captured in battle, often used to decorate such platforms by the ancient Romans

Sanpietrini (or *sampetrini*), small, rectangular flint paving stones used in Piazza San Pietro (hence the name) but also used in numerous old streets and squares of Rome; the name used in past centuries for the workmen employed on the maintenance of St Peter's

Schola cantorum, enclosure for the choristers in the nave of an early Christian church, adjoining the sanctuary

Segmented pediment, rounded (as opposed to triangular) moulding over a window or door aperture

Sinopia (pl. *sinopie*), large sketch for a fresco made on the rough wall in a red earth pigment called sinopia (originating from Sinope on the Black Sea). When a fresco is detached for restoration, it is possible to see the sinopia beneath, which can also be separated from the wall

Silenus, in general terms a satyr, lustful, ugly and partial to wine, often a companion of Dionysus

Skyphos, drinking cup with two handles

Soffit, the underside of an arch or beam

Solomonic column, twisted column, so called from its supposed use in the Temple of Solomon

Spandrel, surface between two arches in an arcade or the triangular space on either side of an arch

Spina, low stone wall connecting the turning-posts (*metae*) at either end of a circus

SPQR, *Senatus Populusque Romanus* ('the Senate and the Roman People'), these letters have represented the Romans since the days of the Republic and are now used to denote the municipality

Stamnos, big-bellied vase with two small handles at the sides, closed by a lid

Stele (pl. *stelae*), upright stone bearing a monumental or commemorative inscription

Stemma (pl. *stemmi*), coat of arms or heraldic device

Stoa, a long, narrow colonnaded building, used as a meeting hall or for public gatherings

Strigil, bronze scraper used by the Romans to remove the oil with which they had anointed themselves

Stylobate, uppermost section of the foundation of a columned temple or other building

Tablinum, the reception or family room in a Roman house

Telamon, (*see Atlantis*)

Temenos, a sacred enclosure

Tepidarium, a room for warm baths in a Roman bath complex

Tessera (pl. *tesserae*), a small cube of marble or glass used in mosaic work

Tetrastyle, of a portico, having four columns on the front façade

Thermae, originally simple Roman baths, later elaborate complexes with libraries, assembly rooms and gymnasia

Tholos, a circular building in the ancient world, sometimes with a beehive-shaped roof, used as a tomb or for ritual purposes

Tondo (pl. *tondi*), circular painting or relief

Transenna (pl. *transennae*) open-work grille or screen, usually of marble, in an early Christian church

Travertine, rock quarried near Tivoli; the commonest of Roman building materials

Tribune, the part of a basilica containing the throne; the throne itself

Triclinium, dining- and reception-room of a Roman house

Triglyph, small panel of a Doric frieze raised slightly and carved with three vertical channels

Triptych, painting or panel in three sections

Trompe l'oeil, literally, a decep-tion of the eye; used to describe illusionist decoration and paint-ed architectural perspectives

Tumulus, a burial mound

Velarium, canvas sheet supported by masts to protect the specta-tors from the sun in an open theatre

Verde antico, green marble from Tessaglia

Volute, a scroll-like decoration at the corners of an Ionic capital; also typically present console-style on the façades of Baroque churches

RULERS OF ANCIENT ROME

Kings of Rome

Romulus	753–716 BC	Tarquinius Priscus	616–579 BC
Numa Pompilius	716–673 BC	Servius Tullis	579–534 BC
Tullus Hostilius	673–640 BC	Tarquinius Superbus	534–509 BC
Ancus Martius	640–616 BC		

Roman Republic (509–27 BC)

Sulla (dictator)	82–78 BC	Julius Caesar (dictator)	45–44 BC
First Triumvirate (Julius Caesar, Crassus, Pompey)	60–53 BC	Second Triumvirate (Mark Antony, Lepidus, Octavian)	43–27 BC
Pompey (dictator)	52–47 BC		

Roman Empire (27 BC–AD 395)

Augustus (formerly Octavian)	27 BC–AD 14	Commodus	180–192
Tiberius	14–37	Pertinax	193
Caligula	37–41	Didius Julianus	193
Claudius	41–54		
Nero	54–68	**Severans**	
Galba	68–69	Septimius Severus	193–211
Otho	69	Caracalla	211–217
Vitellius	69	Geta (co-emperor)	211–212
		Macrinus	217–218
Flavians		Elagabalus	218–222
Vespasian	69–79	Alexander Severus	222–235
Titus	79–81		
Domitian	81–96	Maximinus Thrax	235–238
Nerva	96–98	Gordian I	238
Trajan	98–117	Gordian II	238
		Pupienus	238
Antonines		Balbinus (co-emperor)	238
Hadrian	117–138	Gordian III	238–244
Antoninus Pius	138–161	Philip I	244–247
Marcus Aurelius	161–180	Philip II	247–249
Lucius Verus (co-emperor)	161–169	Decius	249–251
		Gallus and Volusian	251–253

Aemilianus	253	Licinius	308–324
Valerian	253–260	Flavius Severus	306–307
Gallienus	260–268	Maxentius	306–312
Claudius II	268–270	Constantine the Great	
Quintillus	270	(reunites empire)	306–337
Aurelian	270–275	Constantine II	337–340
Tacitus	275–276	Constans (co-emperor)	337–350
Florian	276	Constantius II	
Probus	276–282	(co-emperor)	337–361
Carus	282–283	Magnentius (co-emperor)	350–353
Carinus	282–285	Julian the Apostate	361–363
Numerian (co-emperor)	283–284	Jovian	363–364
Diocletian		Valentinian I (in West)	364–375
(institutes tetrarchy)	285–305	Valens (in East)	364–378
Maximian (co-emperor)	286–305	Gratian	367–383
Constantius Chlorus	305–306	Valentinian II (usurper)	375–392
Galerius	305–310	Theodosius I	378–395

Western Empire (395–476)

Honorius	395–423	Anthemius	467–472
Valentinian III	425–55	Olybrius	472
Petronius Maximus	455	Glycerius	473
Avitus	455–456	Julius Nepos	474–475
Majorian	457–461	Romulus Augustulus	475–476
Libius Severus	461–465		

POPES

Antipopes, usurpers or otherwise unlawful occupants of the pontifical throne are given in square brackets.

1. **St Peter**; martyr; 42–67
2. **St Linus**, of Tuscia (Volterra?); martyr; 67–78
3. **St Anacletus I**, of Rome; martyr; 78–90 (?)
4. **St Clement I**, of Rome; martyr; 90–99 (?)
5. **St Evaristus**, of Greece (or of Bethlehem); martyr; 99–105 (?)
6. **St Alexander I**, of Rome; martyr; 105–115 (?)
7. **St Sixtus I**, of Rome; martyr; 115–125 (?)
8. **St Telesphorus**, of Greece; martyr;125–136 (?)
9. **St Iginus**, of Greece; martyr; 136–140 (?)
10. **St Pius I**, of Italy; martyr; 140–155 (?)
11. **St Anicetus**, of Syria; martyr; 155–166 (?)
12. **St Soter**, of Campania; martyr; 166–175 (?)
13. **St Eleutherus**, of Epirus; martyr; 175–189
14. **St Victor I**, of Africa; martyr; 189–199
15. **St Zephyrinus**, of Rome; martyr; 199–217
16. **St Calixtus**, of Rome; martyr; 217–222
[**Hippolytus**, 217–235]
17. **St Urban I**, of Rome; martyr; 222–230
18. **St Pontianus**, of Rome; martyr; 21 July 230–28 Sept 235
19. **St Anterus**, of Greece; martyr; 21 Nov 235–3 Jan 236
20. **St Fabian**, of Rome; martyr; 10 Jan 236–20 Jan 250
21. **St Cornelius**, of Rome; martyr; March 251–June 253
[**Novatian**, 251–258]
22. **St Lucius I**, of Rome; martyr; 25 June 253–5 March 254
23. **St Stephen I**, of Rome; martyr; 12 May 254–2 Aug 257
24. **St Sixtus II**, of Greece (?); martyr; 30 Aug 257–6 Aug 258
25. **St Dionysius**, of Magna Graecia (?); martyr; 22 July 259–26 Dec 268
26. **St Felix I**, of Rome; martyr; 5 Jan 269–30 Dec 274
27. **St Eutychianus**, of Luni; martyr; 4 Jan 275–7 Dec 283
28. **St Gaius**, of Dalmatia; martyr; 17 Dec 283–22 April 296
29. **St Marcellinus**, of Rome; martyr; 30 June 296–25 Oct 304
30. **St Marcellus I**, of Rome; martyr; 27 May 308–16 Jan 309
31. **St Eusebius**, of Greece; martyr; 18 April 309–17 Aug 309 or 310
32. **St Melchiades** or **Miltiades**, of Africa; martyr; 2 July 311–11

Jan 314

33. **St Sylvester I**, of Rome; 31 Jan 314–31 Dec 335

34. **St Mark**, of Rome; 18 Jan 336–7 Oct 336

35. **St Julius I**, of Rome; 6 Feb 337–12 April 352

36. **Liberius**, of Rome; 17 May 352–22 Sept 366

[**St Felix II**, 355–22 Nov 365]

37. **St Damasus I**, of Spain; 1 Oct 366–11 Dec 384

[**Ursinus**, 366–367]

38. **St Siricius**, of Rome; 15 Dec 384–26 Nov 399

39. **St Anastasius I**, of Rome; 27 Nov 399–19 Dec 401

40. **St Innocent I**, of Albano; 22 Dec 401–12 March 417

41. **St Zosimus**, of Greece; 18 March 417–26 Dec 418

42. **St Boniface I**, of Rome; 29 Dec 418–4 Sept 422

[**Eulalius**, 27 Dec 418–3 April 419]

43. **St Celestine I**, of Campania; 10 Sept 422–27 July 432

44. **St Sixtus III**, of Rome; 3 July (?) 432–19 Aug 440

45. **St Leo I the Great**, of Tusculum; 29 Sept 440–10 Nov 461

46. **St Hilarius**, of Sardinia; 19 Nov 461–29 Feb 468

47. **St Simplicius**, of Tivoli; 3 March 468–10 March 483

48. **St Felix III (II)**, of Rome; 13 March 483–1 March 492

49. **St Gelasius I**, of Africa; 1 March 492–21 Nov 496

50. **St Anastasius II**, of Rome; 24 Nov 496–19 Nov 498

51. **St Symmachus**, of Sardinia; 22 Nov 498–19 July 514

[**Laurentius**, Nov 498–505]

52. **St Hormisdas**, of Frosinone; 20 July 514–6 Aug 523

53. **St John I**, of Tusculum; martyr; 13 Aug 523–18 May 526. Died at Ravenna

54. **St Felix IV (III)**, of Samnium (Benevento?); 12 July 526–22 Sept 530

55. **Boniface II**, of Rome; 22 Sept 530–7 Oct 532

[**Dioscurus**, 22 Sept 530–14 Oct 530]

56. **John II**, of Rome; 2 Jan 533–8 May 535

57. **St Agapitus I**, of Rome; 13 May 535–22 April 536. Died at Constantinople

58. **St Silverius**, of Frosinone; martyr; 8 June 536–11 March 537

59. **Vigilius**, of Rome; June 538 (?)–7 June 555

60. **Pelagius I**, of Rome; 16 April 556–4 March 561

61. **John III**, of Rome; 17 July 561–13 July 574

62. **Benedict I**, of Rome; 2 June 575–30 July 579

63. **Pelagius II**, of Rome; 26 Nov 579–7 Feb 590

64. **St Gregory I the Great**, of Rome; 3 Sept 590–13 March 604

65. **Sabinianus**, of Tusculum; 13 Sept 604–22 Feb 606

66. **Boniface III**, of Rome; 19 Feb 607–12 Nov 607

67. **St Boniface IV**, of Valeria de' Marsi; 25 Aug 608–8 May 615

68. **St Deusdedit I**, of Rome; 19 Oct 615–8 Nov 618

69. **Boniface V**, of Naples; 23 Dec 619–25 Oct 625

70. **Honorius I**, of Campania; 27 Oct 625–12 Oct 638

71. **Severinus**, of Rome; 28 May 640–2 Aug 640

72. **John IV**, of Dalmatia; 24 Dec 640–12 Oct 642

73. **Theodore I**, of Jerusalem (? or Greece); 24 Nov 642–14 May 649

74. **St Martin I**, of Todi; martyr; 21 July 649–16 Sept 655

75. **St Eugenius I**, of Rome; 16 Sept 655–2 June 657

76. **St Vitalian**, of Segni; 30 July 657–27 Jan 672

77. **Deusdedit II**, of Rome; 11 April 672–17 June 676

78. **Donus**, of Rome; 2 Nov 676–11 April 678

79. **St Agatho**, of Sicily; 27 June 678–10 Jan 681

80. **St Leo II**, of Sicily; 17 Aug 682–3 July 683

81. **St Benedict II**, of Rome; 26 June 684–8 May 685

82. **John V**, of Antioch; 23 July 685–2 Aug 686

83. **Conon**, of Thrace; 21 Oct 686–21 Sept 687

[**Theodore**, 22 Sept 687–Oct 687]

[**Paschal**, 687]

84. **St Sergius I**, of Palermo; 15 Dec 687–8 Sept 701

85. **John VI**, of Greece; 30 Oct 701–11 Jan 705

86. **John VII**, of Greece; 1 March 705–18 Oct 707

87. **Sisinnius**, of Syria; 15 Jan 708–4 Feb 708

88. **Constantine**, of Syria; 25 March 708–9 April 715

89. **St Gregory II**, of Rome; 19 May 715–11 Feb 731

90. **St Gregory III**, of Syria; 18 March 731–10 Dec 741

91. **St Zacharias**, of Greece; 10 Dec 741–22 March 752

92. **Stephen II**, of Rome; 23 March 752–25 March 752

93. **St Stephen III**, of Rome; 26 March 752–26 April 757

94. **St Paul I**, of Rome; 29 May 757–28 June 767

[**Constantine II**, 5 July 767–769]

[**Philip**, 768]

95. **Stephen IV**, of Sicily; 7 Aug 768–3 Feb 772

96. **Hadrian I**, of Rome; 9 Feb 772–26 Dec 795

97. **St Leo III**, of Rome; 27 Dec 795–12 June 816

98. **St Stephen V**, of Rome; 22 June 816–14 Jan 817

99. **St Paschal I**, of Rome; 25 Jan 817–11 Feb 824

100. **Eugenius II**, of Rome; 21 Feb 824–27 Aug 827

101. **Valentine**, of Rome; Aug (?) 827–Sept (?) 827

102. **Gregory IV**, of Rome; Oct 827–25 Jan 844

103. **Sergius II**, of Rome; Jan 844–27 Jan 847

[**John**, 844]

104. **St Leo IV**, of Rome; 10 April 847–17 July 855

105. **St Benedict III**, of Rome; 6 Oct 855–17 April 858

[**Anastasius**, 29 Sept 855–20 Oct 855]

106. **St Nicholas I the Great**, of Rome; 24 April 858–13 Nov 867

107. **Hadrian II**, of Rome; 14 Dec 867–14 Dec 872

108. **John VIII**, of Rome, 14 Dec 872–16 Dec 882

109. **Marinus I (Martin II)**, of Gallesium; 16 Dec 882–15 May 884

110. **St Hadrian III**, of Rome; 17 May 884–17 Sept 885

111. **Stephen VI**, of Rome; Sept 885–Sept 891

112. **Formosus**, bishop of Porto; 6 Oct 891–4 April 896

113. **Boniface VI**, of Gallesium; April 896

114. **Stephen VII**, of Rome; May 896–Aug 897

115. **Romanus**, of Gallesium; Aug 897–end of Nov 897

116. **Theodore II**, of Rome; Dec 897

117. **John IX**, of Tivoli; Jan 898–Jan 900

118. **Benedict IV**, of Rome; Jan 900–end July 903

119. **Leo V**, of Ardea; end of July 903–Sept 903

[**Christopher**, of Rome; 903–904]

120. **Sergius III**, of Rome; 29 Jan 904–14 April 911

121. **Anastasius III**, of Rome; April 911–June 913

122. **Lando**, of Sabina; end of July 913–Feb 914

123. **John X**, of Ravenna; March 914–May 928

124. **Leo VI**, of Rome; May 928–Dec 928

125. **Stephen VIII**, of Rome; Jan 929–Feb 931

126. **John XI**, of Rome; March 931–Dec 935

127. **Leo VII**; 3 (?) Jan 936–13 (?) July 939

128. **Stephen IX**, of Germany (?); 14 (?) July 939–Oct 942

129. **Marinus II (Martin III)**, of Rome; 30 (?) Oct 942–May 946

130. **Agapitus II**, of Rome; 10 May 946–Dec 955

131. **John XII**, Ottaviano, of Tusculum; 16 (?) Dec 955–14 May 964

132. **Leo VIII**, of Rome, 4 Nov 963–1 March 965

133. **Benedict V**, of Rome; 22 (?) May 964–23 June 964

134. **John XIII**, of Rome; 1 Oct 965–5 Sept 972

135. **Benedict VI**, of Rome; 19 Jan 973–June 974

[**Boniface VII**, of Rome; 974]

136. **Benedict VII**, of Rome; Oct 974–10 July 983

137. **John XIV**, of Pavia; Dec 983–20 Aug 984)

[**Boniface VII**; for the second time, Aug 984–July 985]

138. **John XV**, of Rome; Aug 985–March 996

139. **Gregory V**, of the family of the Counts of Carinthia; 3 May 996–18 Feb 999

[**John XVI**, of Greece; March 997–Feb 998]

140.**Sylvester II**, of France; 2 April 999–12 May 1003

141.**John XVII**, of Rome; June (?) 1003–6 Nov 1003

142.**John XVIII**, of Rapagnano; Jan (?) 1004–July (?) 1009

143.**Sergius IV**, of Rome; 31 July 1009–12 May 1012

144.**Benedict VIII**, of Rome; 18 May 1012–9 April 1024

[**Gregory**, 1012]

145.**John XIX**, of Rome; April 1024–1032

146.**Benedict IX**, Theophylact, of the family of the Counts of Tusculum; elected (aged 15) for the first time in 1032–deposed in Dec 1044; elected for the second time 10 March 1045–deposed 1 May 1045; elected for the third time 8 Nov 1047–deposed 17 July 1048

147.**Sylvester III**, bishop of Sabina; 20 Jan 1045–10 March 1045. Deposed

148.**Gregory VI**, of Rome; 5 May 1045–20 Dec 1046

149.**Clement II**, bishop of Bamberg; 25 Dec 1046–9 Oct 1047.

150.**Damasus II**, of Bavaria; 17 July 1048–9 Aug 1048

151.**St Leo IX**, of Germany 12 Feb 1049–19 April 1054

152.**Victor II**, of Germany; 16 April 1055–28 July 1057

153.**Stephen X**, of the family of the Dukes of Lorraine; 3 Aug 1057–29 March 1058

[**Benedict X**, of Rome; 5 April 1058–24 Jan 1059]

154.**Nicholas II**, Gérard de Bourgogne; 24 Jan 1059–27 (?) July 1061

155.**Alexander II**, of Milan; 30 Sept 1061–21 April 1073

[**Honorius II**; 1061–1072]

156.**St Gregory VII**, Hildebrand di Bonizio Aldobrandeschi, of Sovana; 22 April 1073–25 May 1085

[**Clement III**; 25 Jan 1080–Sept 1100]

157.**Bl. Victor III**, Desiderio Epifani, of Benevento; elected 24 May 1086, consecrated 9 May 1087–16 Sept 1087

158.**Bl. Urban II**, of Reims; 12 March 1088–29 July 1099

159.**Paschal II**, Rainiero, of Breda; 14 Aug 1099–21 Jan 1118

[**Theodoric**, Sept–Dec 1100]

[**Albert**, Feb–March 1102]

[**Sylvester IV**, 18 Nov 1105–12 April 1111]

160.**Gelasius II**, Giovanni Caetani, of Gaeta; 24 Jan 1118–28 Jan 1119

[**Gregory VIII**, Maurice Bourdain, of Limoges, 8 March 1118–April 1121. Deposed]

161.**Calixtus II**, Gui de Bourgogne, of Quingey; 2 Feb 1119–13 Dec 1124

162.**Honorius II**, Lamberto Scannabecchi, of Fanano (Modena); 15 Dec 1124–13 Feb 1130

163.**Innocent II**, Gregorio Papareschi, of Trastevere; 14 Feb 1130–24 Sept 1143

[**Anacletus II**, Pierleone, a

converted Jew; 14 Feb 1130–25 Jan 1138]

[**Victor IV**, Gregorio da Monticelli, elected 15 March 1138, abdicated 29 May 1138]

164. **Celestine II**, Guido, of Città di Castello; 26 Sept 1143–8 March 1144

165. **Lucius II**, Gerardo Caccianemici dell'Orso, of Bologna; 12 March 1144–15 Feb 1145

166. **Bl. Eugenius III**, Bernardo Paganelli, of Montemagno (Pisa); 15 Feb 1145–8 July 1153

167. **Anastasius IV**, Corrado, of the Suburra, Rome; 12 July 1153–3 Dec 1154

168. **Hadrian IV**, Nicholas Breakspeare, of Bedmond (Hertfordshire, England); 4 Dec 1154–1 Sept 1159

169. **Alexander III**, Rolando Bandinelli, of Siena; 7 Sept 1159–30 Aug 1181

[**Victor IV (V)**, Ottaviano; 7 Oct 1159–20 April 1164]

[**Paschal III**, Guido da Crema; 22 April 1164–20 Sept 1168]

[**Calixtus III**, of Hungary, Sept 1168–29 Aug 1178]

[**Innocent III**, Lando Frangipane of Sezze, 1179–1180]

170. **Lucius III**, Ubaldo Allucingoli, of Lucca; 1 Sept 1181–25 Nov 1185

171. **Urban III**, Uberto Crivelli, of Milan; 25 Nov 1185–20 Oct 1187

172. **Gregory VIII**, Alberto di Morra, of Benevento; 21 Oct 1187–17 Dec 1187

173. **Clement III**, Paolino Scolare, of Rome; 19 Dec 1187–Mar 1191

174. **Celestine III**, Giacinto Bobone Orsini, of Rome; 30 March 1191–8 Jan 1198

175. **Innocent III**, Lotario dei Conti di Segni, of Anagni; 8 Jan 1198–16 July 1216

176. **Honorius III**, Cencio Savelli, of Rome; elected in Perugia, 18 July 1216–18 March 1227

177. **Gregory IX**, Ugolino dei Conti di Segni, of Anagni; 19 March 1227–22 Aug 1241

178. **Celestine IV**, Castiglione, of Milan; 25 Oct 1241–10 Nov 1241

179. **Innocent IV**, Sinibaldo Fieschi of Genoa; 25 June 1243–7 Dec 1254

180. **Alexander IV**, Orlando dei Conti di Segni, of Anagni; 12 Dec 1254–25 May 1261

181. **Urban IV**, Hyacinthe Pantaléon, of Troyes; 1261–1264

182. **Clement IV**, Gui Foulques Le Gros, of St-Gilles; 1265–29 Nov 1268

183. **Gregory X**, Teobaldo Visconti of Piacenza; 1 Sept 1271–10 Jan 1276

184. **Innocent V**, Pierre de Champagny, of the Tarentaise; 21 Jan 1276–22 June 1276

185. **Hadrian V**, Ottobono de' Fieschi, of Genoa; 11 July 1276–18 Aug 1276

186. **John XXI**, Pedro Juliao, of Lisbon; 8 Sept 1276–20 May 1277

187. **Nicholas III**, Giovanni Gaetano Orsini, of Rome; 25 Nov 1277–22 Aug 1280

188. **Martin IV**, Simon de Brion, of Montpincé in Brie; 22 Feb 1281–28 March 1285

189. **Honorius IV**, Iacopo Savelli, of Rome; 2 April 1285–3 April 1287

190. **Nicholas IV**, Girolamo Masci, of Lisciano di Ascoli; 15 Feb 1288–4 April 1292

191. **St Celestine V**, Pietro Angeleri da Morrone, of Isernia; 5 July 1294–13 Dec 1294

192. **Boniface VIII**, Benedetto Gaetani, of Anagni; 24 Dec 1294–11 or 12 Oct 1303

193. **Bl. Benedict XI**, Niccolò Boccasini, of Treviso; 22 Oct 1303–7 July 1304

194. **Clement V, Bertrand de Got**, of Villandraut, near Bordeaux; elected at Perugia 5 June 1305–14 April 1314

195. **John XXII**, Jacques d'Euse, of Cahors; elected at Avignon 7 Aug 1316–4 Dec 1334

[**Nicholas V**, Pietro da Corvara, 12 May 1328–30 Aug 1330]

196. **Benedict XII**, Jacques Fournier, of Saverdun, near Toulouse; 20 Dec 1334–25 April 1342

197. **Clement VI**, Pierre Roger de Beaufort, of Château Maumont, near Limoges; 7 May 1342–6 Dec 1352

198. **Innocent VI**, Etienne d'Aubert, of Mont, near Limoges; 18 Dec 1352–12 Sept 1362

199. **Urban V**, Guillaume de Grimoard, of Grisac, near Mende in Languedoc; 16 Oct 1362–19 Dec 1370

200. **Gregory XI**, Pierre Roger de Beaufort, nephew of Clement VI, of Château Maumont, near Limoges; elected at Avignon 30 Dec 1370–27 March 1378

201. **Urban VI**, Bartolomeo Prignano, of Naples; 9 April 1378–15 Oct 1389

202. **Boniface IX**, Pietro Tomacelli, of Naples; 2 Nov 1389–1 Oct 1404

203. **Innocent VII**, Cosimo de' Migliorati, of Sulmona; 17 Oct 1404–6 Nov 1406.

204. **Gregory XII**, Angelo Correr, of Venice; 30 Nov 1406–4 June 1415

ANTIPOPES

Clement VII, Robert of Savoy, of Geneva; 20 Sept 1378–16 Sept 1394

Benedict XIII, Pedro de Luna, of Aragon; 28 Sept 1394–23 May 1423

Clement VIII, Gil Sanchez Muñoz, of Barcelona; 10 June 1423–16 July 1429

Benedict XIV, Bernard Garnier; 12 Nov 1425–1430 (?)

Alexander V, Pietro Filargis, of Candia; 26 June 1409–3 May 1410

John XXIII, Baldassarre Cossa, of Naples; 17 May 1410–29 May 1415

205. **Martin V**, Oddone Colonna, of Genazzano; elected (aged 50) 11 Nov 1417–20 Feb 1431

206. **Eugenius IV**, Gabriele Condulmero of Venice; elected (aged 48) 3 March 1431–23 Feb 1447

[**Felix V**, Amadeus, duke of Savoy; 5 Nov 1439–7 April 1449]

207. **Nicholas V**, Tommaso Parentucelli, of Sarzana; elected (aged 49) 6 March 1447–24 March 1455

208. **Calixtus III**, Alfonso Borgia, of Xativa, Spain; elected (aged 78) 8 April 1455–6 Aug 1458

209. **Pius II**, Aeneas Silvius Piccolomini, of Corsignano (Pienza); elected (aged 53) 19 Aug 1458–15 Aug 1464

210. **Paul II**, Pietro Barbo, of Venice; elected (aged 48) 30 Aug 1464–26 July 1471

211. **Sixtus IV**, Francesco della Rovere, of Savona; elected (aged 57) 9 Aug 1471–12 Aug 1484

212. **Innocent VIII**, Giovanni Battista Cibo, of Genoa; elected (aged 52) 29 Aug 1484–25 July 1492

213. **Alexander VI**, Roderigo Lenzuoli-Borgia, of Valencia, Spain; elected (aged 62) 11 Aug 1492–18 Aug 1503

214. **Pius III**, Francesco Todeschini Piccolomini, of Siena; elected (aged 64) 22 Sept 1503–18 Oct 1503

215. **Julius II**, Giuliano della Rovere, of Savona; elected (aged 60) 31 Oct 1503–21 Feb 1513

216. **Leo X**, Giovanni de' Medici, of Florence; elected (aged 38) 9 March 1513–1 Dec 1521

217. **Adrian VI**, Adrian Florensz Dedel, of Utrecht; elected (aged 63) 9 Jan 1522–14 Sept 1523

218. **Clement VII**, Giulio de' Medici, of Florence; elected (aged 45) 19 Nov 1523–25 Sept 1534

219. **Paul III**, Alessandro Farnese, of Rome, elected (aged 66) 13 Oct 1534–10 Nov 1549

220. **Julius III**, Giovanni Maria Ciocchi del Monte, of Monte San Savino, near Arezzo; elected (aged 63) 7 Feb 1550–23 March 1555

221. **Marcellus II**, Marcello Cervini, of Montefano (Macerata); elected (aged 54) 9 April 1555–30 April 1555

222. **Paul IV**, Giovanni Pietro Caraffa, of Capriglio, Avellino; elected (aged 79) 23 May 1555–18 Aug 1559

223. **Pius IV**, Giovanni Angelo de' Medici, of Milan; elected (aged 60) 26 Dec 1559–9 Dec 1565

224. **St Pius V**, Antonio Ghislieri, of Bosco Marengo, near Tortona; elected (aged 62) 7 Jan 1566–1 May 1572

225. **Gregory XIII**, Ugo Boncompagni, of Bologna; elected (aged 70) 13 May 1572–10 April 1585

226. **Sixtus V**, Felice Peretti, of Grottammare; elected (aged 64) 24 April 1585–27 Aug 1590

227. **Urban VII**, Giovanni Battista Castagna, of Rome; elected (aged 69) 15 Sept 1590–27 Sept 1590

228. **Gregory XIV**, Niccolò Sfondrati, of Cremona; elected (aged 55) 5 Dec 1590–15 Oct 1591

229. **Innocent IX**, Giovanni Antonio Facchinetti, of Bologna; elected (aged 72) 29 Oct 1591–30 Dec 1591

230. **Clement VIII**, Ippolito Aldobrandini, of Fano; elected (aged 56) 30 Jan 1592–3 March 1605

231. **Leo XI**, Alessandro de' Medici, of Florence; elected (aged 70) 1 April 1605–27 April 1605

232. **Paul V**, Camillo Borghese, of Rome; elected (aged 53) 16 May 1605–28 Jan 1621

233. **Gregory XV**, Alessandro Ludovisi, of Bologna; elected (aged 67) 9 Feb 1621–8 July 1623

234. **Urban VIII**, Maffeo Barberini, of Florence; elected (aged 55) 6 Aug 1623–29 July 1644

235. **Innocent X**, Giovanni Battista Pamphilj, of Rome; elected (aged 72) 15 Sept 1644–7 Jan 1655

236. **Alexander VII**, Fabio Chigi, of Siena; elected (aged 56) 7 April 1655–22 May 1667

237. **Clement IX**, Giulio Rospigliosi, of Pistoia; elected (aged 67) 20 June 1667–9 Dec 1669

238. **Clement X**, Emilio Altieri, of Rome; elected (aged 80) 29 April 1670–22 July 1676

239. **Innocent XI**, Benedetto Odescalchi, of Como; elected (aged 65) 21 Sept 1676–11 Aug 1689

240. **Alexander VIII**, Pietro Ottoboni, of Venice; elected (aged 79) 6 Oct 1689–1 Feb 1691

241. **Innocent XII**, Antonio Pignatelli, of Spinazzola (Bari); elected (aged 76) 12 July 1691–27 Sept 1700

242. **Clement XI**, Giovanni Francesco Albani, of Urbino; elected (aged 51) 23 Nov 1700–19 March 1721

243. **Innocent XIII**, Michelangelo Conti, of Rome; elected (aged 66) 8 May 1721–7 March 1724

244. **Benedict XIII**, Pietro Francesco Orsini, of Gravina (Bari); elected (aged 75) 29 May 1724–21 Feb 1730

245. **Clement XII**, Lorenzo Corsini, of Florence; elected (aged 79) 12 July 1730–6 Feb 1740

246. **Benedict XIV**, Prospero Lambertini, of Bologna; elected (aged 65) 17 Aug 1740–3 May 1758

247. **Clement XIII**, Carlo Rezzonico, of Venice; elected (aged 65) 6 July 1758–2 Feb 1769

248.**Clement XIV**, Giovanni Vincenzo Ganganelli, of Sant'Arcangelo di Romagna (Forlì); elected (aged 64) 19 May 1769–22 Sept 1774

249.**Pius VI**, Angelo Braschi, of Cesena; elected (aged 58) 15 Feb 1775–29 Aug 1799

250.**Pius VII**, Giorgio Barnaba Chiaramonti, of Cesena; elected (aged 58) 14 March 1800–20 Aug 1823

251.**Leo XII**, Annibale della Genga, born at La Genga, near Foligno; elected (aged 63) 28 Sept 1823–10 Feb 1829

252.**Pius VIII**, Francesco Saverio Castiglioni, of Cingoli; elected (aged 69) 31 March 1829–30 Nov 1830

253.**Gregory XVI**, Bartolomeo Cappellari, of Belluno, elected (aged 66) 2 Feb 1831–1 June 1846

254.**Pius IX**, Giovanni Maria Mastai Ferretti, of Senigallia; elected (aged 54) 16 June 1846–7 Feb 1878

255.**Leo XIII**, Gioacchino Pecci, of Carpineto Romano, elected (aged 68) 20 Feb 1878–20 July 1903

256.**St Pius X**, Giuseppe Sarto, of Riese (Treviso); elected (aged 68) 4 Aug 1903–20 Aug 1914

257.**Benedict XV**, Giacomo della Chiesa, of Genoa; elected (aged 60) 3 Sept 1914–22 Jan 1922

258.**Pius XI**, Achille Ratti, of Milan; elected (aged 65) 6 Feb 1922–10 Feb 1939

259.**Pius XII**, Eugenio Pacelli, of Rome; elected (aged 63) 2 March 1939–9 Oct 1958

260.**John XXIII**, Angelo Roncalli, of Sotto il Monte, Bergamo; elected (aged 77) 28 Oct 1958–3 June 1963 (beatified 2000)

261.**Paul VI**, Giovanni Battista Montini, of Brescia; elected (aged 65) 21 June 1963–6 Aug 1978

262.**John Paul I**, Albino Luciani, of Belluno; elected (aged 65) 26 Aug 1978–29 Sept 1978

263.**John Paul II**, Karol Wojtyla, of Wadowice (Krakow), Poland; elected (aged 58) 16 Oct 1978–2 April 2005

264.**Benedict XVI**, Joseph Ratzinger, of Markt am Inn (Passau), Germany; elected (aged 78) 19 April 2005

INDEX

More detailed or explanatory references (where there are many references listed), or references to an artist's masterpiece (where it is not listed by name) are given in bold. Numbers in italics are picture references.

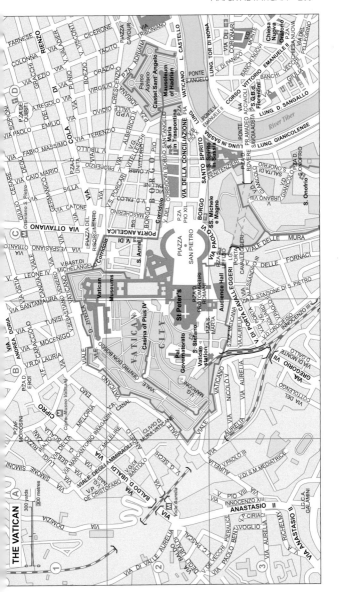

THE VATICAN

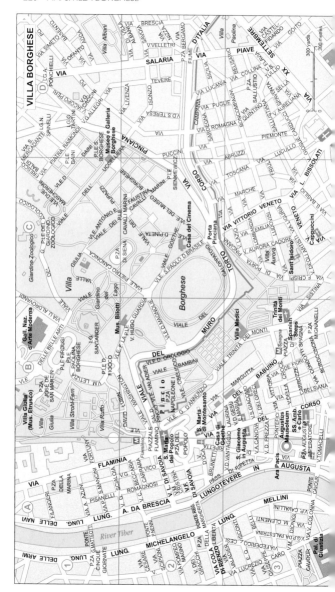

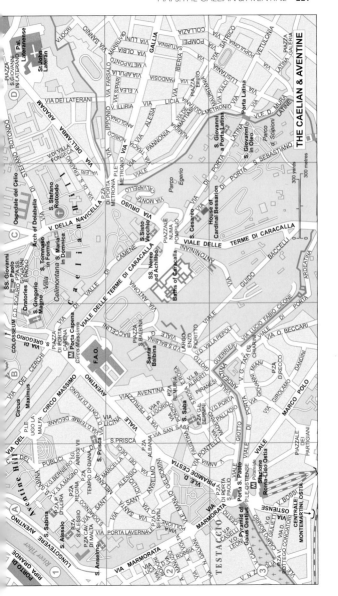

THE CAELIAN & AVENTINE

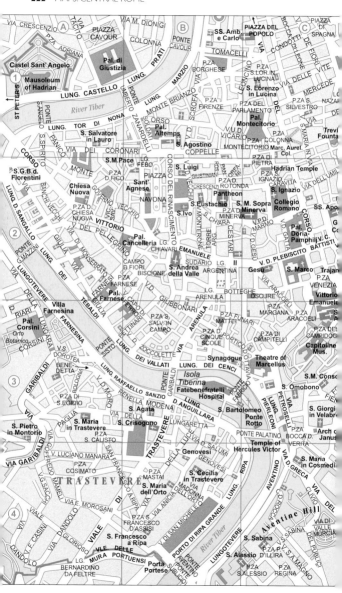

contd. from p. 2

Edited by Annabel Barber; Editorial assistant Sophie Willats

Layout and design: Anikó Kuzmich
Maps by Dimap Bt; Floor plans by Imre Bába
Architectural line drawings: Gabriella Juhász & Michael Mansell RIBA

Photo research, editing and pre-press: Hadley Kincade
Photographs by Andrea Federici: pp. 60, 78; Bill Hocker: pp. 33, 142;
Thomas Howells: pp. 17, 148, 156; Mark Mansfield: p. 106; Phil Robinson: pp. 83,
126; Sophie Willats: p. 58; Annabel Barber: pp. 13, 21, 25, 28, 29, 46, 49, 51, 79,
89, 113, 114, 147; The Art Archive/Musei Capitolini Rome/Gianni dagli Orti: p. 13;
The Art Archive/ Museo Nazionale Palazzo Altemps, Rome/Gianni dagli Orti: p. 70;
The Art Archive/Alfredo dagli Orti: p. 116; Wikicommons: p. 16; Alinari Archives,
Florence: pp. 37, 45, 97, 103; Bridgeman/Alinari Archives: p. 144; © 2008. Photo
Scala, Florence/Fondo Edifici di Culto–Ministero dell'Interno: p. 43; Courtesy of
the Fondo Edifici di Culto–Ministero dell'Interno: p. 54; © 2006. Photo Scala,
Florence/Luciano Romano: p. 95; © 1990. Photo Scala, Florence: pp. 67, 87, 154;
© 1990. Photo Scala, Florence/Fondo Edifici di Culto–Ministero dell'Interno:
p. 108; Luisa Ricciarini/TopFoto: p. 63; The Granger Collection, NYC/TopFoto:
p. 65; © adam eastland/Alamy/Red Dot: p. 73; © Saverio Maria Gallotti/Alamy/Red
Dot: p. 82; © imagebroker/Alamy/Red Dot: p. 119; © Bildarchiv Monheim GmbH/
Alamy/Red Dot: p. 124; © Massimo Listri/Corbis/Red Dot: p. 92; ©istockphoto.
com/mmac72: p. 85; ©istockphoto.com/fotoVoyager: p. 93; ©istockphoto.com/
compassandcamera: pp. 101, 110; ©istockphoto.com/e-person: p. 134;
©istockphoto.com/juuce: p. 138; JuleBerlin/www.stockexpert.com: p. 104;
imagestalk/www.stockexpert.com: p. 155.

Cover photograph: Fragment from a colossal statue of Constantine (photo: Thomas
Howells); Frontispiece: detail of the Garden Room from the Villa of Livia at Prima
Porta (photo: Mark Mansfield)

Acknowledgements
The author is especially indebted to Marco Fe' d'Ostiani,
who provided much generous help.
The editor wishes to thank Luigi de Simone Niquesa, Martin Davies
and Niels Koopman.

Printed in Hungary by Dürer Nyomda Kft, Gyula

ISBN 978–1–905131–30–3